MW00440229

Praise for *The Trump Administration*
and International Law

"As one of the most preeminent and learned legal scholars of our time, Harold Hongju Koh leverages his prior government experience to provide a penetrating analysis of the threat posed by the Trump Administration to a law-governed international society. His insights are invaluable, as are his comments about the harmful effects of the Trump 'strategy' and the counterstrategy opportunities that lie ahead. A must read for all who are concerned about U.S. national security and future world order."

—**John O. Brennan**, Assistant to the President for Homeland Security and Counterterrorism (2009 to 2013) and Director of the Central Intelligence Agency (2013 to 2017)

"Harold Hongju Koh, a brilliant and influential scholar of international law, has delivered here a timely, deeply reasoned warning of how much is at stake in the struggle between the Trump Administration and 'Kantian' global order, that is, an international society governed by reason, science, and law. Neither despairing nor encouraging, Koh's analysis of Trump's initial disruptions—and the counterstrategies so far mounted against him—clarifies how, among other things, the future of human rights protections in the United States and beyond lies in the balance. This sobering but practical-minded book will be of great help to policymakers, activists and scholars as they struggle against diverse attacks on postwar international liberalism."

—**Steve Coll**, Dean, Graduate School of Journalism, Columbia University, Pulitzer Prize–winning writer, *The New Yorker*

"Harold Hongju Koh always has been a courageous, prescient voice on the big issues facing the community of humankind. This important book provides strategies to blunt Donald Trump's attempt to dismantle the system of international rules and norms that developed over decades and for buttressing these fundamental elements of our interconnected world. This book is required reading for all who think seriously about the rule of law and a source of hope for those who care."

—**John Sexton**, President Emeritus, New York University

"As the Trump presidency comes ever closer to gutting the internal foundations of our democracy, we should celebrate Harold Hongju

Koh's deeply informed and wisely reasoned demonstration that the transnational legal process offers undimmed hope for progress."
—**Laurence H. Tribe**, Carl M. Loeb University Professor,
Harvard Law School

"At a moment when the U.S. government is straying wildly from its historic commitments to human rights and the rule of law, Harold Hongju Koh provides a welcome response. In this timely and important book, Koh describes how advocates are using the courts and other fora to challenge many of the most egregious assaults on our constitutional system and our democracy. Ultimately this is a hopeful book, showcasing the many innovative ways that patriotic Americans are fighting back and preserving core principles that will be key to our future."
—**Michael Posner**, former Assistant Secretary of State for
Democracy, Human Rights and Labor, Obama Administration

"In this searingly clear analysis of the Trump Administration's challenge to international law, Yale Professor and former State Department Legal Adviser Harold Hongju Koh makes the compelling, reassuring claim that the vast density and depth and inherent drag of existing international order can act as an effective countervailing force against even the most irresponsible of international actors—that 'the law' as an organic totality is more powerful than particular rules."
—**Philip Allott**, Professor Emeritus of International Public Law at
Cambridge University and Fellow of Trinity College Cambridge

"President Trump partakes of a tradition of American exceptionalism and isolationism, but does so in a strikingly undisciplined manner. Prof. Koh argues convincingly that, so far, the President's sputtering attempts to undermine the institutions, regimes and alliances of the post–World War II order have been largely ineffective. International and U.S. domestic law, and their institutions, have proven 'sticky.' They have not been easily displaced or overturned. Here is cause for a modicum of hope. However, Koh recognizes that President Trump may be less cause than effect, with a widespread anti-globalist nativism spreading in autocracies and illiberal democracies. Globally, law and institutions urgently require strategic reinforcement."
—**Stephen J. Toope**, Professor of Law and Vice-Chancellor,
University of Cambridge

THE TRUMP ADMINISTRATION
AND INTERNATIONAL LAW

THE TRUMP ADMINISTRATION AND INTERNATIONAL LAW

Harold Hongju Koh

The Trump Administration and International Law. Harold Hongju Koh.
© Oxford University Press 2019. Published 2019 by Oxford University Press.

OXFORD
UNIVERSITY PRESS

Oxford University Press is a department of the University of Oxford. It furthers the
University's objective of excellence in research, scholarship, and education by
publishing worldwide. Oxford is a registered trademark of Oxford University Press in
the UK and certain other countries.

Published in the United States of America by Oxford University Press
198 Madison Avenue, New York, NY 10016, United States of America.

© Oxford University Press 2019

Library of Congress Cataloging-in-Publication Data
Names: Koh, Harold Hongju, 1954– author.
Title: The Trump administration and international law / Harold Hongju Koh.
Description: New York : Oxford University Press, 2019. | Includes bibliographical
references and index.
Identifiers: LCCN 2018024105 | ISBN 9780190912185 ((hardback) : alk. paper)
Subjects: LCSH: International law—United States. | United States—Foreign
relations—2017– | Trump, Donald, 1946- —Influence.
Classification: LCC KZ3410 .K64 2018 | DDC 341.0973—dc23
LC record available at https://lccn.loc.gov/2018024105

1 3 5 7 9 8 6 4 2

Printed by Sheridan Books, Inc., United States of America

Note to Readers

This publication is designed to provide accurate and authoritative information in
regard to the subject matter covered. It is based upon sources believed to be accurate
and reliable and is intended to be current as of the time it was written. It is sold with
the understanding that the publisher is not engaged in rendering legal, accounting,
or other professional services. If legal advice or other expert assistance is required,
the services of a competent professional person should be sought. Also, to confirm
that the information has not been affected or changed by recent developments,
traditional legal research techniques should be used, including checking
primary sources where appropriate.

*(Based on the Declaration of Principles jointly adopted by a Committee of the
American Bar Association and a Committee of Publishers and Associations.)*

To my Family,
For making everything possible

CONTENTS

CONTENTS

Introduction: Trumping International Law?

As you read these words, the U.S. administration of Donald J. Trump has been in office for nearly two years, a tumultuous period that has disrupted many things, including the world of international law. Our experience thus far has raised a haunting question: will the Trump administration's many initiatives permanently change the nature of America's relationship with international law and its institutions?

To answer that question, one must consider two others. First, is there a *counterstrategy* that those who resist Trump's broader approach can jointly and severally apply to increase the odds that America's existing legal obligations will be faithfully executed? Second, looking past the daily skirmishing and even beyond the Trump administration, what is ultimately at stake? Can across-the-board resistance—strategically applied—prevent the slow backsliding of our postwar system of global governance into a far nastier, more brutish world, less respectful of democracy, human rights, and the rule of law?

I approach these questions after four decades as an international and constitutional law professor, including several decades as a human rights lawyer and one decade serving the U.S. government as a lawyer and policymaker. On the day after Trump's

The Trump Administration and International Law. Harold Hongju Koh.

stunning election in November 2016, I was asked: "Can the rest of us—America and the world—still win, if Donald Trump loses?" My instinctive answer: "Yes, because Donald Trump does not own the process by which international law is made and maintained."

This book expands on that answer. Chapter 1 opens by arguing that there *is* a counterstrategy of effective resistance—the same theory that I have been applying for most of my professional career, both as a scholar and as a practitioner: *transnational legal process*.[1] Chapters 2 through 5 describe how this counterstrategy has played out during the first years of the Trump administration, in such areas as immigration and human rights; attempts to "resign without leaving" such international arrangements as the Paris Climate Deal and trade agreements; bilateral actions involving countries of concern, such as North Korea, Russia, and Ukraine; and in the conduct of America's ongoing wars. In each of these areas, I argue, transnational actors both inside and outside the United States have employed techniques of transnational legal process to mitigate the Trump administration's efforts to break, stretch, or violate international law. This counterstrategy, I argue, has proven both an appropriate and largely effective response to curb the Trump administration's excesses and to preserve America's constitutional obligations to comply with binding international standards.

These policy episodes further reveal that far more is at stake in today's reality show of *Trump vs. World* than the string of unending political scuffles we daily watch unfolding on cable television. I close by arguing that what is really at stake is a much larger, deeply consequential struggle between competing visions of a future world order. That struggle is far bigger than America or Donald Trump, who is as much evidence and product of that battle as he is a cause. Since World War II, the leading democratic nations of the world have collectively worked toward an admittedly imperfect, but adequately functioning, Kantian vision of a law-governed international society. Trump's motley array of instincts and impulses has been uniformly directed toward disrupting this vision.

How successfully we collectively resist the dark impulses revealed by the early days of the Trump administration thus reflects far more than an exercise in ordinary politics. It will determine whether—as we enter the mid-twenty-first century—history will remember Trump's election as a grim pivot toward a more cynical, Orwellian system of global governance dominated by realist great-power spheres of influence. As the next years unfold, our challenge will be to preserve and improve upon this Kantian vision and to resist those who would discard it, of whom Donald Trump is only the most visible.

Chapter 1

Trump's "Strategy" and the Counterstrategy of Resistance

A. TRUMP'S "STRATEGY"

Does Donald Trump have a visible strategy toward globalism? We now know that this mercurial president acts based not so much on strategy as on instinct and impulse. But make no mistake, those instincts and impulses point in the same general direction: Wherever possible, disengage from globalism. Undermine international institutions and resign from global leadership. Reverse what Barack Obama did and what a President Hillary Clinton would have done. When in doubt, adopt an isolationist "hard power" posture. And if challenged, defend the president's legal right to act with extreme claims of presidential power that demand broad deference from Congress, the courts, our allies, media, and nongovernmental organizations.

Trump's means to achieving these ends have become equally predictable. Make radical shifts with little or no notice. "Flood the zone" with relentless initiatives so that the world quickly forgets yesterday's surprise because of this morning's tweet. When confounding a settled wisdom, call the truth itself into question by challenging media reports as "fake news" and denigrating settled knowledge, especially scientific expertise. Diminish diplomacy as

The Trump Administration and International Law. Harold Hongju Koh.
© Oxford University Press 2019. Published 2019 by Oxford University Press.

a soft-power tool by demoralizing and gutting the career bureaucracy. And cloak discriminatory actions in the veil of presidential power and "national security process," which his underlings advise us "will not be challenged."[1]

Still, we must acknowledge an inner logic underlying Trump's rhetoric that viscerally touches real and deep American fears. In Trump's worldview, the rush to globalization has left the American working class behind, particularly those who believe their jobs have been taken by immigrants. The United States has lost competitiveness vis-à-vis other countries, in what he perceives to be a zero-sum game. Because the United States has enough trouble dealing with its own problems, he contends, it should not needlessly waste energy judging or solving the problems of others. In his view, the United States now bears too much of the burden of international leadership, which should instead be shared or offloaded. To respond to Trump's approach, any successful counterstrategy must not only respond to his immediate means and ends but also address these deeper populist currents into which he has plainly tapped. It is to that counterstrategy that I now turn.

B. TRANSNATIONAL LEGAL PROCESS

This book argues that notwithstanding its resonance in some quarters, Trump's strategy—systematic disengagement from nearly all institutions of global governance—is failing to achieve its desired goals. The reason is *transnational legal process*. International law is no longer just for nation-states or national governments. What Jeremy Bentham once called "inter-national law"—the law between and among sovereign nations—has evolved into a hybrid body of international and domestic law developed by a large number of public and private transnational actors. These sovereign and nonsovereign actors include our allies; states, municipalities, and localities of the United States; government bureaucracies; the media; courts; nongovernmental organizations (NGOs); intergovernmental organizations (IGOs); and committed individuals. I have argued that these many actors make and remake transnational law—the hybrid law that combines domestic and international, public and private law—by generating *interactions* that lead to *interpretations* of international law that become *internalized* into, and thereby binding under, domestic law (in this case, United States law). These internalized rules create default patterns of international law-observant behavior for all participants in the process. Those default patterns become routinized and "sticky" and thus difficult to deviate from without sustained effort.

The central insight of this analysis is that most compliance with law—including international law—comes not from coercion but from *patterns of obedience*.[2] Even all alone at 2 o'clock in the morning, most of us still stop for a red light. Why? Because most legal compliance does not owe to the fact that a police car is sitting behind you. The prime reason why law-abiding people do not regularly steal from each other is not because it is illegal, or because they fear detection, but because they have internalized a norm—probably learned from their parents, in school, or at places of worship—that ethical and law-abiding people do not steal. Internalized norms, not coercion, are the main drivers of legal obedience.[3] Most legal obedience, I would argue, comes from ✗ such norm internalization.

Norm internalization can come from many sources, the most prominent being religion, the paradigmatic internalized norm set. Once norms have been internalized by individuals and institutions, they become habits that, once learned, are not easily abandoned. Just as boats sail between riverbanks established by decades of flowing water, and new travelers almost invariably observe established traffic lanes, human and institutional behavior tends to follow default patterns set by internalized norms.

But neither are default habits immutable. With concerted effort, they can be changed. In my own lifetime, many people used to smoke regularly indoors, discard plastics in regular trash bins, and leave their seat belts unbuckled. But if as you read this, you are drinking from a plastic bottle, you have probably internalized a different habit, which is to throw recyclables into a recycling bin. Why? Because everywhere you go you encounter a sign, read a warning, see a recycle bin, are confronted by a friend or family member, or are forced to answer a challenge—all interactions that make clear that what you once did out of laziness or indifference no longer represents appropriate behavior. Most likely, you now recycle because a history of such interactions has encouraged you gradually to internalize a different normative interpretation. A period of socialization over time has now taught you to think it is *right* to recycle. A series of interactions has clarified a new norm of desirable behavior that you have come to accept as part of your internal value set. If most compliance comes from obedience, and most obedience comes from norm-internalization, then most norm-internalization comes from triggering such *interactions*, which lead to *interpretations*, which then lead to *internalizations*.

C. AN OUTSIDE–INSIDE COUNTERSTRATEGY

So how does this academic theory become political counterstrategy? If asked, "Do you believe in the power of transnational legal process?" I would answer—like my old teacher Abe Chayes's Southern Baptist minister—"Believe in it? I've seen it done!"

Throughout my career, I have seen this strategy applied repeatedly by players both inside and outside of the government. As a human rights lawyer, I tried to apply it myself from outside the government; as a government official, I tried to apply it from inside.

Nongovernmental actors traditionally apply the "outside strategy"—"interaction–interpretation–internalization"—to generate interactions that force interpretations that promote internalizations of international norms even by resisting governments. Lawsuits represent the paradigmatic example: if a government policy becomes illegal, an outside nongovernmental group can sue (generate an interaction) that yields a judicial ruling (an interpretation) that the government defendant must then obey as a matter of domestic law (norm-internalization).

The "inside strategy," which I applied during my decade as a government official, I call "engage–translate–leverage," or, simply, using international law as "smart power." In hindsight, call this "the Obama–Clinton doctrine." President Barack Obama tried to apply this foreign policy philosophy throughout his presidency. Upon taking office in 2009, Obama said that "[a] new era of engagement has begun," emphasizing that "living our values doesn't make us weaker. It makes us safer, and it makes us stronger."[4] That approach was urged upon him—and would have been continued had she become president—by Secretary of State Hillary Rodham Clinton, who argued: "We must use what has been called smart power, the full range of tools at our disposal—diplomatic, economic, military, political, legal, and cultural" to achieve better policy outcomes.[5]

A smart-power strategy means first that, given the choice, the United States—and other like-minded states—should choose engagement over unilateralism. When faced with a foreign policy problem, the United States should not proceed alone but rather seek to engage with other countries and adversaries around common values, in search of diplomatic solutions that can be embedded within durable international law principles.

Second, a strategy of "international law as smart power" suggests that wherever possible, the United States should choose a persuasive legal *translation* based on existing law over denying the applicability of law altogether. If a country faces an entirely new situation—for example, problems that simply did not exist when the international laws of war were first drafted, such as drone warfare or cyberconflict—a tempting, but wrong, approach would be simply to deny the applicability of law, i.e., to ask the "Tina Turner question": "What's law got to do with it? What's law but a sweet old-fashioned notion?" Since we now face a new technological situation, some might reason, we must be in a "law-free zone" where we can do whatever we want. Under this reasoning, there is no law to apply because we are in a "legal black hole," and thus may pursue whatever option power politics dictates that best serves our perceived self-interest.

But the wiser, smart-power alternative is for a government to apply what Montesquieu called the "spirit of the laws," or a "translation approach."[6] True, we may not always have a set of established legal rules that maps perfectly onto the new and unanticipated factual circumstance, but we can still make a good-faith effort to translate from the spirit of existing rules of law (e.g., the laws of war) to new situations (e.g., drones or cyberconflict).[7] As a policy matter, the translation approach is superior because law-abiding nations strive to act based not just on power or expedience but rather by cabining new activity within recognizable legal frameworks.

On reflection, there is a world of difference between these alternatives. Claiming that we face a "black-hole" situation—where there is no law to apply—is qualitatively different from acknowledging that existing rules do not exactly cover this new situation. In the former case, we are saying we can make up our own rules and no third party can judge us. But if we try in good faith to *translate* the spirit and intent of existing laws to govern new or unforeseen circumstances, we acknowledge the need to join with others committed to the rule of law to frame a new set of rules for emerging cases. In time, those new rules can eventually enjoy international consensus and legal legitimacy. So if a more "law-friendly" path exists, we should follow it. Doing so will keep the law on our side, keep us on the moral high ground, and preserve the vital support of our allies and international institutions as the crisis proceeds.[8]

[handwritten margin note: How long does this take? Possible research idea.]

The third element of the inside strategy is a commitment to *leveraging* international law as smart power to achieve sustainable policy solutions. This means blending legal arguments with other tools—including military force, diplomacy, development, technology, markets, and international institutions—to achieve complex foreign policy outcomes that cannot be achieved without the legitimacy that international law bestows: examples include the Dayton Peace Accord, the New START Treaty, or the Paris Climate Change Agreement.

Take, for example, the classic study *The Rise and Fall of the Great Powers* by my Yale colleague historian Paul Kennedy.[9] History teaches, Kennedy argued, that any great power that tries repeatedly to dominate the world with hard military or economic force will eventually find that force exhausted. Great powers tend to overexert their hard power and fall into a situation of "imperial overstretch," plagued by external debt, national weariness, and internal dissension. They try to do too much with too little, seeking to motivate the actions of others with tools of coercion rather than persuasion. But in the real world, most international cooperation comes not from coercion but from joint action motivated by shared values. As we have seen in recent years, even a global superpower like the United States possesses only a limited amount of hard power that can be overtaxed—for example, by simultaneous military campaigns in Iraq, Afghanistan, and Syria.

The more successful, durable approach, political scientist Joseph Nye argues, is for wise nations to seek to influence the world through "smart power"[10]—a combination of "hard" and "soft" power that gains legitimacy from espousing international law and common values. If a nation squanders its reputation for legitimacy, it devalues its greatest asset in exercising global leadership. That is why nations try to make and keep—not gratuitously break—international rules: because those rules hold together the fabric of our multilateral relationships with our allies, international organizations, and other standing institutions of international law.

Relate this to Verdier + voeten's Article on CIL

A moment's reflection tells us that the two transnational legal process strategies are complementary. The outsider's strategy of using "interaction–interpretation–norm internalization" to promote international legal compliance by resisting governments can be combined with the insider's strategy of "engage–translate–leverage" to embed and preserve respect for international law *within* U.S. governmental bureaucracies. Interaction promotes engagement; interpretation generates translations; and norm-internalization enables lawful options to be leveraged with other policy tools into more creative, nuanced, and durable policies. Thus, these two strategies working together—an outside strategy implemented by committed nongovernmental activists and an inside strategy pursued by governmental officials committed to the rule of law[11]—can lead a nation into a pattern of sustained default compliance with international law that makes quick deviation from these rules far more difficult than casual observers might predict.

D. THE EMERGING TRUMP PHILOSOPHY

What does all this have to do with a new, willful president arriving at the White House with a radical agenda to change how America engages with the world? In its first years, the Trump administration took a strikingly reactionary foreign policy approach. He renounced the approach taken not only by such Democratic presidents as Bill Clinton and Barack Obama, and former Democratic presidential candidates and Secretaries of State Hillary Clinton and John Kerry, but also by such past internationalist Republican presidents as George H.W. Bush and Richard Nixon.

Trump's antiglobalist philosophy broadly rejects the Obama-Clinton approach—"engage–translate–leverage"—in favor of "disengage–black hole–hard power." Wherever possible, Trump's instinct seems to be to disengage—unilateralism, or, as he calls it, "America First." The Trump approach does not value concerted efforts to translate existing legal rules but rather claims that there are no rules that bind our conduct. Under this worldview, the United States should act based on its perceived national interests, not international rules: an approach grounded on perceived *national rights*, not the universal rights on which this country was founded and that form the foundation of modern international human rights law. Finally, the emerging Trump approach seems to rest almost entirely on hard power, offering no visible strategy for bilateral and multilateral diplomacy or any attendant role for the State Department.[12] Trump and his team have shown little or no inclination to combine hard and soft power into a more nuanced approach nested in multilateral diplomacy that would allow America to leverage the legitimacy of lawful options into a creative set of proactive solutions to pressing international problems.

But as the chapters that follow will demonstrate, the various ways in which the Trump administration has announced its disengagement from global governance have thus far proven largely ineffective. This is precisely because the United States has become so deeply enmeshed with the laws, norms, and institutions of international law. In an increasingly integrated, globalized world, a nation-state can no more resign from the global system than an individual can resign from the human race. As Americans have learned since Trump's election—and the British have learned since their tumultuous June 2016 Brexit vote—like it or not, our societies are all deeply enmeshed in that globalized system, over which we exercise limited influence, even as it governs us.

To be sure, the United States of America—and its president in particular—are powerful players in the making and unmaking of international law. But upon inspection, the wide-ranging counterstrategy of damage control surveyed in the chapters that follow has spawned a de facto path of least resistance. Under that default, the United States under Trump rarely exits, but rather *stays in and underperforms* in existing international regimes. As Chapter 3 argues, the default outcome of Trump's blustering has tended to be "*resigning without leaving*": the United States remains within existing international institutions but with dramatically reduced influence. While that may be a suboptimal state of affairs, it has the virtue of being curable, at a future time when Trump no longer controls the two houses of Congress or has been supplanted by a more enlightened successor U.S. administration.

E. TRANSNATIONAL LEGAL PROCESS
   AS ROPE-A-DOPE

So will Donald trump international law, or vice versa? The theory above suggests that no player in the transnational legal process—not even the most powerful one—can single-handedly discard the rules that we have been following for some time. If players outside and inside the government enforce existing legal constraints in a way that makes policy changes and institutional exits too difficult or politically costly, a mercurial president like Donald Trump may decide to just "move on"—i.e., claim that he has "checked the box" on a political promise, in order to shift focus to other issues that he and his political base care about more, such as health care repeal or infrastructure reform.

If all of this seems too academic, recall "rope-a-dope," the famous counterstrategy developed by our greatest pugilistic strategist, Muhammad Ali. Faced in Zaire by George Foreman—a much younger, stronger, seemingly invincible champion—Ali settled upon a brilliantly simple counterstrategy. He surprised everyone by retreating to the ropes and letting the champion pound him, taking pains only to avoid getting knocked out himself. For many rounds, Ali let his opponent "punch himself out," until, at the end, Ali finally came off the ropes and knocked out his now-exhausted and weakened opponent.

The analogy here should be clear. If the Trump administration threatens to violate international law, actors outside the federal government can apply the external strategy of "interaction–interpretation–internalization" to hold it accountable. Those opposing President Trump's policy initiatives on legal grounds can deploy the outside strategy in the various fora available to them to resist those initiatives. By so doing, they force Trump to punch himself out by expending energy and capital on initiatives that do not meaningfully advance his or his party's interests or chances at re-election. Meanwhile, U.S. bureaucrats committed to international rules can continue to pursue the inside strategy of engage–translate–leverage to maintain default compliance with existing norms, unless explicitly directed to do otherwise. Outside activists can work with other players who are checking the White House to generate interactions via direct democracy, citizen mobilization, litigation, advocacy, and resistance. If the federal government fails to follow international law, states and localities—as both outsiders and insiders—can step up to help fill the gap.

This doesn't follow as directly

This struggle will continue until one side or another gets exhausted. But make no mistake: those in today's New American Resistance are making much the same strategic bet as Ali made in Zaire: that over time, the energetic aggressor who loudly launches multiple ineffectual initiatives to change the status quo will force little real change. *The winning counterstrategy may be simply to resist, absorb punishment, parry where possible, and strategically counterpunch* until Trump and his administration finally get so tired, exhausted, and frustrated from all the flailing around, that they find themselves getting politically "knocked out": by the Special Counsel, by congressional investigations, by the 2018 midterm elections, or the 2020 presidential re-election bid.

Admittedly, in the game of "rope-a-dope," both sides pay a fearful price. Even while the nominal winner—Ali, in the Zaire fight—may win the fight, in the process he may endure the kind of battering that weakens his fabric and leaves him unglued in the long run. The parallel, broader danger is that Trump's relentless disdain for international law may undo the "stickiness" of our standing rules and institutions by "ungluing" the elements of administrative and transnational governance that maintain obedience to international rules. Especially when understood as part and parcel of Brexit and the global resurgence of Orwellian authoritarianism—discussed in Chapter 6—Trump may prove less a cause than a symptom of a much broader global counterassault on the postwar Kantian order. Left unchecked, that counterassault is arguably spreading a wave of global authoritarianism that could potentially generate a transnational transference of lawlessness flowing through the very same channels of transnational legal process that foster compliance.

check this chp.

While these are real and serious concerns, as yet, I hope they are premature. In the pages that follow, I argue that so far, transnational legal process *is* working, but harder times lie ahead. If Trump's stated goal is to unglue the reflex to coordinate domestic and international legal processes, our counterstrategy should be to *strengthen* that connection. Trump's anti-globalist rhetoric may seek to sever the link between the domestic and the international. But in a modern age of globalization, the interactive link between domestic and global law can be no more easily severed than the link between local cause and global effect. Transnational legal process enmeshes us all. That process is much bigger than Trump. He does not and cannot own it, because we all do.

F. INTERTWINED CONSTRAINTS: LAW, POLICY, AND POLITICS

Some might read the case studies that follow as too loosely mixing international and domestic law, and law, policy, and politics in discussing the constraints that impede impetuous presidential change. But one of my core claims is that these strands of constraint are inherently intertwined. When discussing the impact of transnational legal process on government behavior, it is both un-realistic and counterproductive artificially to split off legal from policy and political constraints. In real life, these three kinds of constraints invariably overlap and are often used in combination to check action destructive of legal stability.

Although international lawyers tend to say, "let's carefully dis-tinguish between law and policy," in reality, it is rarely so clear-cut. Law, policy, and politics pose interconnected constraints in foreign affairs decision making. Some policy options may not be available as a matter of law. Some options—which government lawyers tend to call "lawful, but awful"—may be legal, but not prove wise as a matter of policy. Still other options might seem desirable as a matter of both law and policy, but when actually tried, prove just not to be politically available. As they famously say in the Broadway musical *Hamilton*, sometimes "you don't have the votes."

Admittedly, law and policy differ as tools to promote the stickiness of internalized international norms. Executive branch policies usually do not bind future administrations as powerfully as do executive branch determinations about the applicability of international legal rules. Yet one reason not to obsess unduly over the distinction between law and policy is that often, norms ini-tially articulated as policy for political reasons affect legal rulings and over time themselves harden into law. Under Ronald Reagan, for example, the United States famously declined to ratify the 1982 U.N. Convention on the Law of the Sea, but recognized much of it as governing U.S. practice and eventually as customary international law. The same could be said for the United States' slow embrace of the Universal Declaration of Human Rights or the Vienna Convention on the Law of Treaties, both of which it now treats as customary international law.

As the case studies that follow show, the very process of turning politics into policy and then into soft and hard law lies at the very core of transnational legal process. As I have described elsewhere, the goal of transnational legal process is to internalize norms socially, politically, and legally, but the precise sequence in which these internalizations occur will differ from case to case.[13] This sequencing is perhaps best illustrated by the case of the Travel Ban, to which I now turn.

Chapter 2

The Counterstrategy Illustrated: Transnational Legal Process in Action

The "rope-a-dope" counterstrategy outlined above is not hypothetical. Rather, it describes the broader counterstrategy of "transnational legal process" that we have witnessed playing out across the broad spectrum of U.S. foreign policy during the first years of Donald Trump's presidency. At the risk of trying to describe a landscape from a moving train, the next four chapters illustrate this rope-a-dope in action, by discussing many interactions over a broad array of issue areas. The two case studies described in this chapter illustrate both the outside and the inside strategies at work.

Donald Trump was inaugurated as president on January 20, 2017. The next day, millions marched in protest at Women's Marches in cities around the world, chanting, "This is what democracy looks like." Then came the executive orders, starting with the Travel Ban.

The Trump Administration and International Law. Harold Hongju Koh.
© Oxford University Press 2019. Published 2019 by Oxford University Press.

A. IMMIGRATION AND REFUGEES

Perhaps the most visible face of the Trump administration's international policies has been its harsh stance on immigration, including three successive Travel Bans; an order seeking to strip all federal funding from so-called sanctuary cities;[1] and strict border controls, as illustrated by repeated calls for a Wall (allegedly to be paid for by Mexico, but in fact calling for billions of U.S. taxpayer expenses). The administration ended temporary protected status (TPS) for sixty thousand Hondurans, forty-six thousand Haitians, twenty-five hundred Nicaraguans, and two hundred thousand Salvadorans. Trump's team declared its hostility toward refugees, the courts, and "chain migration"; announced plans to cut legal immigration in half with "skills-based immigration" that would eliminate the visa lottery[2]; and unveiled an aggressively maximalist penchant for deportation, even of "Dreamers."[3] At the international level, citing concerns about U.S. sovereignty, the administration ended participation in the Global Compact on Migration. Perhaps its most revealing tactic was its adoption of "shock-and-awe" raids in schools, businesses, and homes, including a strikingly heartless policy (discussed in the Afterword) of separating migrant parents from their children, in an effort to encourage "self-deportation." Most glaring, in April 2017 and 2018, Trump demonstrated a dissonant willingness to drop bombs out of professed sympathy for the very same Syrian children that his administration has refused to admit into the United States.

On January 27, 2017, President Trump signed his most visible executive order. For ninety days, his Travel Ban 1.0 blocked entry into the United States by citizens of seven predominantly Muslim countries (adjusted in March to six and in September to six majority-Muslim countries plus North Korea and Venezuela).

The Ban initially barred individuals with valid visas and green cards from those countries from re-entering the United States.[4] For 120 days, the Ban suspended entry of all refugees into the United States, and for an indefinite period of time barred all Syrian refugees. This Travel Ban amounted to a thinly disguised Muslim Ban, not least because on the campaign trail, candidate Trump had repeatedly promised to impose just such a measure.[5]

On its face, such a policy seemed blatantly illegal. First, under international law, such a ban facially violates two treaties to which the United States has long been a party: the Refugee Convention,[6] which requires that "[t]he Contracting States shall apply the provisions of this Convention to refugees without discrimination as to race, religion or country of origin," as well as the International Covenant on Civil and Political Rights, which states that "[a]ll persons are equal before the law and are entitled without any discrimination to the equal protection of the law."[7] Second, these norms have been internalized into the domestic law of the United States, a country founded on religious freedom. Even a sanitized Muslim Ban discriminates against one religion for the benefit of others, in violation of the First Amendment's Establishment Clause. Such a broad ban has never been authorized by statute; to the contrary, key immigration laws expressly forbid exclusion based on national origin. Third, as a matter of policy, the Ban was both over- and underinclusive. While none of the countries from which people were excluded had ever actually produced a terrorist who had killed anyone on U.S. soil, other countries that had (e.g., Saudi Arabia, from which most of the 9/11 attackers hailed) were not on the list.[8]

Fourth, the president had repeatedly called for "extreme vetting." What he seemed not to appreciate is that the United States *already had* a system of extreme vetting, conducted on an intensive, individualized basis. Far from being ineffective, that system has been working, as demonstrated by the fact that no individual vetted through the rigorous system regulating the entry of refugees has committed a fatal terrorist act inside the United States for more than forty years.[9] The new administration proposed instead to replace individualized vetting with categorical exclusions based on national and religious stereotypes. But under the Constitution, group-based exclusions are illegal when based on such crude categorizations. Such stereotyping offends a basic American article of faith: that people are judged not by where they are from, or by the color of their skin, or by whom they worship, but by the content of their individual character. As I learned in government from many sad hours of studying terrorist profiles, some proven terrorists fit no group stereotype, while other individuals who may fit some stereotype could prove upon closer examination to be gold-star fathers of heroic American soldiers.

Fifth, the Travel Ban emerged from a grossly defective and arbitrary governmental process. As it was rushed into operation, the executive order was not vetted by knowledgeable governmental lawyers, the incoming secretaries in the Departments of Defense and Homeland Security, or most of the key legislators who oversee counterintelligence and homeland security issues.[10] Sixth, and most glaringly, the sudden, overbroad Travel Ban responded to no new national security threat, a fact that I confirmed with a number of former government colleagues who had served in the most sensitive national security positions until Inauguration Day, January 20, 2017. They all agreed that they knew of no new security threat—and the new administration had identified none—that warranted shifting so abruptly toward an overtly discriminatory policy only seven days later.

As transnational legal process kicked in, the Ban came under swift and furious legal challenge. An Iraqi interpreter who had worked with and supported U.S. forces in Iraq was one of the first people stopped pursuant to the Ban, at John F. Kennedy Airport. His counsel, a Yale Law School immigration clinic supervised by my colleague Michael Wishnie, provoked an interaction that led to a legal interpretation: they successfully filed for a temporary restraining order in the U.S. District Court for the Eastern District of New York, then asked the new Rule of Law Clinic that I had just organized at Yale to develop a factual declaration on behalf of former national security officials. We found a large number of former national security officials of both political parties ready to swear in court that the Travel Ban bore no rational relation to any compelling governmental interest.[11]

As the actions broadened to include a suit brought by the state of Washington in Washington federal court, our Yale Law School Rule of Law Clinic filed first a joint declaration and then an amicus brief on behalf of ten former national security officials: former Secretaries of State Madeleine Albright and John Kerry, former Secretary of Defense Leon Panetta, former Secretary of Homeland Security Janet Napolitano, four former heads of the CIA (including two Republicans, Michael Hayden and John McLaughlin), and the most recent national security adviser and her two deputies (Susan Rice, Avril Haines, and Lisa Monaco). A number of these amici were still serving in the U.S. government just one week before this order issued and swore that they saw no emergent national security threat that justified the sudden policy change. Our filings confirmed that the Travel Ban would likely harm our counterterrorism and law enforcement efforts, because it was based not on any known national security threat but rather on illegal stereotypes and prejudice.

This outside pressure soon combined with internal resistance. The initial ban had been imposed virtually without State Department input. When it was publicly announced, a thousand career State Department officials swiftly signed a dissent channel cable that said: "this ban stands in opposition to the core American and constitutional values that we, as federal employees, took an oath to uphold;" the cable declared: "we are better than this ban."[12] Remarkably, it then became evident that the White House had announced the Ban without actually knowing whether the Justice Department was prepared to defend it in court. When ordered to do so, Acting Attorney General Sally Yates refused, for which she was fired and accused by the president of having "betrayed the Department of Justice."[13] In short order, more than thirty cases were filed before the First, Second, Fourth, and Ninth Circuits. As the legal battles progressed, the intelligence community and other parts of the bureaucracy apparently engaged in unprecedented leaking, providing more factual grist for the lawsuits.[14] As the cases unfolded, despite the president's usual advantage in immigration litigation regarding entry, court after court blocked the executive order. Finally, the administration simply retracted Travel Ban 1.0, stating its intent to review and re-release the Ban in due course.

In the meantime, other players in the transnational legal process joined the fray. Such allies as Germany's Angela Merkel, Canada's Justin Trudeau, Britain's Theresa May, France's Emmanuel Macron, Australia's Malcolm Turnbull, and many other members of the G-20 all raised the issue directly in early conversations with the new president.[15] Pressed by such groups as Veterans for American Ideals,[16] U.S. military service members protested, particularly when it became clear that our Iraqi military allies were being barred from entry. One of the commanding generals of the Iraqi forces, Talib al Kenani, marveled, "I'm a four star general, and I'm banned from entering the U.S.?" Eventually such political pressure led to Iraq being removed from the list.[17]

Domestic actors came forward. Democratic members of Congress—joined by such Republican legislators as Senators John McCain, Lindsey Graham, Bob Corker, Marco Rubio, and Tim Scott, as well as House Homeland Security Chair Mike McCaul and Representative Charlie Dent—all criticized the order.[18] Unexpected Republican voices—including such unlikely names as the Koch brothers, former Vice President Dick Cheney, and former Justice Department lawyer John Yoo—all opposed the Ban, suggesting that the decision had driven a wedge between Trump and his traditional conservative allies.[19] Fifteen state attorneys general protested not just the Travel Ban but also Trump's plan to build the Wall, to renew deportations, and to punish sanctuary cities.[20] Dozens of cities and counties filed an amicus brief supporting the individual and subnational plaintiffs.[21] Forty-seven universities, including my home university, Yale, spoke out against the Ban,[22] and 163 tech companies filed an amicus brief protesting how the Travel Ban would affect their workers.[23]

Within hours, the resistance had spread beyond the courts to the streets. Because the initial lawsuit filed by Yale's immigration clinic took the unusual form of a habeas class action, every immigrant class member blocked at the airport could say they were entitled to a writ of habeas corpus procured by their own lawyer. Armed by the Internet, more than four thousand volunteer lawyers across America rushed to their nearest international airport, showing officials court orders that they had downloaded to their cellphones and iPads and filing habeas petitions based on legal templates that our students had uploaded to the world wide web.[24] As taxi, Uber, and Lyft drivers delivered lawyers to the airports, they became new centers of protest, with spontaneous demonstrations erupting at dozens of airports only one week after the widespread demonstrations in the city streets.

Acts of solidarity broke out all across America, including individual protests, group marches, and community candlelight vigils. Popular culture joined in: the Museum of Modern Art and its exhibits displayed art by individuals from the excluded countries; *Saturday Night Live* and late-night comedians attacked the Ban; traditional and social media highlighted the human impact of the Ban's separation of families; and stories were virally shared on Facebook, Twitter, Snapchat, and other social media outlets. Even Super Bowl commercials told sympathetic stories about immigrants who had come to America to make good.[25] Interest groups took turns staging major demonstrations, including a Climate March, a March for Science, a Day Without Immigrants (when New York diners could not get a meal in less than three hours), and a Day Without Women (when little got done anywhere).

By March 2017, the president had issued a revised Travel Ban 2.0,[26] which maintained the original Ban's basic features. Our Rule of Law Clinic converted our initial national security declaration into an amicus brief—now signed by fifty former officials—that would eventually be filed at the Supreme Court. Our argument was simple: "It doesn't matter how much lipstick you put on that pig; it's still a pig." A Muslim Ban, however packaged, is still a Muslim Ban. We argued that the revised order was "ill-conceived, poorly implemented and ill-explained."[27] We again pointed out that there was no national security justification for this sudden change of policy, which attacked humanitarian values while threatening U.S. jobs.[28] The revised Ban would endanger our troops in the field, jeopardize counterterrorism partnerships and domestic law enforcement, and enrage the very Muslim-American communities whose help the U.S. government needed in order to find radicalized individuals who might commit terrorist attacks within the United States. Even if one's goal were extreme vetting, the existing individualized system was plainly better at vetting than an undifferentiated group Ban.

Even before Travel Ban 2.0 went into effect, it was again blocked by district courts in the Fourth and Ninth Circuits.[29] In the first skirmish before the Supreme Court over a stay of the Ninth Circuit's injunction, Chief Justice Roberts and Justice Kennedy joined the liberal justices—Breyer, Ginsburg, Sotomayor, and Kagan—in a Solomonic *per curiam* opinion from which Justices Thomas and Alito, and new Justice Neil Gorsuch, vociferously dissented.[30] Initially, the merits of the case were scheduled to be argued before the Supreme Court in October 2017. But just weeks before that argument, the administration issued yet a third version of its Ban (3.0), dropping one country (Sudan) from the list while adding several others. This caused the Court to strike the case from its October 2017 argument calendar.[31]

On its face, Travel Ban 3.0 suffered from the vice of original sin. It followed the same template as the prior two bans, continuing the same overbroad, blanket approach that the lower courts had previously enjoined, and was still visibly based more on national stereotypes than on intense individualized vetting. The revision's tweaks seemed designed mainly to lessen the impression that the Ban was targeting Muslim-majority countries. Chad, a predominantly Muslim country, was later dropped after its inclusion clearly harmed an important counterterrorism partnership. The third ban added North Korea, although only a tiny number of North Koreans enter the United States every year, most of them refugees. And a few Venezuelan officials were targeted for sanctions, although apparently not because of any identifiable terrorist activity.[32] The abrupt change led the Supreme Court to declare both circuit court judgments vacated and moot.[33]

Yet within days, district courts in both the Fourth and Ninth Circuits again enjoined Travel Ban 3.0, and the appellate courts affirmed that ruling. The Supreme Court again granted review, setting the case for argument in April 2018.

When Travel Ban 3.0 finally reached the Supreme Court on the merits, the government's core defense had become "national security process." The solicitor general argued that Travel Ban 3.0 had resulted from a worldwide multi-agency review that had recommended entry restrictions only on countries that had failed to provide enough information for their nationals to be vetted.

But in fact, the record made clear that the Trump Administration had produced a ban in search of, rather than in response to, a bona fide national security threat. Prior immigration bans based on national security policies had: (1) responded to specific, credible threats based on individualized information, (2) rested on the best available intelligence, and (3) been subject to thorough interagency review. The three sweeping Travel Bans rested not on such carefully tailored grounds, but were instead: (1) overbroad, blanket entry bans based on national origin that were (2) not supported by any intelligence cited by the government and that (3) had been issued in the absence of careful interagency policy and legal review by national security and foreign policy officials. Although the government sought the kind of traditional judicial "deference owed to the Executive's foreign-policy and national-security judgments," in fact, the executive's national security and foreign policy experts played little or no role at all in the development of the first travel ban. The second and third iterations of that ban then mirrored the first so closely in form and substance that any additional "national security process" could hardly dispel this original sin. Having so visibly failed to consult governmental expertise when putting the initial ban together, Trump could not credibly claim a compelling need for judicial deference to that expertise as the prime reason to sustain the ban.

In fact, overwhelming evidence demonstrated that the proclamation's overbroad suspension of travel not only had failed to advance our national security or foreign policy interests but had seriously damaged those interests. Remarkably, in the fifteen months during which the litigation raged, the government could not produce a single sworn declaration from an executive official willing to defend either the national security–based need for the orders or the truncated "national security process" that led to their adoption. The question thus starkly posed was whether—as *Marbury v. Madison* put it—it was "the province and duty of the judicial department to say what the law is" or to act as the government's national security rubber stamp.[34] In its final form, the case pointedly asked whether the government could shield Travel Ban 3.0 from meaningful judicial review by cloaking discrimination in a thin veil of "national security."

As the Afterword details, in June 2018, the Supreme Court issued a grievously wrong 5–4 decision declining to preliminarily enjoin the Travel Ban 3.0. But transnational legal process will continue. Although the Supreme Court declined to invalidate the Ban on its face, the lower courts—which were almost universally hostile to the ban—could still find it discriminatory as applied. The *Trump* court found that U.S. persons had standing to challenge the ban, that the core issues were effectively justiciable, and remanded to the lower courts so the litigation can proceed while the Ban operates. Many plaintiffs, including lawful permanent residents, asylum seekers, refugees, students, and children can now be expected to press Travel Ban 3.0's elaborate system of exemptions and waivers in an effort to test whether that program is real. If waivers are granted, the discriminatory impact of the ban will be mitigated;

if they are broadly denied, the discriminatory nature of the ban will be reaffirmed and could be the basis for a permanent injunction.

Other transnational actors will invoke transnational legal process to contest and limit the impact of the court's ruling. As they did after losing the Haitian interdiction case at the Supreme Court a quarter century ago, litigants will surely seek out international fora to make arguments against the travel ban based on international law.[35] European countries will need to think hard about whether giving assistance in implementing the ban through air travel to the United States runs up against their international law responsibilities to respect religious freedom. Universities and corporations that prominently challenged the ban may choose technical workarounds that allow remote employment and enrollment from within countries hostile to the ban. Should Congress change hands in November 2018, the Court's ruling, which rested on statutory grounds, could be legislatively overruled. A new Congress could enact legislation defining and expanding how the exemptions and waivers are to be implemented, or simply bar the Department of Homeland Security from using any funding to implement the travel ban. Or, Congress could explicitly modify the immigration law to proscribe the executive from issuing nationality-based bans on immigration. If only the House changes hands, it could enact bills to which a narrowly divided Senate would be forced to react. And if the ban persists until 2021, a new president could undo it with the stroke of a pen.

Beneath it all, the question lingers: how much does Donald Trump really care about the Muslim Ban? Even if the Court ends up sustaining Travel Ban 3.0, hasn't he already spent too much capital on a counterproductive policy that he does not really need, and that has needlessly alienated many who otherwise might have been willing to work with him? The Battle of the Ban has cost Trump dearly. It has alienated him from his bureaucracy, stamped

Read source material on Haitian Interdiction case [handwritten margin note]

his administration as xenophobic, and driven a wedge between his fragile coalition of Trumpites and traditional Republicans. Every piece of capital he has spent on this issue has weakened his hand on other immigration issues, including Deferred Action for Childhood Arrivals (DACA) reform, and diverted energy from the core agenda that actually interests his coalition: Obamacare repeal (which has repeatedly failed), jobs, regulatory rollback, and infrastructure reform.

The point is that the Supreme Court's ruling is only the beginning, not the end, of the Travel Ban story. The bruising "Battle of the Ban" has only galvanized Trump's legal opposition and hardened and educated the Resistance. In the process, it has helped to shrink Trump's coalition to its base, leaving precious little capital to support his core issues.

B. HUMAN RIGHTS

During my adult life, as a law professor, Legal Adviser, and Assistant Secretary of State for Democracy, Human Rights, and Labor, I have heard every American secretary of state—Democratic or Republican—speak out in support of human rights.[36] But when asked about human rights in other countries, Trump's first secretary of state, Rex Tillerson, repeatedly said at his confirmation hearing that he was "not ready to judge."[37] But how can any responsible U.S. official not be ready to judge, for example, whether innocent people in the Philippines can be summarily executed by their authoritarian president, Rodrigo Duterte?[38] Secretary Tillerson also announced his intention to support American interests, but not American values. He stated, remarkably, that an overreliance on values "creates obstacles to our ability to advance our national security interests [and] our economic interests."[39] By so saying, he reaffirmed Trump's prioritizing of national over universal rights and overlooked decades

Get a copy of this speech

of bipartisan U.S. policy repeatedly confirming that advancing global human rights values is in fact a core American interest.[40]

Since then, the administration has plainly lost sight of the many ways in which the United States has traditionally relied on alliances and cooperation with our rights-respecting democratic allies to help advance our broader national security interests.[41] In his short, ineffective period as secretary of state, Tillerson declined to appear at the announcement of the State Department's annual Human Rights Report.[42] The new administration refused to engage with respect to human rights or to speak out in support of universal human rights values in diplomacy with North Korea, China, Russia, Saudi Arabia, and Turkey. U.N. Ambassador Nikki Haley called the U.N. Human Rights Council "corrupt," and in June 2018, the administration announced that the United States would withdraw from that body.[43] The United States no longer appears to defend its conduct at the Inter-American Human Rights Commission. And there has been a blatant, disturbing softness on human rights in the Middle East, particularly with respect to Saudi Arabia, Egypt, Bahrain, and Turkey, where President Trump congratulated President Erdoğan even after visibly irregular elections and an attack by Turkish guards on demonstrators outside the Turkish embassy in Washington, D.C. Most recently, it has even been reported that the State Department plans to drop altogether the promotion of democracy and human rights from its mission statement.[44]

Perhaps the most visible proposed human rights rollback was candidate Trump's statement that "[if I am elected, w]e'll use waterboarding and a hell of a lot worse than waterboarding."[45] Shortly after the election, the press leaked a draft national security executive order that called for reinstating the discredited program of interrogation of high-value alien terrorists, to be operated outside the United States, presumably at revived "black sites"— former offshore detention facilities operated by the C.I.A.[46]

Campaign statements and draft executive orders are not law. Congress has repeatedly forbidden torture by treaty and statute.[47] Those laws include an anti-torture treaty, the Geneva Conventions,[48] and the Uniform Code of Military Justice (UCMJ).[49] As Judge Henry Floyd of the Fourth Circuit recently noted, "While executive officers can declare the military reasonableness of conduct amounting to torture, it is beyond the power of even the president to declare such conduct lawful."[50] Nor does it matter that Al Qaeda and the Islamic State (IS) have not signed the Torture Convention or the Geneva Conventions. The United States is bound to foreswear torture because the treaty specifies a minimal standard of humane treatment that America must unilaterally obey, whether or not the terrorists have agreed.[51]

Ironically, what has ended up nullifying Trump's own rhetoric is his penchant for appointing to civilian national security positions former generals who have internalized these principles forbidding torture. All U.S. military officers take an oath to obey not any particular president but rather the Constitution and laws of the United States of America. American soldiers are trained to follow the Geneva Conventions and learn to internalize the norms against torture. The U.S. military has long recognized that enforcing a norm against torture as a universal right serves its national interests, by protecting its own citizens and soldiers when they are captured. The norm of humane treatment to which Americans have committed themselves binds the country, as a defining element of its national identity, whether others agree to follow it or not. For that reason, Senator John McCain declared that Trump's campaign statements "must not go unanswered because they mislead the American people about the realities of interrogation, how to gather intelligence, what it takes to defend our security, and, at the most fundamental level, what we are fighting for as a nation."[52]

In 2013, upon leaving the State Department, I left behind a memo explaining why it is "*not legally available* to policymakers to claim" that the Convention Against Torture does not apply outside the United States.[53] In 2015, the Obama administration made this point explicit in its presentation before the Committee Against Torture in Geneva, stating that the torture ban applies "in all places, at all times, with no exceptions."[54] And the Counterterrorism Frameworks Report that the Obama administration issued during its last days in office stated that "[t]orture and cruel, inhuman, or degrading treatment or punishment (CIDTP) are categorically prohibited under domestic and international law, including international human rights law and the law of armed conflict. These prohibitions exist everywhere and at all times."[55]

In his farewell counterterrorism speech, President Obama declared these mandates without qualification: "We prohibited torture, everywhere, at all times—and that includes tactics like waterboarding."[56] These prohibitions reflected a simple scientific fact: that at a cellular level, each and every tactic used in torture for the purpose of extracting information—sleep deprivation, temperature change, waterboarding, food restriction—inhibits, rather than improves, memory, confession, and truth-telling.[57] What renders torture particularly pointless is that it simply does not work for its own intended purposes, so much so that these should be called *impaired*, not "enhanced," interrogation tactics.[58] As President Obama explained during his campaign, "[t]orture is how you create enemies, not how you defeat them. . . . how you get bad information, not good intelligence. Torture is how you set back America's standing in the world, not how you strengthen it."[59]

These and other arguments were made in public and private letters from dozens of former military leaders to all of President Trump's key senior national security officials—many of them themselves former military. In the end, in an array of statements made around the time of their appointments, all of those officials publicly pledged *not* to follow an order to torture anyone.[60] In their confirmation hearings, General James Mattis, now secretary of defense; Chief of Staff John Kelly, formerly secretary of Homeland Security; Mike Pompeo, formerly CIA Director and now secretary of state; and Jeff Sessions, attorney general, all said that they would not follow an order to torture.[61] And when the torture issue revived again with a fury during the CIA Director confirmation hearings of Gina Haspel—who had presided over a black site and helped supervise destruction of waterboarding tapes—she said under oath that she did "not believe that torture works." In exchange for her eventual confirmation, she offered her "personal commitment, clearly and without reservation, that under my leadership, C.I.A. will not restart such a detention and interrogation program."[62]

In the end, even a willful president cannot implement a command that his subordinates will not obey. So despite Trump's rhetoric, the draft torture order was never issued or enacted into law, and his subordinates are bound by law not to execute a torture order. What all this shows is that, once internalized, the anti-torture norm is not so easily ousted. And by refusing to execute illegal orders, career military play perhaps their most critical role: maintaining fidelity to the rule of law to promote longer-term societal stability, even while they accept a new administration's political direction.

In short, established normative patterns do not swiftly change just because political power has changed hands. Taken together, the battlefields of immigration and torture, respectively, show how the outside strategy of litigation and the inside strategy of bureaucratic resistance to norm change work and interact.

But how much confidence can we have in this? Given that for a number of years we did torture?

Chapter 3

Resigning Without Leaving

A. CLIMATE CHANGE

Donald Trump's rhetoric has thus far met a similar fate in the realm of climate change. In a June 2017 Rose Garden ceremony, the administration announced with great fanfare its "intent to withdraw" from the 2015 Paris Agreement on Climate Change, the landmark treaty establishing national reduction targets for greenhouse gas emissions for all member states. The Paris Deal was negotiated under the auspices of the U.N. Framework Convention on Climate Change (UNFCCC), a treaty with 196 state parties to which the Senate gave its advice and consent in 1992.

The evolution of the Paris Deal graphically illustrated the engage–translate–leverage framework applied by the Obama–Clinton approach to international law as smart power. Led by Special Climate Envoy Todd Stern, the Obama administration did not withdraw—as the George W. Bush administration previously had done from the 1997 Kyoto Protocol—but rather *engaged* repeatedly with countries around the world to frame the global deal. The Obama administration engaged at the annual Conference of Parties meetings in Copenhagen, Cancun, Durban and Paris with the G-20; with the countries of the Major Economies Forum and BASIC (Brazil, South Africa, India, and China), especially China; and in scores of other bilateral meetings with countries large and small. Instead of treating

The Trump Administration and International Law. Harold Hongju Koh.
© Oxford University Press 2019. Published 2019 by Oxford University Press.

climate change as an area without law, the United States *translated* from norms inchoate in the rigid, legally binding, top-down Kyoto architecture. But the Copenhagen approach declined to specify internationally negotiated emissions targets that applied only to developed countries, instead following a much more informal, politically binding, bottom-up blueprint infused with stronger norms and with greater symmetry between the duties of developed and developing nations. This intense, creative diplomacy allowed the Obama administration to *leverage* these principles into an innovative architectural design that required a "double trigger" acceptance by at least fifty-five parties of the UNFCCC, accounting for at least 55 percent of greenhouse gas emissions. In short order, those accessions led to the Paris Agreement, which entered into force with more than one hundred fifty parties on November 4, 2016, just four days before the election of Donald Trump.

Trump's 2017 announcement of his "intent" for the United States to "withdraw" from the Paris Agreement was again driven by a philosophy of "disengage–black hole–hard power." But his rhetoric launched little meaningful legal action—for the simple reason that his announcement did not *legally* disengage. International law makes clear that U.S. presidents cannot simply delete prior signatures from treaties. President George W. Bush had earlier demonstrated the futility of announcing a withdrawal under terms not designated by an international agreement when he tried to "unsign" the Rome Statute, which established the International Criminal Court. The "unsigning" letter the Bush administration sent to the United Nations—authored by current National Security Adviser John Bolton—had uncertain effect under customary international law, meaning that the U.S. signature remained on the Rome Statute, with arguably unchanged legal force. This allowed the United States to re-engage with the

Rome Statute parties when the Obama administration came into office.[1] The Paris Agreement recognizes withdrawal only under the terms specified in the Agreement's text, which plainly declare that a party cannot give notice of withdrawal to the U.N. Secretary General until "three years from the date on which this Agreement has entered into force."[2] Since the Paris Agreement entered into force on November 4, 2016, the earliest date that the United States could even give such legal notice would be November 4, 2019. That notification would then take another full year to take legal effect, meaning that Trump cannot legally withdraw the U.S. from the Agreement until November 4, 2020, the day *after* the next U.S. presidential election.

Until then, Trump's withdrawal announcement has no more legal meaning than one of his tweets. To be clear, the United States has not "virtually" or "preemptively withdrawn" or otherwise formally disengaged in any way as a party from the Paris Agreement. At this writing, the U.N. Treaty Depositary page on the Paris Agreement still lists the United States as a party.[3] While the State Department website indicates that it has notified the U.N. Depositary of its "intent to withdraw," a "media note" makes clear that the United States has done nothing more than communicate "the U.S. intent to withdraw from the Paris Agreement as soon as it is eligible to do so, *consistent with the terms of the Agreement*."[4] Far from having left, in the words of the coalition of Paris supporters, "We Are Still In."[5] Trump has resigned but has not left. But America's commitment to fighting climate change—unlike Trump's—is not so easily reversed. Under similar circumstances, the United States was in arrears of its United Nations dues for many years, but never quit its membership and eventually came back into compliance: a pattern that could equally be followed here.

As a legal matter, Trump's "withdrawal" announcement has no more legal force than an employee's empty threat to leave his job in three years' time. Trump initially claimed that he plans to "renegotiate" better terms, but the other 190 state parties have no incentive to renegotiate a weaker agreement with a flailing American administration that may already be voted out of office when the time comes to complete its withdrawal. In August 2017, Ambassador Haley informed the U.N. Secretary-General of the United States' intent "to exercise its right to withdraw from the Agreement [u]nless the United States identifies suitable terms for reengagement," whatever those words might mean.[6] In its August 2017 statement, the State Department further announced that the United States would continue to participate in the annual UNFCCC Conference of Party (COP) meetings, where, as a prospectively exiting party, the U.S. delegation's influence is now greatly diminished. If the United States continues to participate in the Paris process and remains a state party for the balance of Trump's first term, it has not meaningfully withdrawn; it has only reduced its own influence by identifying itself as a voluntary lame duck. So while President Trump proclaimed that his withdrawal announcement represented a reassertion of America's sovereignty, in reality, he has unilaterally surrendered influence over the agreement to China and the other BASIC countries, which have recently reaffirmed their Paris commitments and will continue to push the United States to keep its own.[7]

While Trump has committed an egregious self-inflicted wound by preemptively announcing his intent to withdraw from the Paris Agreement, for the next two years, there is little reason to treat his withdrawal announcement as either definitive or final. Since the announcement, the administration has sent confusing messages to U.S. allies as to whether it will actually follow through when the time comes.[8]

Meanwhile, bureaucratic stickiness and external litigation have slowed the domestic dismantling of America's Paris commitments. Many elements of the original Paris Agreement compliance plan have already been internalized into the federal administrative agenda by Obama's Quadrennial Energy Review and are not so easily ousted.[9] The Trump administration's March 2017 Climate Executive Order calls for reversing course on the Clean Power Plan (CPP), an agency rule that implements the U.S.'s Paris commitments through interstate cap-and-trade and by states building fewer coal-burning plants while creating greater capacity for renewable energy. The Environmental Protection Agency's (EPA) authority to implement the CPP was stayed 5–4 by the Supreme Court in 2016 (with the late Justice Scalia in the majority).[10] At this writing, the D.C. Circuit en banc is still deciding whether the EPA has the authority to implement the CPP.[11] Meanwhile, the court has pointedly reminded the government that the EPA has an "affirmative statutory obligation to regulate greenhouse gases."[12]

The EPA has issued a proposal to undo the CPP and consider a weaker replacement in line with the agency's revised reading of the Clean Air Act.[13] But because the EPA is still reviewing comments to its proposed reinterpretation of the Act,[14] all options remain on the table—including ultimately keeping the CPP in place. An overt effort by the Trump administration to discard the plan would undoubtedly trigger new fights about notice-and-comment rulemaking before the D.C. Circuit, which will rule on the legality of any new proposed agency action. In such litigation, environmental groups could well claim that the president has failed faithfully to execute continuing U.S. international legal obligations under the Paris Accords. In such a suit, any appeals to special "*Chevron* deference" to agency action by the courts would be compromised by the fact that the very same agency, under different presidents, has now offered competing interpretations of the exact same Clean Air Act provisions.

Domestic litigation has also pushed back against the Trump administration's other attempted rulemaking changes. When Trump's EPA proposed relaxing the Obama administration's fuel economy standards, seventeen states and the District of Columbia quickly sued to block the rollback.[15] Regardless of the outcome of this lawsuit, Obama's standards are locked in until 2021, at which point a new president may be in office.[16] States and localities have filed numerous actions against major fossil-fuel companies for public nuisance, seeking oil company document disclosure, and trust funds to pay for the damages caused by sea-level rise. Our Children's Trust—which represents children who will be affected by climate change—has filed a series of suits against the federal and some state governments claiming that their substandard stewardship of the atmosphere has violated the public trust.[17]

Meanwhile, empowered by a special EPA waiver of the Clean Air Act's preemption of state motor vehicle emission standards, California has announced that it intends to retain the more-stringent Obama-era standards.[18] Because other states are free to do the same, the EPA may need to compromise on a new national standard, or else automakers will still need to satisfy the Obama-era targets in the thirteen California-standard jurisdictions, which account for more than a third of the automobile market.[19] Former EPA Administrator Scott Pruitt had stated that he was not considering revoking California's waiver "at present," but media reports indicate that the agency's fuel economy proposal will conclude that the waiver allows California to regulate emissions but not in ways that also relate to fuel economy.[20] This understanding of the waiver would effectively eliminate California's power to independently regulate tailpipe carbon emissions;

however, two federal courts have previously rejected this narrow interpretation.[21] Should the EPA revoke or "reinterpret" California's Clean Air Act waiver, the state will surely sue.

Substantial domestic resistance has also arisen against the Trump administration's efforts to deregulate non-carbon greenhouse gases. When Trump's EPA tried to stay enforcement of the Obama administration's already-final methane standards for new and modified oil and gas sites, claiming that its decision to do so was immune from judicial review, the court found that action to be "arbitrary and capricious" and an ineffective revocation that exceeded the agency's authority under the Clean Air Act.[22] The court went on to rule that the EPA would have to initiate full rulemaking procedures to stay or undo the regulation and until then was required to enforce the Methane Rule.[23] Litigation also continues in defense of the EPA's authority to regulate hydrofluorocarbons, with a new agreement to control these compounds recently concluded in Kigali, Rwanda.[24] In short, the domestic internalization of international climate norms remains sticky, and not so easily altered by Trump's EPA.

If, in November 2019, the administration should unilaterally give notice of its intent to withdraw from the Paris Agreement, new litigation will almost certainly ensue to invalidate that notice, arguing that the president lacks constitutional power to withdraw from the Agreement without congressional participation. The judicial precedent most on point remains the Supreme Court's summary disposition nearly four decades ago in *Goldwater v. Carter*.[25] *Goldwater* dismissed without oral argument a group of senators' challenge to the president's unilateral decision to terminate a bilateral mutual defense treaty with Taiwan in accordance with its terms as part of the recognition of the government in Beijing. But on closer examination, *Goldwater* is a very thin reed on which to rest a broad pronouncement of unilateral presidential power to terminate multilateral treaties that have international legal force. There was no majority opinion in *Goldwater*. The justices splintered around a number of rationales, and only one justice reached the merits. Two justices voted that the case should be argued, not decided summarily; another justice asserted that the case was not ripe because the political branches had not yet reached "constitutional impasse"; four justices found that it was a political question. Only one justice voted on the merits to uphold the president's treaty termination power, based on the peculiar fact that that case—unlike climate change—involved recognition of foreign governments, an issue over which the president plainly exercises textual plenary constitutional power.[26]

In the years since *Goldwater v. Carter*, several lower courts have followed its lead by finding nonjusticiable suits questioning executive power to unilaterally withdraw from treaties.[27] But in an important recent decision, *Zivotofsky ex rel. Zivotofsky v. Clinton*, the Supreme Court declined a similar political question challenge to an assertion of the president's recognition power in the face of a contrary congressional statute, calling the political question doctrine a "narrow" exception to the general rule that the judiciary has the "responsibility to decide cases properly before it." Chief Justice Roberts's opinion for the Court reduced the political question test to its two "textual" elements, ruling that a political question exists only "[1] where there is a textually demonstrable constitutional commitment of the issue to a coordinate political department; or [2] a lack of judicially discoverable and manageable standards for resolving it.'"[28]

Under *Zivotofsky*'s narrowed political question test, treaty termination is not a decision "textually committed" by the Constitution to a branch other than the judiciary. Article II of the Constitution authorizes the president to "make" treaties with advice and consent of the Senate, but no constitutional text expressly gives authority to any branch to unmake such treaties. Nor is there a "lack of judicially discoverable and manageable standards for resolving" the question. The Court need only decide whether the president's solitary action is legally sufficient to terminate an international treaty obligation, which is the law of the land. If the Court can decide on the merits in such landmark separation of powers cases as *Marbury v. Madison, The Steel Seizure Case, Myers v. United States, INS v. Chadha, Morrison v. Olson,* and *Zivotofsky* itself,[29] why can't it decide on the merits whether the president's unitary withdrawal from a multilateral treaty is constitutionally sufficient to bind other branches—and the world? That would certainly be a political *case,* but would not make the contested legal issue a *political question.* As Chief Justice Roberts noted in *Zivotofsky,* enforcing the separation of powers "is what courts do." In *Zivotofsky,* the question was whether a statute enacted by Congress unconstitutionally encroached on the president's foreign affairs powers. The parallel question here would be whether the president's attempted unilateral termination unconstitutionally encroached on *Congress's* foreign affairs powers. To decide this question, a court need only apply traditional judicially manageable tools of constitutional interpretation—examining text, structure, and historical evidence about the nature of the law and constitutional powers at issue.

Much of the debate in *Goldwater* concerned justiciability. The justices asked whether Congress as a whole had challenged the president's action, and if not, whether the plaintiffs had standing to bring the action, and whether the case was genuinely ripe for decision, absent what Justice Powell deemed a true "constitutional impasse." While debate continues over what degree of congressional opposition it would take to confer congressional standing, there seems little doubt that after the Court's decision in *Massachusetts v. EPA,*[30] states and localities suffering from diminished coastlines due to rising sea levels would have standing to challenge a national climate change policy decision that encourages a rise by accelerating the melting of the polar icecaps. Such a rise would constitute injury in fact and would be redressable through EPA action for purposes of the Supreme Court's current environmental standing test stated in *Lujan v. Defenders of Wildlife*.[31]

Some commentators have made much of the fact that the president has unilaterally terminated a number of international agreements since the 1930s, and a few dozen since *Goldwater*.[32] But just because Congress acquiesced in the president's termination of a number of agreements that Congress did not care about tells us little about what would happen if Congress were actively to contest such a withdrawal. Given that there are currently no statutory provisions that require the president to notify Congress of a treaty termination or withdrawal, it would be odd to treat activity of which Congress may not even have been aware as accepted customary constitutional practice. By way of comparison, in *INS v. Chadha*, the Court famously invalidated the legislative veto, even though 295 legislative vetoes had been inserted into nearly 200 statutes in the preceding half-century.[33]

Obviously, the United States is not the only country in which this issue has arisen. The British Supreme Court in the Brexit litigation recently held that the U.K. government may not use its executive prerogative powers to trigger Article 50, the withdrawal provision of the Treaty of the European Union, but instead must seek parliamentary approval if fundamental rights are affected.[34] The Court held that prior parliamentary approval of the United Kingdom's withdrawal from the European Union was needed because Brexit would require fundamental constitutional changes, including repealing the 1972 EU Act, which expressly allowed for E.U. treaties to take effect within U.K. domestic law, a law that the executive would not have the power to effect unilaterally. If the United States were to seek to withdraw from the Paris regime—not to mention another international organization like the United Nations or the World Trade Organization, whose rules are strongly internalized into U.S. law—termination would similarly necessitate unwinding many domestic statutes that the president could not terminate alone.

Similarly, the High Court of South Africa recently held that the executive branch could not unilaterally withdraw from the Rome Statute of the International Criminal Court without parliamentary approval.[35] In response, the South African government complied with the court's order and revoked the instrument of withdrawal. As has been widely discussed, some U.S. Supreme Court justices—particularly Justices Breyer, Ginsburg, and Kennedy—have been influenced by constitutional practice in other democratic countries. Indeed, Justice Breyer has recently written a book arguing in favor of this practice.[36] If the constitutional issue raised by *Goldwater* were relitigated in the context of withdrawal from the Paris Climate Agreement, we could expect the reasoning of these and other comparative law precedents to be urged upon the U.S. Supreme Court.

The real question is whether American courts would really stand mutely by if Donald Trump, by tweet, sought unilaterally to withdraw the United States not just from the Paris Agreement but from the United Nations, the International Monetary Fund, the World Bank, the World Trade Organization, and NATO. If the president, acting alone, could unilaterally disengage from most of our international commitments, that practice could potentially transform the entire post-World War II world order. While the treaty termination issue arises most vividly in the context of the Paris Climate Agreement, at a time when we have a president and national security adviser avowedly hostile to international agreements, the implications of this constitutional issue obviously extend as well to international organizations (e.g., the U.N. Charter), international tribunals (e.g., the International Court of Justice, where the United States is currently defending an action brought by Iran), mutual security organizations (e.g., NATO, which Trump has repeatedly and severely criticized), and trade agreements (multilateral, such as the WTO, where China has now sued the United States; regional, e.g., NAFTA; and bilateral, e.g., the Korea-U.S. Free Trade Agreement). Standing alone, the summary disposition in *Goldwater* is simply too thin a precedent, and too off-point and under-reasoned, to treat as settled law governing all of these situations.

If, in November 2019, the administration actually chooses unilaterally to give notice of its intent to withdraw from Paris, the real legal battle will finally begin. New litigation brought by states and "Big Green" groups would almost certainly ensue, arguing that the president lacks constitutional power to withdraw from the Paris Agreement without congressional participation. For the reasons suggested above, the outcome of such a lawsuit would not be a foregone conclusion. And even if a domestic litigation challenge to withdrawal ultimately proved unsuccessful, the litigation could still last more than a year, potentially pushing the national decision of whether to complete the withdrawal past Trump's presidency.

If and when the Court finally decides this issue on the merits, it may well conclude that there should not be a single "transsubstantive" rule governing termination of international agreements. The Court could well conclude that the degree of congressional participation should depend on the subject matter of the agreement at issue. Some commentators have argued that President Trump's threat to terminate or withdraw from NAFTA would be barred by Congress's authority to regulate foreign commerce under the Commerce Clause, an argument that equally extends to withdrawing from a climate change agreement with sweeping implications for domestic and foreign commerce.[37]

Meanwhile, since Trump's Paris announcement, those resisting Trump's initiatives have gone beyond rope-a-dope to affirmative, alternative climate action. Many U.S. climate stakeholders other than the federal government—such as states and localities and private clean energy entrepreneurs—have intensified their efforts toward meeting the Paris targets. These alternative stakeholders will almost surely generate an alternative plan of litigation and emissions reduction designed to keep U.S. emissions within striking distance of the promised U.S. Nationally Determined Contribution.

Widespread support for climate change solutions continues to grow among other transnational actors as well. Through the "Under2 MOU" (Under 2 Degrees Celsius Memorandum of Understanding) coalition, states, provinces, regions, and cities around the world have pledged the common goal of reducing greenhouse gas emissions to 80–95 percent below 1990 levels by 2050.[38] Already the governors of California, New York, and Washington have formed the United States Climate Alliance, a coalition that will bring together U.S. states to uphold the Paris Agreement and take further climate action.[39] Similarly, through the Compact of Mayors, six hundred global cities have pledged to reduce greenhouse gas emissions by nearly one billion tons annually by 2030. California alone could bring us five percent of the way to our global pledge, which is to cut our emissions by 26–28 percent below 2005 levels by 2025.[40] And emissions trading among subnational entities to distribute emissions reductions could begin, consistent with the domestic mitigation and internationally transferred mitigation outcomes provisions of Paris Articles 4.2 and 6.[41]

Although President Trump claims the Paris Agreement would provide other countries with an economic edge over the United States, business leaders now believe instead that future economic prosperity is best advanced by remaining in and supporting the Paris Agreement. Coal jobs will continue to be scarce. Default patterns have shifted toward clean energy and cannot be undone overnight. New power plants are much more likely to use cheap gas or renewables. The Breakthrough Energy Coalition, pioneered by Bill Gates, will invest $1 billion in companies that provide affordable clean energy.[42] Through the "We Mean Business" Coalition, 471 companies with over $8 trillion in market capitalization have undertaken more than 1,000 climate action commitments.[43] For this same reason, hundreds of major companies and investors—including DuPont, eBay, Nike, Unilever, Levi Strauss & Co., Hilton, Adobe, Apple, Facebook, Google, and Hewlett Packard—have publicly urged President Trump to remain in the Paris Agreement, joined even by some oil and gas companies, such as Shell and Exxon Mobil.[44]

Thus, while the Trump administration waffles, the global community can just keep doing what it is doing. It can disregard as legally meaningless the Trump administration's prospective "withdrawal" from the Paris Agreement and instead look to these subnational actors' and business leaders' efforts to meet the U.S.'s pledged greenhouse gas emissions reductions.[45] Even if the United States should fall into arrears on emissions reductions or Green Climate Fund contributions, as it has done in the past with respect to its U.N. dues, these other domestic and international stakeholders can exert pressure to force this administration and the next to make up the difference.

Simply put, the rope-a-dope seems to be working. Trump's claimed withdrawal from the Paris Agreement marked just the beginning of the transnational legal process story. The outside strategy of "interaction–interpretation–internalization" is playing out even as we watch. Inside the government, the Trump plan to undo Paris is encountering bureaucratic obstacles. While the "disengage–black hole–hard power" faction won the day in June 2017, since then, within the Trump administration, the "engage–translate–leverage" approach has made a comeback.

Ironically, Trump's effort to withdraw has been stymied not just by career bureaucrats but also by his own political appointees— such as Energy Secretary Rick Perry and now-departed Secretary of State Tillerson, National Security Adviser H.R. McMaster, and economic adviser Gary Cohn. All of these officials favored "engaging" (i.e., keeping a seat at the table) and "translating" (i.e., reading ambiguities in the treaty to permit lower U.S. environmental performance) over overt withdrawal, which they correctly saw as losing leverage within the ongoing COP process. Even as a lame duck, the United States has continued to attend ongoing international meetings in an apparent effort to try to get better conditions at the margins of the Paris Agreement. Thus, even if in the end the administration tries to withdraw in accordance with the Agreement's terms, it will not be breaking international law, but rather treating the Paris Agreement as bona fide international law that the United States has already internalized to a surprising degree.

The lesson, in short, is that the Trump administration does not own our climate policy. We all do. The Paris Agreement was a bold global bet that developed and developing nations would all cooperate to reduce greenhouse gas emissions through incentives to develop clean energy. The environmental community and the many transnational actors committed to cleaner energy are far bigger than Donald Trump. His administration remains visibly divided on this issue, and he has personally demonstrated little meaningful commitment or capacity to follow through on any of his public statements. If the federal government does not live up to its Paris commitments, many other players can and are stepping up to fill the gap. As Trump's policies and credibility fray on many fronts, his so-called Paris "withdrawal" may be just another one of them. Only time will tell whether, with concerted effort and aggressive innovation—in Humphrey Bogart's words—"we'll always have Paris."[46]

B. TRADE DIPLOMACY

A parallel story could be told about President Trump's calamitous trade diplomacy, which has disrupted alliances, potentially sparked trade wars, stalled freer trade, and left the United States on the sidelines of major trade liberalization initiatives. In a telling 2017 speech, German Foreign Minister Sigmar Gabriel asserted that "[t]he international law codified in the Charter of the United Nations . . . is in crisis" in no small part because Trump "perceives Europe in a very distanced way, regarding previous partners as competitors and . . . even as . . . economic opponents."[47]

Upon entering office, Trump acted on that perception to instigate three unilateral moves. First, he announced the United States' withdrawal from the Trans-Pacific Partnership (TPP), a multilateral trade pact with eleven Pacific nations, of which the Obama administration had been a major architect. After Trump's exit, many assumed that the TPP would collapse without U.S. participation, but the other parties—principally Australia, Canada, Chile, and Japan—continued the partnership anyway. They renegotiated parts of the TPP to remove some of Washington's demands and in March 2018 signed the Comprehensive and Progressive Agreement for Trans-Pacific Partnership (CPTPP, or TPP-1). Under this new agreement, Canadian and Australian

ranchers will now be able to sell beef more cheaply in Japan because of new tariff reductions that American ranchers will not
enjoy. Meanwhile, smaller trading countries such as Malaysia
and Vietnam—which had aspired to preferential access to the
U.S. trade market—have accepted instead improved market access to the other large CPTPP economies.

When it had become irrevocably clear that the CPTPP was going
forward without the United States, Trump inquired as to whether
America could rejoin the same pact he had prematurely abandoned.
After being publicly mocked for his "off-again, on-again" position,
Trump announced that the United States would not be part of the
CPTPP, at least for now. Yet here, too, the international law rules
that Trump had dismissed now limited his freedom. Embedded
in the revised agreement are provisions that both prevent the
United States from formally starting negotiations to join until
2019 and give each current member a de facto veto, as all 11 other
partners must agree whether to admit a new member to the club.
Anticipating the possibility of an eventual American return, the
11 member countries never deleted—only "suspended"—about 20
key provisions originally advocated by the United States—most
notably, stronger intellectual property protections. But the United
States still would not likely embrace the deal without reopening
negotiations on such sensitive issues for existing members as
truck tariffs, auto-part sourcing, and agricultural products such as
rice, which are mainly produced in the U.S. states that voted for
Trump in 2016. Right now, existing CPTPP members seem to have
little appetite for complex renegotiations, and are well positioned
to extract concessions from Trump as the price of America's attempt at belated reentry.

Second, Trump initially announced that he would withdraw
from the North American Free Trade Agreement (NAFTA) with
Canada and Mexico and the Republic of Korea–U.S. Free Trade

Agreement (KORUS). But after facing intense opposition from his own Departments of Agriculture and Commerce, which feared the impact on their domestic constituencies, Trump shifted to a hasty plan to "renegotiate" the agreements without advance buy-in from the other partners. As with the Paris Agreement, the other parties to NAFTA had little incentive to renegotiate a less-favorable agreement with a flailing American administration. Both Canada and Mexico have thus far largely rebuffed Trump's aggressive demands to update the NAFTA on such thorny issues as automotive content, dairy, dispute resolution, government procurement, and a sunset clause, putting off until 2018 a renegotiation that Trump's White House had originally announced would be completed by 2017. Trump's political imperatives have now placed his negotiators in an electoral bind, as only by trading speed for substance can they produce a quickly renegotiated agreement in principle in enough time for Trump to take credit for it in the 2018 elections.[48]

By June 2018, Trump was hinting that he no longer intended to withdraw from NAFTA, but instead planned to deal separately with Canada and Mexico to restructure the agreement, even though NAFTA's provisions plainly require all three countries' concurrence for any revisions. During a few dizzying days at the 2018 Quebec G-7 summit, Trump refused to endorse a joint statement with his closest trade allies, charged their trade policies with threatening U.S. national security, and questioned why Russia was still being excluded from the G-7, before making the baffling claim—after himself imposing aggressive tariffs—that he could support a G-7 partnership that had no tariffs, barriers, or subsidies. As Congress began preparing bipartisan legislation to reassert its authority over trade policy, Trump insulted Canadian Prime Minister Justin Trudeau as "weak" and "dishonest" before flying off to Singapore to praise North Korean dictator Kim Jong-un as a "very talented man" with a "great personality." In Singapore, Trump left the North Korean media with the impression that he favored sanctions relief, despite Congress having passed sweeping legislation stiffening North Korean sanctions only the prior year.[49]

With South Korea, Trump's room to maneuver proved even more limited, because he underestimated the deeply interconnected nature of U.S. trade and national security policy. His need for Pacific allies to help contain North Korean nuclear adventurism forced him to reverse his early courtship of Taiwan and his initial threats to sharply reduce Chinese imports.[50] Flip-flopping on his early condemnation of China as a "currency manipulator," Trump went to Beijing to give China "great credit" for "being able to take advantage of another country for the benefit of their citizens."[51] And in early negotiating rounds, the Koreans met Trump's threats to annul or renegotiate the KORUS by boldly suggesting that if it came to that, South Korea was ready to annul first.[52] By late March 2018, a bilateral agreement in principle was finally reached after a hasty negotiation that—despite Trump's rhetoric—ended up producing only modest changes.[53]

As his third unilateral move after entering office, Trump launched a series of punitive measures against other nations' purportedly unfair trade practices.[54] He followed by announcing startlingly aggressive tariffs on steel and aluminum imports—supposedly, like the Travel Ban, issued in the name of national security. Blurring the traditionally separate national security and trade policy streams, Trump invoked national security to call for auto tariffs on Mexico, Canada, Japan, and Germany, presumably to gain greater leverage for NAFTA renegotiations. But he undermined his own credibility almost immediately, by granting a series of retreats, exemptions, and short-term waivers (with respect to the metal tariffs) after the various affected trading partners pushed back.[55] At the same time, he overlooked a genuine national security threat and triggered bipartisan congressional resistance by calling for leniency for ZTE, a Chinese telecommunications company that had pleaded guilty to and paid billions in penalties for violating U.S. sanctions on Iran and North Korea.

Ironically, the short-term impact of these various measures has been to expand, not shrink, the U.S. trade deficit in goods. The three biggest categories of imports that the Commerce Department sought to punish in 2017—Chinese steel and Canadian aircraft and lumber—all notably backfired. Trump's threat to curb steel imports triggered a 20-percent surge in the same through the first nine months of 2017 relative to the same period one year earlier.[56] The Commerce Department's decision to impose lumber duties of as much as 24 percent in response to what it deemed unfair Canadian provincial subsidies floundered when hurricanes devastated the American South, creating unexpected demand for building materials and pushing lumber prices up, not down.[57] When Trump backed Boeing's claim that it had been harmed by Canadian subsidies on Bombardier's C Series jet, the independent, bipartisan U.S. International Trade Commission— composed of George W. Bush and Obama appointees—voted unanimously against that claim, effectively invalidating the nearly 300 percent tariff that Trump's Commerce Department had wanted to impose.

The area of trade diplomacy again shows how deeply the United States has become enmeshed in multilateral trade regimes and the myriad ways in which other participants in those regimes can exercise reciprocal power, through both international law and politics. Exiting these regimes is neither immediate nor easy, and will be sharply contested by other transnational players. False factual charges are quickly countered, and unilateral actions not based on sound evidence receive swift rebuttal. While Trump has consistently sought to scapegoat NAFTA for bleeding American jobs, for example, his own cabinet has resisted, particularly because economists have extensively chronicled the extent to which Trump has overstated NAFTA's cost in terms of lost American jobs.[58]

Similarly, Trump baldly asserted that the "World Trade Organization [WTO] . . . [has] taken advantage of this country like you wouldn't believe. . . . [A]s an example, we lose . . . almost all of the lawsuits in the WTO. . . ." Yet almost immediately, multiple commentators stepped forward to respond that in fact, the United States has prevailed before WTO dispute-settlement panels on more than 90 percent of the adjudicated issues.[59] Trump imposed his unilateral steel and aluminum tariffs without invoking the consultation-and-grievance procedures required by the WTO's dispute settlement rules. By so doing, Trump offended the very allies whom the United States needs to help with the China trade problem. In April 2018, China filed a complaint at the World Trade Organization over the U.S.'s decision to impose tariffs on some $50 billion of Chinese goods. And even while Trump has continued asserting that the WTO has been a disaster for the United States, far from boycotting that organization, the United States has filed its own new case at the WTO to try to halt Beijing's policy regarding China's protection of intellectual property rights.[60]

Thus, despite Trump's simplistic tweet—"Trade wars are good and easy to win"[61]—the global response to his various unilateral actions has proven the opposite. Increasingly, internationally traded products comprise components assembled in multiple countries, which renders the very notion of a bilateral "trade deficit" hard to measure. Trade liberalization is now less a policy choice than an essential means to secure manufacturing efficiency for the growing number of companies who manufacture locally but source globally. Ironically, by invoking national security interests as justification for imposing blanket tariffs on steel and aluminum, Trump is only inviting both a WTO panel defeat and specious invocations of the same national security argument by Russia, China, and others to defend their own dubious trade practices.

As in other areas, the Trump administration has offered mainly empty threats to resign from, without really leaving, key trade agreements. That tactic has simply created more "lose–lose" situations, stalling preexisting deals and alienating existing trade partners without creating new ones. In nearly every available venue for trade liberalization, the United States has gone from leader to bystander, losing in the process past allies, future leverage, and immediate benefits from freer trade. Of the 35 trade pacts currently under consideration worldwide, the United States is a party to just one. An economist for George W. Bush's White House recently observed that Trump mistakenly thinks that "if the U.S. said stop, this [global trade] process would come to a halt"; but in fact, "[t]he world just moves on without us."[62] Former trading partners have now gone beyond simply bemoaning the loss of United States leadership to banding together against Trump as a common foe. In Latin America, for example, Trump seems ironically to have done more than any economic factor to spur commercial integration in opposition to his initiatives.

With respect to those trade agreements where the United States has not excluded itself from participation, yet cannot muster the leverage for meaningful renegotiation, its likely default will now be to stay in and underperform. While that outcome may be curable down the road by a successor administration, the wear of playing "rope-a-dope" against Trump's trade impulses is becoming more and more apparent. Improvised American unilateralism in the face of embedded trade multilateralism greatly damages the United States' reputation as a reliable treaty partner and diminishes its long-term capacity to exercise leadership

Another good pt to bring into Intro HK / help to frame current historical moment.

within those treaty arrangements in times of genuine global economic crisis.

C. THE IRAN NUCLEAR DEAL

Much the same story could be told about the Iran Nuclear Deal, which candidate Trump threatened to "rip up" and President Trump repeatedly called "the worst deal in history."[63] The July 14, 2015 Joint Comprehensive Plan of Action (JCPOA) envisioned actions by Iran, the International Atomic Energy Agency (IAEA), and the allies known as the P5+1 (the five permanent U.N. members—the United States, the United Kingdom, France, China, and Russia—plus Germany, with a European Union representative speaking for the three European countries).[64] After extended negotiation, Iran agreed to specified limits on its nuclear development program in exchange for the P5+1's joint relaxation of domestic and international sanctions that had been imposed through the United Nations.

Once again, the Iran Nuclear Deal illustrated the Obama–Clinton "engage–translate–leverage" "smart-power" framework in action. The Obama administration *engaged* with Iran, the P5+1, the United Nations, and the IAEA. It *translated* Iran's desire to maintain a civil nuclear program into a deal that verifiably cut off Iran's pathways to a nuclear weapon. That deal allowed Iran to engage in certain peaceful nuclear activities, all without endorsing a legal right to enrich, gaining in exchange unprecedented monitoring access for the IAEA. The Obama team then *leveraged* that core bargain first by strengthening sanctions in June 2010,[65] followed by gradually lifting national and multilateral sanctions and increasing international inspection to achieve an outcome that probably could not have been attained through military force. The JCPOA verifiably reduced Iran's stockpiles of enriched uranium by 98 percent, forcing shipment of twenty-five thousand pounds out of the country. The Plan increased the "breakout" time that it would take for Iran to acquire a bomb from two to three months to at least one year, reduced the number of Iran's installed centrifuges by two-thirds, prevented Iran from producing weapons-grade plutonium, and verified the country's compliance with robust IAEA monitoring and inspection.

On May 8, 2018, shortly after John Bolton became national security adviser, Trump announced that the United States would withdraw from the Deal, "instituting the highest level of economic sanction" on Iran and on "[a]ny nation that helps Iran in its quest for nuclear weapons."[66] But as with other accords, now that Trump has resigned, the question remains: "Will he really leave?" At this writing, the JCPOA remains fragile, but functioning.[67] True to his default, Trump has resigned but not yet left, and America is still in but underperforming. The other parties initially all responded to Trump's action by saying that they still intended to comply with the Deal. While the Plan's future is in considerable jeopardy, as with the Paris Climate Deal, the carefully constructed regime of cooperation has become the focal point for all interested stakeholders' expectations. As with other Trump exits, after the withdrawal announcement, what comes next?

In critical respects, the JCPOA is both a product and a generator of transnational legal process. The key political commitments in the deal—which are multilateral, sequential, and enforced by existing domestic sanction authorities—have already been fulfilled. In January 2016, Iran dismantled much of its nuclear program, in accordance with its agreement with the P5+1. The United States and the European Union removed their nuclear-related domestic sanctions, and the U.N. Security Council lifted similar sanctions under Resolution 2231, which terminated and replaced past resolutions. Under domestic and international law, the Deal is a politically, not legally, binding arrangement, implemented on the U.S. side largely through executive branch waivers of nuclear-related sanctions. The legislative waiver provisions require the president to certify every 120 days whether Iran is in compliance with the Deal, regularly reminding Trump of his continuing val-idation of an agreement that he had constantly disparaged. The statutory deadlines painted Trump into a corner, reminding him every four months that he either had to eat his words, or refuse to waive sanctions and jeopardize the accord. Similarly, the deal required the IAEA to monitor adherence to international law by certifying quarterly that Iran is in compliance with the JCPOA, which it has now done ten times. In May 2018, the IAEA once again confirmed "that the nuclear-related commitments [of the JCPOA] are being implemented by Iran."[68]

In September 2017, President Trump attacked the Iran Nuclear Deal before the United Nations, even while again certifying Iran's compliance with the deal.[69] One month later, Trump continued to waive the sanctions but refused to certify the accord on the grounds that the sanctions suspended were not proportionate to Iran's progress. By so doing, Trump tried to avoid having to make the decision whether to withdraw from or renegotiate the agree-ment, instead shifting the burden to U.S. allies to broker a new deal and pushing to Congress the decision whether or not to reim-pose sanctions.[70] But as with repealing Obamacare, the Republican Congress was skeptical of imposing new sanctions without a better deal in place. All the key Republicans—particularly House Speaker Paul Ryan and Senate Foreign Relations Committee Chair Bob Corker—came to see ripping up the deal as not worth the downsides, perhaps hoping that the Iranians would eventually create greater cause for a claim of breach.[71] While Israeli Prime

Minister Benjamin Netanyahu repeatedly attacked the deal, some leading Israelis—including former Defense Minister Ehud Barak—advocated staying in as a peaceful alternative that has "blocked Iran's path to a nuclear weapon, and prevented the emergence of an arms race in the Middle East."[72]

On May 8, 2018, Trump changed course and announced that he would no longer waive U.S. statutory sanctions. But his action has only triggered a new round of transnational legal process. Should the Iranians continue to keep their part of the bargain, the Trump administration would be hard-pressed to explain why they replaced with nothing, a multilateral deal that seemed to have been working.[73] The other partners to the deal—the Europeans, the Russians, and the Chinese—will not default on their political obligations just because Donald Trump wants to tear the deal up.[74] Nor will they return to unilaterally reimposing sanctions on Iran. Even under the uncertainty created by Trump's threats, Europe's trade with Iran nearly doubled in 2016.[75] Under the umbrella of intergovernmental cooperation, Iran's economy has been slowly recovering. Iran has made deals to expand its oil fields, build cars, buy anti-aircraft systems from Russia, and purchase dozens of aircraft from European and American companies. Consistent with the deal's sanctions relief, the United States had released its hold on—and cannot quickly reclaim—tens of billions of dollars in frozen Iranian oil revenues.[76] Gradual re-enmeshment of the foreign and Iranian banking sectors continues.[77] Thus, even without U.S. participation, the network of trade deals being struck between the allies' businesses and Iran's may well continue.

Trump claimed he was withdrawing to force the other parties back to the negotiating table. But that cannot happen if the other JCPOA participants refuse to renegotiate. Even if talks were now reopened, the Trump administration could hardly get a better deal, simply because the United States could no longer invoke as leverage the crushing multilateral sanctions that brought Iran to the table in the first place. Following the TPP model, the Europeans responded to Trump's announcement by proposing that America's absence be used not to end the Deal, but rather to expand it beyond nuclear weapons capacity to cover more ballistic activity, the post-2025 period, and broader issues of stability in the Mideast. In theory, the European stakeholders could negotiate long-term investment or energy partnerships with Iran, hoping that in time the mercurial Trump will use a deal primarily renegotiated by others as an excuse to reenter.

In short, Trump is forcing his European allies to choose between siding with America and siding with Iran. If the Europeans bet on Iran, then, as with Cuba, the United States could find itself trying ineffectually to enforce unilateral sanctions on Iran without partners. If the United States aggressively enforces secondary sanctions against European companies doing business in Iran, we could see a replay of the regulatory wars that followed President Reagan's extraterritorial sanctions on the Soviet pipeline, which ended up pitting the United States against its closest European allies.[78] European governments could well revive blocking legislation that prohibits compliance with U.S. judgments and administrative determinations implementing extraterritorial sanctions, which could lead to a transatlantic trade war. European companies would have to decide whether to scale back their still-modest trade and investment in Iran or risk jeopardizing their access to the far larger U.S. market. The United States would be seen not simply as abandoning its allies but also as penalizing their companies for relying upon an agreement that was working. Again, the greatest cost would be immeasurable damage to America's reputation for global leadership and compliance with international law, undermining perceptions of U.S. responsibility and reliability.

Were the JCPOA now to collapse, the access of the IAEA to conduct "eyes-on" inspections inside Iran would also disappear, and that agency would no longer be in a position to verify the exclusively peaceful nature of Iran's program. In the worst-case scenario, Iranian officials could claim breach by the United States, start enriching uranium again, and restart their program for building a bomb, without IAEA "eyes-on" to monitor their activities. Iran could go on to withdraw from the Treaty on the Nonproliferation of Nuclear Weapons, essentially inviting U.S. or Israeli military action and dramatically destabilizing the region.

Alternatively—and the uneasy status quo for now—is that Iran could choose to keep fulfilling its JCPOA nuclear commitments in order to keep benefiting from the continued lifting of U.N. and E.U. sanctions. Trump's renewed unilateral sanctions will cover a much smaller percentage of trade than did the original sanctions, and Trump's May announcement did not mention triggering the "snapback" mechanism of Resolution 2231, which allows any P5 member to reimpose the comprehensive U.N. sanctions, without a vote by the U.N. Security Council, by claiming a violation of the JCPOA. What probably constrained Trump from triggering this mechanism is that the other stakeholders will not likely agree that such a violation has occurred. While the JCPOA technically permits a Security Council Permanent Member who wields a veto to singlehandedly force reimposition of prior Security Council sanctions, the standard for action is whether "the JCPOA Participant State believes [another's action] constitutes significant non-performance of commitments under the" agreement, a standard that Iran has probably not breached. And, if the United States withdraws from the Deal, it might no longer qualify as a "JCPOA Participant State" authorized to trigger the snapback clause. In addition, Iran could plausibly argue that the United States has no good-faith basis for charging breach, as Iran ceased performing only in response to the U.S.'s unilateral withdrawal announcement.[79] And even if the U.N. sanctions that were in place before the deal were legally reimposed, the other Security Council members, particularly China and Russia, would not likely enforce them.

The irony, of course, is that all of these legal provisions were designed based on the assumption that Iran, not the United States, would be the first to breach the Deal. In sum, Trump has created yet another "lose–lose" situation, blowing up a pre-existing deal without creating a new one, losing in the process allies, leverage, and a guaranteed ability to monitor Iran's nuclear program.

Between outright collapse and unsteady continuation lies a third possibility: that, as with the Paris Agreement, following unilateral U.S. renunciation, the JCPOA could die a "death by a thousand cuts." Reimposition of U.S. sanctions could actively discourage third-country investment while at the same time allowing Trump to overread Iranian conduct to place a hair-trigger on snapback sanctions in response to claimed Iranian breaches. The easing of sanctions had led Iranian civil society to see its own hardline leaders as the main obstacle to economic and social progress—but Trump has now resurrected the United States as The Great Satan, who can easily be blamed as the source of all of Iran's problems. Reformist Iranian President Hassan Rouhani won re-election in May 2017 by staking his reputation on the economic benefits of the deal. So perversely, renunciation by hardliners in Washington will only strengthen the hand of the hardliners in Tehran—including the Islamic Revolutionary Guard Corps. Trump has needlessly diverted his political capital from the real task of mobilizing a broad international effort to contain the adventurism of the

Revolutionary Guards to a new round of battles with America's closest allies about a nuclear deal they all still support.[80]

So even after Trump's withdrawal announcement, smart-power diplomacy continues, but now without the United States as a part of it. As the Kremlin's spokesperson recently put it, the Iran deal was not a U.S. construct, but rather "the result of a consensus among many parties" that may be seen as "either good or bad, but it is the only one that reflects this consensus."[81] The goal of this new intense round of public and private negotiating will not be regulating Iran's misbehavior so much as ensuring that Trump's intemperate withdrawal does not trigger a permanently destabilizing moment.

What all of this reminds us again is that it is often easier to resign than to leave, and that multiparty deals do not automatically collapse when one party reneges. Multilateral agreements are sticky, and global governance regimes are path-dependent. As these regimes develop, they take on lives of their own—building consensus about what sets of norms, rules, principles, and decision-making procedures should apply in particular issue areas. Intricate patterns of layered public and private cooperation develop, and formal lawmaking and institutions eventually emerge. These patterns create stiff paths of least resistance from which new political leaders can deviate only at considerable cost. All Trump has done is force that process of engage–translate–leverage to shift its focus from Iran, and to take place without him and about him.

Perhaps most important, the Iran deal shows that Trump's strategy of disengage–black hole–hard power leads nowhere. The United States' best option for keeping Iran free of nuclear weapons continues to be the smart-power strategy of engage–translate–leverage. In the words of the two lead American negotiators on Iran, the best approach remains "keep[ing] the world's powers united and the burden of proof on Iran[. . . :] relentless [multilateral] enforcement; enhancing sanctions that punish Iran's non-nuclear misbehavior, including its missile program and sponsorship of terrorism; working closely with Arab partners to deter Iran's meddling in their internal affairs; and making plain our concerns with Iran's domestic human rights abuses[, while] using the diplomatic channel we opened with Iran, after 35 years without such contact, to avoid inadvertent escalation."[82]

Trump claims that his withdrawal will take until at least the end of 2018 to fully implement. Until then, the United States will stay in the Iran Deal and underperform. But as the next chapter shows, Trump has once again underestimated the deep interconnectivity of our global commitments. By conveying that the United States is leaving the Iran Deal, he has given Iran's hardliners greater cause to be the first mover in actually breaking the deal. Instead of staying in step with his allies, he has set in motion a process that threatens to make them adversaries. Transnational legal process continues, but his actions have now made the United States, not Iran, the target of that process.

Having checked the "resign" box, Trump now seems inclined to claim that he has finally taken strong symbolic action against Iran and turn his real attention elsewhere (while continuing to demonize Iran rhetorically). But given the immense stakes in Korea, one could hardly imagine a less opportune moment for America's president to denigrate the kind of denuclearization diplomacy that has peacefully eliminated 98 percent of a country's enriched uranium stockpiles. Nor is this a good moment to give our adversaries reason to question America's willingness to keep its nuclear deals. After all, Kim Jong-un's commitment to carry forward his unspecified June 2018 Singapore pledge to pursue complete denuclearization turns fundamentally upon Trump's willingness to complete his own part of the bargain. So as with the Paris Agreement, Trump has given notice, but for now, the multilateral regime continues. The Iran Nuclear Deal may well survive in some form, if only to keep the North Koreans at the negotiating table. If our allies preserve or even expand the Iran Deal without U.S. leadership, it could become yet another international agreement—like the TPP—that in time Trump ends up applying to rejoin.

Chapter 4

Countries of Concern

A. NORTH KOREA

As the inception of the Trump administration began, Vice President Mike Pence solemnly intoned that "the era of strategic patience [with North Korea] is over."[1] But what precisely could that mean: that we have now entered an era of strategic *impatience*? Trump's first secretary of state, Rex Tillerson, announced that, with regard to North Korea, "all options are on the table," presumably including military force.[2] Then, in a frightening display of saber-rattling, Donald Trump issued a statement from his vacation home threatening "fire, fury and frankly power the likes of which this world has never seen before."[3] He repeated that threat at the U.N. General Assembly, strangely calling Kim Jong-un "Rocket Man" and threatening to "totally destroy" a country with whom we are not at war and that is populated by more than 25 million people, most of them civilians.[4]

As a Korean-American, I have visited North Korea three times, most recently in 2000 on an extended trip as Assistant Secretary of State for Democracy, Human Rights, and Labor with then-Secretary of State Madeleine Albright. My personal observation found the North Korean leadership to be extreme, but certainly not suicidal, and plainly rational enough to understand how counterproductive it would be to invite a massive military attack by

The Trump Administration and International Law. Harold Hongju Koh.
© Oxford University Press 2019. Published 2019 by Oxford University Press.

the United States. Since then, by all accounts, the North Korean nuclear weapons program has become too advanced and sophisticated to be defeated by either ballistic missile defenses or simple cybercommands. And unless we are willing immediately to sacrifice hundreds of thousands of Korean and American lives to both nuclear and conventional artillery attacks, there is no viable military option, especially at this fragile moment soon after South Korea's recent emergence from the political turmoil of presidential impeachment.

Because events in the Korean peninsula change hourly—in what at some moments has looked like a "Cuban Missile Crisis in slow motion"[5]—it is obviously perilous to make predictions about what will happen next. With his reckless nuclear rhetoric, Trump threw a wild card into the mix, to which the enigmatic Kim Jong-un could too easily have overreacted. That created a volatile prospect: that the two egotistical, mercurial leaders might engage in a volatile game of nuclear "chicken" that would serve no one's best interest. That anxiety spiked during a chilling 38-minute false alarm in January 2018, when much of Hawaii misperceived itself as under North Korean attack, followed a few days later by another false alarm in Japan. Either or both of these false alarms could have triggered a mistaken "reactive" nuclear response by Trump, Kim, or both.

By any measure, sporadic exchange of angry threats is a poor substitute for direct communication between potential nuclear adversaries. Moreover, the history of nuclear diplomacy teaches that no nation has ever surrendered its nuclear weapons under threat. To the contrary, those countries that have surrendered their arsenals—most prominently, Iran and Libya—have done so only when confronted by concerted, unified multilateral diplomacy coupled with proposed relief from sanctions.[6] A recent historical review found that over the last quarter century, North Korean provocations have usually declined when diplomatic engagement with the United States has increased. All of this suggests that the only way out of the North Korean crisis is more intensive diplomatic dialogue backed by containment and sanctions. The most obvious route to discourage further North Korean nuclear missile testing is to coax the North Koreans to accept a new iteration of the Six Party Talks—the historic multiparty discussions among the Koreas, Russia, China, Japan, Taiwan, and the United States that resulted from North Korea's 2003 withdrawal from the Nuclear Non-Proliferation Treaty. Indeed, until those talks were abruptly discontinued in 2009, they modeled just the kind of multiparty diplomatic dialogue that later generated the Iran Nuclear Deal.

While Trump's bellicose rhetoric muddied the waters, it never really altered America's main policy alternative for North Korea: a sustainable diplomatic settlement achieved by applying international law as a tool of smart power: engage–translate–leverage.[8] Fortunately for Trump, the election of South Korea's new President Moon Jae-in, a pro-dialogue human rights lawyer whose family originally hailed from the North, created a new prospect: parallel negotiations with the North, with Moon as "good cop," and with Trump as "bad cop." In practical terms, Moon's initiative allowed South Korean diplomatic experts to reach out directly to their North Korean counterparts in order to soften Trump's bluster. The 2018 Pyeongchang Winter Olympics then created a fortuitous opportunity to capitalize on North Korea's interest in bilateral diplomacy. This led to the surprise announcement that Trump would meet Kim Jong-un in Singapore in June 2018, a meeting advanced by the secret Pyongyang visit of then-CIA Director Mike Pompeo, which Trump first cancelled, but ultimately held on schedule with little advance preparation. At that meeting, which was laden with images but light on substance, Trump and Kim issued a vague joint declaration whereby Kim made no specific commitments, said nothing about human rights, and left unclear what the actual action plan was for moving "toward"—the key word in the declaration being "toward"—"complete denuclearization" of the peninsula, an unspecified pledge that North Korea has given five times since 1992.[9] While there will surely be many more twists and turns before this historical episode finally concludes, a basic outline has now emerged. In the space of just a year, without openly sounding retreat, Trump has effectively conceded that America's only realistic option in North Korea is negotiating and abiding by a deal to promote the country's denuclearization. Ironically, that option looks a lot like the "terrible" Iran Nuclear Deal from which Trump just withdrew.

Here again, policy realities have gradually pushed America's approach to North Korea back into a more traditional pattern. Trump initially roiled diplomatic waters by declaring that he would consider recognizing Taiwan, but he was soon schooled by Beijing that he needed Chinese cooperation if he wanted to put pressure on Pyongyang to pursue diplomatic discussions. After criticizing his first secretary of state for encouraging direct talks between the United States and the North,[10] Trump shifted secretly to precisely the same course: sending his second secretary-to-be to prepare just such talks. In his 2018 State of the Union address he concentrated his rhetoric on North Korea's human rights abuses, limiting his policy discussion to an amorphous pledge to pursue a "campaign of maximum pressure," whatever that might mean. He then dropped that rhetoric when he met Kim face to face.[11] Despite his hawkish "fire and fury" remarks, Trump reverted to supporting renewed economic sanctions of the kind voted on by the U.N. Security Council in August 2017, only to imply that sanctions relief might be soon forthcoming if North Korea continued dialogue. And Trump initially engaged in more visible bilateral military cooperation with South Korea, which forced him (as noted in the last chapter) to give considerable ground in order to achieve rapid renegotiation of the KORUS Free Trade Agreement, only to suggest after Singapore that such joint military exercises were in fact unduly provocative.

In April 2018, President Moon and Kim Jong-un concluded a surprisingly warm "getting to know you" summit in Panmunjom, replete with many powerful symbolic elements. North Korea's leader stepped into the South for the first time since the Korean War. The two leaders planted a tree the same age as the divided countries, aligned clocks in the North and South, signed a Panmunjom Declaration proclaiming "a new era of peace," and agreed to unite divided families. But their headline was jointly "confirm[ing] the common goal of realizing, through complete denuclearisation, a nuclear-free Korean peninsula."[12] With that, the two leaders set the stage for the high-stakes bilateral Singapore meeting between Kim and Trump in June 2018.

By every measure, Kim seems to have "won" that initial encounter, a reality to which Trump seemed entirely oblivious. While Trump's supporters claim that his belligerent threats brought Kim to the negotiating table, the reality is far more complex. In the preceding two years, Kim had assembled chips for the poker game to come by rapidly developing an intercontinental ballistic capability. A cave-in at the mountain site where the tests were conducted apparently required Kim to pause testing anyway. Kim plainly calculated that in the next phase of the poker game, de-escalation, like escalation, could be used as a tool to extract reduction in economic sanctions. He also grasped that embracing symbolic diplomacy, first at the Olympics and then with Moon, would visibly signal North Korea's "reasonableness" in a way that would help China pressure the United States to soften sanctions, thereby limiting Trump's freedom to keep threatening preemptive use of nuclear force.

Securing the first-ever diplomatic meeting between a North Korean leader and a sitting American president represented a historic coup for Kim. He won instant legitimacy while making no real concessions, and can now play Trump and Moon against each other by talking denuclearization with the former and peace with the latter. In addition, he has the good luck of negotiating with relative novices, given that some of the most experienced "Korea hands" have already left the U.S. government's diplomatic corps.[13] All of this bought Kim more time to rebuild his pile of poker chips by agreeing to vaguely worded joint declarations that do not bind him to concrete, verifiable steps as a matter of international law. In both 2000 and 2007, the two Korean capitals made joint peace commitments of far greater specificity, each of which North Korea violated within five years.[14]

As denuclearization diplomacy proceeds, the only meaningful measure of its success is how quickly, concretely, and transparently it ensures the removal or destruction of Kim Jong-un's nuclear arsenal. But in Singapore, Kim neither gave up nor promised to give up any of his 60 or so nuclear weapons or ballistic missiles, and offered no concrete steps or timeline for either goal. Nor, strikingly, was anything apparently said about curbing North Korean transfers of chemical weapons or cyberattacks on the U.S. grid. Such cyberattacks had led—nearly all observers agree—to the 2014 Sony hack and the 2017 Wannacry ransomware attack that disabled hundreds of thousands of computers in some 150 countries. These attacks graphically demonstrated that North Korea's cyberforces have greater potential than its intercontinental ballistic missiles immediately to cripple U.S. civilian infrastructure. Nor did the United States get Kim to declare a full inventory of North Korea's existing nuclear arsenal or to accept a framework for international inspection and verification.

Instead, in exchange for Kim's nonactions, Trump embraced North Korea's and China's view that joint U.S. military exercises with

South Korea are "very provocative" "war games" and apparently raised the prospects of both sanctions relief and withdrawing some of the nearly 30,000 American troops in South Korea. That troop presence has long served as a trip wire to ensure U.S. security guarantees to the South. These loose statements will have two perverse effects. First, when combined with Trump's looming tariffs war with China, they embolden China to ease up on sanctions, eroding leverage before any of North Korea's arsenal is dismantled. Second, when coupled with Trump's isolation at the 2018 G-7 meeting, they force America's Asian allies—particularly Australia, Japan, Taiwan, and South Korea—to reconsider their own security relationships with China and North Korea. Despite having given up something for nothing, Trump nonetheless declared the Singapore summit a great success and remarkably claimed that North Korea was no longer a nuclear threat. Yet as the Afterword chronicles, within weeks, follow-on Pyongyang talks foundered; U.S. intelligence falsified Trump's boast by determining that in fact, North Korea had increased its fuel production for nuclear weapons at multiple secret sites.

Despite its vociferous initial criticism of the Obama–Clinton North Korea strategy, as the Singapore process unfolds, the Trump administration will have little choice but to revert to a variant of the Obama administration's past policies. As the Iran Nuclear Deal shows, an engage–translate–leverage approach would combine at least five elements: (1) containment through renewed sanctions;[15] (2) deterrence through coordinated U.S.-Republic of Korea military cooperation; (3) intense multilateral diplomacy with a special focus on North Korea's horrifying human rights record;[16] (4) an accelerated surveillance and cybersabotage program; and (5) enhanced diplomatic pressure by China. All of this should be done with an eye toward getting away from parallel sets of bilateral talks, instead reviving something like the Six Party Talks as an ongoing multilateral diplomatic forum for confidence-building and discussing nonzero-sum trades.

Ironically, in Singapore, Trump relaxed nearly all of these elements. He prematurely floated the idea of sanctions relief, suddenly adopted the Chinese line criticizing American "war games" with South Korea, softened his human rights challenge, and extracted no concrete concessions or meaningful promises regarding denuclearization. But in the months ahead, under political pressure from allies and both sides of the political aisle, Trump's position will surely stiffen and most likely will end up looking like a variant of the prior Obama policy.

Unfortunately, the diplomatic option in North Korea has little chance of real success if the Iran Nuclear Deal finally collapses. Trump's Singapore statements nowhere noted the irony that the vague joint declaration that he was heralding offered nothing approaching the detail or enforcement mechanisms of the Iran Nuclear Deal, from which he had just walked away, despite its demonstrable elimination of 98 percent of Iran's enriched uranium. If Trump insists on walking away from a real denuclearization deal with Iran—a complying country that does not yet have nuclear weapons—why should North Korea ever agree to comply with any nascent paper declaration with Trump that would verifiably dismantle its far more extensive nuclear arsenal?[17]

Nor can the United States meaningfully achieve its goal of complete North Korean denuclearization without an enforceable international legal commitment ensuring greater International Atomic Energy Agency (IAEA) visibility into North Korean nuclear activities. Without regular IAEA access and monitoring, North Korea's ad hoc promises to allow external observers to see one closed missile site give no meaningful assurances that other sites are not fully operational. Nor can the United States persuade Kim Jong-un to stick to any binding commitment—or use its smart power to encourage Russia, China, and our European allies to keep up the pressure on him—unless all of those nations believe that the United States will stick by that deal.

So by backing out of the Iran Deal, Trump again seems to have played into Kim's hands, and given him another bargaining chip. As negotiations unfold, North Korea could now cite Trump's Iran withdrawal as reason to walk away and keep developing the operational capability to reliably deliver nuclear warheads to the U.S. mainland. More likely, Kim could conclude that his weapons cache, unlike those given up by now-toppled regimes in Tehran and Tripoli, will both keep him in power and give him continuing sway at the diplomatic poker table. He could thus still enter into lengthy talks with Trump and Moon, but in the end claim that he has insufficient guarantees about American intentions to warrant completing denuclearization. This tack would allow Kim both to blame Trump and to slow development of his intercontinental delivery capabilities, while still hanging on to the rest of his nuclear and missile force capabilities. Now blessed by America, the North Korean nuclear program would become a permanent reality.

In fact, Trump has many possible bargaining chips that would feed Kim's ego but cost the United States and South Korea little or nothing. These include transborder reunification of elderly North and South Korean citizens (which Moon and Kim have already begun discussing), return of remains of prisoners of war and those missing in action, further joint participation in global sporting and cultural events à la the Pyeongchang Olympics, an American Interests Section in Pyongyang (similar to the one long maintained in Havana), an emergency communications channel (or "hotline") to reduce bilateral uncertainty about actions on both sides of the border, and more freezes or reductions in joint U.S. military exercises with the South, which could be done with little negative impact on joint military readiness.[18]

Simply put, Singapore marks only the beginning of a lengthy process, and not necessarily a promising one. Going forward, Trump's North Korea negotiators will have little choice but to flesh out the Singapore Joint Declaration in greater detail, with more timelines, benchmarks, and concrete steps. Instead of rejecting, they will need to build on, the model of the Iran Nuclear Deal. At the outset that Deal required Tehran to eliminate 98 percent of its enriched uranium and to keep the rest of its enrichment below weapons-grade, to decommission its plutonium reactor, and to dismantle and mothball two-thirds of its centrifuges. Stage One of a similar North Korea negotiation would entail an interim "freeze, inspection, and staged rollback" agreement that trades staged lifting of sanctions for North Korean transparency to genuine international verification.[19] If negotiations deepen, the parties could move to Stage Two: comprehensive discussion of both peace and denuclearization in a multilateral setting. Stage Two could barter staged sanctions relief, high-level visits, international recognition, and humanitarian food and energy aid in exchange for greater transparency. IAEA inspectors must monitor the entire nuclear supply chain—from mining through enrichment and reprocessing—to ensure a genuine, sequenced standstill and rollback of the North Korean nuclear program.[20] But all of this will require far more care and commitment than Trump or his political team have exhibited thus far with regard to the building of international legal architecture.

Ironically, Trump is most likely to succeed if he, like Hillary Clinton and Barack Obama, abandons ad hoc bilateral "headline diplomacy." Instead, he must pursue a carefully negotiated global diplomatic solution that builds a binding legal regime firmly rooted in international law. Trump cannot meaningfully engage with North Korea without relying on all of the "smart-power" elements that he has always disparaged: careful planning, sustained multilateral diplomacy, self-conscious international legal regime-building, and reliance on the State Department's still-extensive bureaucratic memory on North Korea. Simply put, Trump's best "new" policy would be to double down on the old. All of his policy's twists and turns have now clearly abandoned his self-proclaimed strategy of "maximum pressure." So in the end, perhaps the best name for this "new" policy would be "renewed strategic patience."

B. THE RUSSIAN FEDERATION

All seventeen investigating U.S. intelligence agencies and the U.S. Senate Intelligence Committee now agree that Russia "hacked" the 2016 U.S. presidential election. These investigative bodies found that Russia's President Putin did so with an eye toward "undermin[ing] public faith in the U.S. democratic process, denigrat[ing] Secretary Clinton, and harm[ing] her electability and potential presidency." They "further asses[sed that] Putin and the Russian Government developed a clear preference for President-elect Trump."[21] In this setting, "hacking the election" meant distinct but coordinated cyberefforts by different entities associated with the Russian government. These efforts included conducting information operations by deploying bots, trolls, and automation multipliers operated by Russia's Internet Research Agency to steer discussion on social media platforms like Facebook and Twitter. Such operations were apparently combined with active cyberintrusions by Russian operatives against the computers of the Democratic National Committee and Clinton campaign chair John Podesta.

The multiple investigations currently proceeding—principally those led by the bipartisan Senate Intelligence Committee and by Special Counsel Robert Mueller and other prosecutors[22]— have also focused on direct campaign contacts between Russian nationals and Trump campaign staff. Two staff members, George

Papadopoulos and former National Security Adviser Michael Flynn, have already pleaded guilty to lying to federal investigators about these contacts. An amicus brief filed by Yale Law School's Rule of Law Clinic on behalf of thirty-six Russia hands and former intelligence officials recently documented how Russian intelligence has traditionally used "active measure campaigns" not just in the 2016 elections but in a whole "range of activities that include written or spoken disinformation, the spreading of conspiracy theories, efforts to control the media, the use of forgeries, political influence campaigns, the funding of extremist and opposition groups, and cyberattacks" to achieve Russian political ends.[23] A hallmark of these Russian active measure campaigns has been their reliance on intermediaries or "cut outs" inside a country like the United States—including "the unwitting accomplice who is manipulated to act in what he believes is his best interest"—to "amplify the scope and reach of Russian influence efforts, while hiding their involvement and preserving a degree of deniability."

To be sure, the ongoing investigations also focus, inter alia, on claims of money laundering and obstruction of justice. But while it is too early to tell precisely what violations of domestic criminal law may have occurred, Mueller has already indicted a web of Russian conspirators, laying a legal foundation for future charges against others who were aware of the conspiracy and took overt actions to further it. At this writing, we also know from public information that Trump's former campaign chair, Paul Manafort, has been indicted on thirty-two counts—including conspiracy and possible money laundering for Russians—and that there were multiple contacts between various Russians and senior members of the Trump campaign.[24]

While we are still learning the full story, the broader foreign policy question is how lawfully to prevent exactly the same Russian hacking from afflicting our next set of elections. This is a nonpartisan issue that could well recur, in the United States or abroad, as early as the 2018 midterm elections.[25] If these actions were illegal, how can we fight them with the tools of international law?

Although the international law of cyberspace is in its infancy,[26] even if the Russians did not actually manipulate polling results, coercive interference in another country's electoral politics—including the deliberate spreading of false news—constitutes an intervention that violates international law. The most prominent group of nongovernmental experts writing on cyberwar and cybersecurity has declared that "[i]llegal coercive interference could include manipulation of elections or of public opinion on the eve of elections, as when online news services are altered in favo[]r of a particular party, false news is spread, or the online services of one party are shut off."[27] An external attempt to distort the information that voters possess when they go to the polls also violates the human rights of the electors under the International Covenant on Civil and Political Rights.[28]

Given these manifest violations, the recommended policy response would again be to engage–translate–leverage. Ideally, the United States would diplomatically *engage* the Russians to secure acknowledgment that their actions were illegal, *translate* from emerging cyberlaw and existing human rights law to articulate the precise international norms violated, then seek to internalize those norms into domestic law in order to *leverage* from that legal interpretation regarding illegal cyber-intrusions to a policy outcome whereby the United States and other nations could monitor Russian forbearance from future hacking misadventures.

Before he left office, President Obama began that process with a calibrated response under international law: expelling a number of Russian diplomats and closing spy facilities within the United States. Shortly after the 2016 election, the Obama administration issued a legal interpretation. Without mentioning Russia by name, my successor as State Department Legal Adviser publicly cautioned that "a cyber operation by a State that interferes with another country's ability to hold an election or that manipulates another country's election results would be a clear violation of the rule of non-intervention."[29] Had Hillary Clinton become president, the obvious next question would have been whether the United States should now use its cyberassets to punish Russian hackers directly, such as by trying to knock them offline or damaging their hardware, once the United States had met its burden of proof for attributing proxy acts to official Russian actors.[30]

Instead, the Trump administration's "Russia sanctions slow-walk" undermined efforts to leverage Obama's initial moderated response into a broader political outcome. Repeatedly calling the various investigations a "witch hunt," President Trump regularly threatened to retract or modify President Obama's response to the hacking.[31] His reluctance even to acknowledge that the hacking had occurred gave critical cover to Putin, who refused to accept responsibility for his illegal actions. As a result, the Russian hack stands in the way of addressing other aspects of bilateral U.S. policy toward Russia going forward, including Iran, Ukraine, Syria, the Islamic State, and the human rights issues surrounding Putin's brutal treatment of demonstrators and what one commentator called a "trail of dead Russians."[32]

But once again, Trump does not own this transnational legal process story. Congress responded to these startling facts by passing, with overwhelming veto-proof margins, a sweeping Russian sanctions bill—the "Countering America's Adversaries Through Sanctions Act" (CAATSA)—which the president was reluctantly compelled to sign.[33] The Russian sanctions have effectively internalized international law's condemnation of Russian cyber-actions. It required the U.S. State Department to penalize foreign governments and companies doing business with Russia's defense and intelligence sectors, list oligarchs close to Putin's government, and detail possible consequences of imposing penalties on Russia's sovereign debt. Under this law, sanctions may only be delayed or waived if the administration presents Congress with affirmative evidence that Russia is making progress in reducing cybermeddling. Russia vowed an aggressive pushback against the new congressional sanctions.[34] As successive statutory deadlines came and went, however, the Trump administration declined to impose additional sanctions on Russia, insisting instead without evidence that the mere "threat" of sanctions was already acting as an effective deterrent against future Russian adventurism.

Apart from public political pressure, Congress has few remedies to enforce a sanctions law that it has already enacted. In theory, Congress could pass veto-proof mandatory sanctions without waiver provisions, but it has been traditionally reluctant to leave the president without any sanctions safety valve. But as with the South African sanctions bill of the mid-1980s—which passed by veto-proof margins in both houses—the threat that Congress would introduce more such legislation finally spurred several rounds of executive sanctions against Russia in the spring of 2018. In March, the administration finally announced that it would target new sanctions against Russian companies and individuals who had mounted cyberattacks intervening in the 2016 election, including individuals indicted by Special Counsel Mueller. In April, the administration followed with penalties against twenty-four private and public members of Putin's inner circle. Under pressure from allies, the administration then responded to Russian use of nerve agents against a former Russian spy living in Salisbury, England, by expelling sixty Russian diplomats and intelligence officers and closing Russia's Seattle consulate. The Trump administration also approved the sale and transfer to Ukraine of the anti-tank Javelin missile systems, which Putin had opposed and the Obama administration had not authorized. And after Trump pulled back U.N. Ambassador Nikki Haley's April 2018 announcement that the United States would join multilateral sanctions against Russia for its apparent complicity in Bashar al-Assad's chemical attacks on his own civilians in Syria, the administration finally put out word that yet another round of sanctions might be forthcoming.[35] As one Moscow watcher noted, we are witnessing a "growing, rather paradoxical reality, in which Trump as an individual continues to act glaringly conciliatory to Putin, yet his Administration repeatedly takes measures that are arguably more hostile to Putin than those enacted under Obama."[36]

So even if—for whatever reason—Trump does not want to punish Moscow, transnational legal process is nevertheless forcing his hand. The president is deeply embedded in legal frameworks of foreign policy response, just as the United States is deeply embedded in global legal frameworks. Despite Trump's persistent pro-Russian rhetoric, congressional action, independent prosecutors, and the imperative for solidarity with close allies are all making it impossible for Trump to simply stand pat on Russian sanctions. At the same time, the international law prohibition against complicity in the use of chemical weapons is further driving the United States to act with its allies as part of a collective response.

While these are important developments, we should not overstate how much tit-for-tat retaliation is genuinely possible between these two old Cold War rivals. In a post-Cold War world, the United States and Russia are repeat players in a great many thorny global situations. Even within a badly strained relationship, they will have little choice going forward but to remain deeply engaged with one another. In the months ahead, the United States and Russia will continue to battle in the shadows of espionage, in cyberspace, and in the frightening new world of social media information manipulation. But like it or not, Trump and the Russians remain jointly enmeshed in the transnational legal process. In both the military and diplomatic arenas, they will still need one another to help address such complex foreign policy challenges as Iran, the Islamic State (IS), Syria, and Ukraine.

C. UKRAINE

Ukraine is another country where, despite blatant Russian intervention, a hard-power response does not appear to be a live option. As with the hacking of the American election, the Russian central command—using local proxies and shielded by implausible claims of deniability—again committed a systematic pattern and practice of violating sovereignty and human rights, in brazen defiance of international law.

Starting in 2014, Russia seized, occupied, and purported to annex Crimea. As occupation authorities, Russian proxies pursued a campaign of promoting ethnic Russian dominance, and punishing the Crimean Tatar and ethnic Ukrainian populations for their refusal to accept the annexation. Russia ousted Ukraine from exercising its legal rights as a coastal state by seizing living and nonliving resources in Crimean waters—including platforms, infrastructure, fisheries, and underwater cultural heritage—and expropriating and interfering with investments in Ukraine. In eastern Ukraine, Russia sponsored illegal armed groups as they launched a campaign of violence, terror, and intimidation designed to seize control from the legitimate authorities. And in August 2014, Russian-supported terrorists shot down 298 civilians—including three infants—the majority of them Dutch, aboard Malaysian Airlines Flight MH17 as it transited Ukrainian airspace. Whether operating overtly through an occupation regime or indirectly by arming proxies and sponsoring their campaign of intimidation, Russia has displayed a brazen disrespect for the human rights not just of the Ukrainian people but of the world at large.

With then-Vice President Joe Biden taking the lead, the Obama administration sought to pursue an engage–translate–leverage strategy: *engaging* with the European Union and the Organization for Security and Cooperation in Europe in direct dialogue regarding Ukraine, *translating* norms of nonintervention to make it clear that the United States considered Russia's invasion of Ukraine and its seizure of oil reserves in Crimea blatantly illegal, and *leveraging* these elements into a broader "Minsk II" diplomatic process aimed at securing a fairer long-term outcome that is more respectful of Ukraine's democracy and human rights.

When Russia brushed these efforts aside, Ukraine took matters into its own hands and triggered its own set of global interactions designed to generate legal interpretations that could ultimately be internalized into Russian domestic conduct.[37] When the Obama administration left office, the Trump administration ceased robust engagement with Russia on Ukraine, and Ukraine's efforts to seek international justice took on new meaning. Just before Trump's inauguration, Ukraine brought an application against Russia before the International Court of Justice in The Hague (ICJ), alleging that Russia had violated the International Convention for the Suppression of the Financing of Terrorism[38] with its actions in eastern Ukraine, particularly in allowing the Buk missile that shot down MH17 to enter Ukraine in 2014. The lawsuit further alleged that Russia had engaged in systematic discriminatory actions in Crimea against Crimean Tatars and ethnic Ukrainians in violation of Russia's obligations under the International Convention on the Elimination of All Forms of Racial Discrimination (CERD).[39]

The international lawsuit alleged that Russia had turned these two solemn treaties on their head, placing itself above the law. Far from suppressing the financing of terrorism, Russia had supported it by transferring vast amounts of dangerous weapons and other support to groups known to engage in terrorist acts against civilians. Far from eliminating all forms of racial discrimination, Russian occupation authorities had openly employed multiple forms of discrimination in Crimea: promoting ethnic Russian dominance and punishing the Crimean Tatar and ethnic Ukrainian populations for refusing to accept as legitimate Russia's purported annexation of the territory.

In April 2017, the International Court of Justice issued an order for provisional measures against Russia that made clear its expectations that, during the litigation, Russia would honor the Terrorism Financing Convention, the CERD, and its diplomatic commitments in the Minsk II process, which include stopping the flow of weapons to illegal groups in Ukraine.[40] In the face of a flagging multilateral diplomatic process and the Trump administration's striking passivity toward Russian adventurism, Ukraine has thus been able to deploy transnational legal process as part of its own broader rule-of-law response to Russian aggression.

A judgment from the ICJ could help strengthen a collective response to Russia's actions and delegitimize Putin's actions, making implementation of the Minsk II process more likely. At the same time, Ukraine has filed additional legal challenges concurrently with its ICJ litigation. These include a suit condemning the seizure of Crimean oil reserves, platforms, infrastructure, fisheries, and underwater cultural heritage before the International Tribunal for the Law of the Sea (ITLOS) in Hamburg, as well as investor–state arbitrations under a bilateral investment treaty contesting expropriation and illegal interference by Russia with investments in Ukraine.[41]

While it is too early to tell whether these international lawsuits will succeed, at least they have allowed Ukraine to seize back the initiative. Ukraine has used international law to put Russia on the defensive, to demand explanations, and to fill some of the vacuum left by the Trump administration's public refusal to challenge Putin's violations of international law. In late July 2018, following Trump's disastrous Helsinki Summit with Putin, a harried Trump administration finally issued a declaration calling on Russia to end its illegal occupation of Crimea. But by bringing these transnational claims, Ukraine had already said that neither Trump nor Russia controls transnational legal process. By bypassing Trump and directly contesting Russia's actions before various global tribunals capable of determining their legality, Ukraine has confronted Russia on legal ground and reasserted itself as an independent player within the transnational legal process.

Chapter 5

America's Wars

Seventeen years after September 11, 2001, the United States' armed conflict in Afghanistan and against Al Qaeda and its associated forces has become America's longest war. That war has now lasted thirteen years longer than the Civil War or World War II, and nearly nine years longer than the Revolutionary War. So much ink has been spilled about the "Forever War"—and such related topics as torture, Guantánamo, and drones—that one can hardly remember what the world was like before September 11.

As State Department Legal Adviser during the Barack Obama administration, I worked daily to ensure that the post-9/11 war stayed within legal limits. But I soon became convinced that the larger, more critical project was bringing the Forever War to an end. For America, peace should be the norm and war the exception. Condoning a state of perpetual war would mark a gross deviation from our constitutional and international norms. When I returned to private life in early 2013, I began giving public statements calling for our political leaders to make a concerted effort in that direction.[1] In a wide-ranging speech delivered at the National Defense University in May 2013, President Obama expressly embraced that goal, saying we need to "continue to fight terrorism without keeping America on a perpetual wartime

The Trump Administration and International Law. Harold Hongju Koh.
© Oxford University Press 2019. Published 2019 by Oxford University Press.

footing."[2] But with Donald Trump's election, that goal has lost its White House sponsor.

This chapter addresses three questions. First, how, during a Trump presidency, can the United States finally end its long-running battle against Al Qaeda and the Islamic State? Second and more fundamentally, how can it end the parade of mutating conflicts that leads to Forever War in Afghanistan? Third and most vexing, what can international law do to address the continuing nightmare in Syria, which triggered the refugee crisis that destabilized Europe, arguably caused Brexit, and may have contributed to Trump's own election?

A. AL QAEDA AND IS

Return with me for a moment to September 18, 2001, one week after the fall of the Twin Towers in New York City. Suppose the president of the United States had given the following speech:

> My fellow citizens of America and the world: we have just suffered the worst attack on our soil since Pearl Harbor. A week ago, more than 3,000 innocent people were killed just for going to work. This was an obscene human rights violation. We must respond firmly and lawfully, consistent with our values. Today, Congress passed the 2001 Authorization for the Use of Military Force (AUMF), which authorizes me to go to war against Al Qaeda, the Taliban, and associated forces. Our aim must be to defeat Al Qaeda and its partners and to prevent them from proliferating and attacking our homeland.
>
> So here is what we will not do, and here is what we must do. We will not do anything foolish, illegal, or inconsistent with American values. We will not violate foreign

sovereignty or international law. We will not claim that we are in a Global War on Terror. We are in a particular battle with a particular foe that just attacked us—Al Qaeda—so we must defeat it in time. But we will not invade Iraq. We will not torture anyone. We will not open offshore prison camps like Guantánamo. We will not create military commissions because our existing civilian and military courts can do the job. But here is what we must do. We must incapacitate— by capture if possible, by killing if necessary—Osama bin Laden and his senior operational leaders—several hundred in all—who pose a direct threat to the United States. We will use law enforcement methods when they are available and military measures when they are not. We will take every available step to prevent civilian casualties. But we will also use every technological method lawfully available to us, including drones.

In using these tools, we will work closely with our allies. We will be as transparent as we can be: we will keep Congress and the public fully informed. We will adhere to domestic and international law, and where that law is murky, we will work hard to clarify the governing international norms. We will isolate extremists and reach out to moderate Islam. And in all cases, we will respect our Constitution, international law, and the human rights of those who so grossly violated them.

This will not be easy. It will take time, and it will cost lives. Not everything will be public. But I pledge that this will be both a bipartisan and a global effort. We will not turn this into a political football. This is the World against Al Qaeda, not the United States against the World. Unlike other wars, from which we could walk away, this is a conflict we must win if our families are to live in our homeland free from fear. Let us all hope this is over very soon. Please give us your support.

Sadly, this was the road not taken. What this thought experiment shows is how badly America mismanaged its response to 9/11. Instead of acting firmly and surgically against Al Qaeda, the United States squandered global goodwill by invading Iraq, committing torture, opening Guantánamo, flouting domestic and international law, and undermining civilian courts. By taking the wrong path, the George W. Bush administration sacrificed legitimacy and took its eye off the ball, leaving its successors to pick up the pieces.

Although some critics claim that the Obama administration's approach to counterterrorism mirrored George W. Bush's, in fact Obama visibly shifted to a more nuanced "smart-power" strategy toward counterterrorism. Obama pledged that the United States would fight terrorism by *engaging* with its allies, *translating* from the existing laws of war in an effort to integrate lawful targeting and detention into an overarching strategy of smart power, and *leveraging* limited uses of force with strong legal tools, such as diplomacy, development, and cooperative law enforcement in search of broader diplomatic solutions. Within this broad collective "smart-power" response to terrorism, he asserted, drones are not a strategy, but rather a legally available tool.

Because torture is always illegal, in conducting this more limited conflict, the Obama administration showed an absolute commitment to the humane treatment of Al Qaeda suspects. No one claimed that the Obama administration conducted torture, waterboarding, or enhanced interrogation tactics. But within a smart-power strategy, the use of drones in wartime could be lawful, depending on the precise facts regarding how they are used. It is thus profound error to suggest that we need to "keep lawyers off the backs of the generals." It is precisely the legal advice the generals are getting that ensures that they are engaged in lawful acts of war, and not illegal acts of summary execution.

President Obama got off to a promising start with his January 2009 executive orders ending torture, his vow to close Guantánamo, his 2009 Nobel Prize speech, and his 2010 National Archives speech in which he affirmed his commitment to follow the laws of war. In early 2010, I gave my first speech as State Department Legal Adviser to the American Society of International Law outlining the basic legal standards the U.S. government applied to such actions, and in the years that followed, other Obama officials followed.[3]

In these public statements, the Obama administration abandoned George W. Bush's open-ended claim of a "Global War on Terror." If such a global war rages, arguably no law applies, because the United States is authorized to use force anywhere, against anyone in self-defense. Instead, the Obama administration expressly acknowledged that its authority under domestic law derives from acts of Congress, not just the president's vague constitutional powers. And under international law, following Bush's second-term position, the Obama administration further recognized that U.S. actions are constrained by the laws of war. So rather than treating this conflict as a black hole, Obama's administration worked to translate the spirit of those laws and to apply them to this new situation. Under Obama's framework, the United States no longer described itself as generally at war with "terror," but rather as engaged in much narrower armed conflict in which drones and other tools are used to dismantle specific nonstate transnational networks that have directly attacked and threatened the United States, such as Al Qaeda and the so-called "Islamic State."

But in the years that followed, progress was slow. The Obama administration visibly failed to complete its eight-year effort to close Guantánamo. Nor did it end the use of military commissions in favor of trying leading terrorists only in civilian courts. Obama announced plans to withdraw all troops from both Iraq and

Afghanistan, but they are still in those countries today. And with the rise of terrorist groups like the Islamic State (IS), the armed conflict spread to new geographic regions. At this writing, U.S. armed forces remain engaged in active conflict across the globe: particularly in Afghanistan, Iraq, Syria, Yemen, and parts of Africa, against Al Qaeda and its partners, as well as IS.

Nor, at the outset, was the Obama administration sufficiently transparent—to the media, to Congress, and to our allies—about the legal standards and decision-making process that it applied to its use of drones. The inevitable release of necessary pieces of the administration's public legal defense came too little and too late. This spurred a left-right coalition—running from Code Pink to Rand Paul—to speak out against the drone program, fostering the perception that the program was illegal, unnecessary, and out of control. The public lost track of the real issue, which was never drone technology per se, but rather the need for transparent, agreed-upon domestic and international legal process and standards.

After all, cutting-edge technologies are often deployed for military purposes, but whether or not they are being used lawfully depends on whether they are deployed consistently with the laws of war. It makes as little sense to attack the technology of drones as it does to attack the technology of other remote precision weapons that were novel in their time, such as spears, catapults, or guided missiles. Indeed, because drone technology is highly precise, if properly controlled to minimize civilian casualties, it could prove *more* lawful and consistent with human rights and humanitarian law than the alternatives. Ironically, even as we argue about the law governing drone technology, that technology is rapidly being supplanted by even more technologically advanced tools of war, such as cyberwar or more advanced robotics, for which the governing legal standards are even more murky.

In May 2013, President Obama made an important course correction in a wide-ranging speech delivered at the National Defense University ("NDU speech").[4] He committed himself to ending the Forever War by: (1) disengaging from Afghanistan; (2) closing Guantánamo; and (3) disciplining drones. His speech made clear that the administration's counterterrorism strategy viewed "kill and capture" as only a small part of a broader engage–translate–leverage strategy. "In the Afghan war theater," the president said, "we must—and will—continue to support our troops until the transition is complete at the end of 2014 [by continuing] to take strikes against high value Al Qaeda targets, but also against forces that are massing to support attacks on coalition forces. . . . [But b]eyond the Afghan theater," the president clarified, "we only target Al Qaeda and its associated forces."[5]

Even then, he made clear, the use of drones would be heavily constrained by four principles. First, that America adheres to the principle of "capture over kill." Second, that the United States must conduct this conflict with full respect for international law and state sovereignty. Third, that under the international law of *jus ad bellum* (the law of going to war), the doctrine of self-defense may at times be invoked to use force—based on a necessarily elongated notion of "imminence"[6]—against those senior operational leaders who present a "continuing and imminent threat" of striking against the United States.[7] And fourth, that as a matter of *jus in bello* (the law applied in war), in any use of force, there must be a "near-certainty that no civilians will be killed or injured."[8] The president further committed himself to maintaining a clear, lawful, and workable framework to govern *detention* of Al Qaeda and its associated forces at Guantánamo and elsewhere. He promised *transparency and consultation* with Congress and allies and to consider future workable proposals to extend oversight of lethal actions taken outside of active war zones. Each of these key principles—a smart-power strategy, legal frameworks to govern drones and detention, and a commitment to transparency, consultation, and oversight—marked a significant advance over past policy.

Initially, President Obama detailed these policies in classified presidential policy guidance. But when leaving office in December 2016, the Obama administration embedded these principles into a comprehensive "legal and policy frameworks" document, designed to govern how the various U.S. practices developed during the previous eight years could be squared with the international laws of war.[9] In short, he relied on both policy *and* legal frameworks to promote the stickiness of internalized international norms. By so doing, Obama apparently counted on the future "hardening" over time of norms first articulated as policy into binding legal rules: the notion at the core of transnational legal process. In March 2011, the Obama administration had similarly issued a little-noticed announcement of support for two important components of the international legal framework mandating humane treatment in armed conflicts: Additional Protocol II and Article 75 of Additional Protocol I to the 1949 Geneva Conventions.[10] While in 2011, the Obama administration could not bring itself to say outright that these provisions constituted customary international law, as time has passed, these policies have hardened to now effectively bind the U.S. government as a matter of customary international law.

Of course, the Obama administration was far from perfect. My goal is not to whitewash its blemishes, but to suggest that in this area, Obama got three big things right. First, as the next section discusses, Obama committed himself to bringing the Forever War to an end.

Second, he articulated a better general strategy of "international law as smart power"—engage–translate–leverage—than

Trump's destructive approach of "disengage–follow national interests–go it alone." As Secretary Hillary Clinton made clear on the tenth anniversary of September 11, in the short-term, we have an inescapable need for "precise and persistent force [that] can significantly degrade . . . al-Qaida. So we will continue to go after its leaders and commanders, disrupt their operations and bring them to justice. . . . attack its finances, recruitment, and safe havens."[11] But our longer-term objective must be what she called a "smart-power" approach: using force for limited and defined purposes within a much broader nonviolent frame, with our broad objective being to use diplomacy, development, education, and people-to-people outreach to challenge Al Qaeda's "ideology, counter its propaganda, and diminish its appeal, so that every community recognizes the threat that extremists pose to them and . . . deny them protection and support. And we need effective international partners in government and civil society who can extend this effort to all the places where terrorists operate."[12]

Third and most fundamentally, Obama saw the lawfulness of American actions as critical to the global legitimacy of U.S. counterterrorism policy. During its eight years, the Obama administration became more willing to bind itself to a more transparent, more rigorous, more fact-based set of legal rules to govern the post-9/11 conflict. President Obama left office having acknowledged that under traditional laws of war, the United States is obliged to follow both the law of initiating war (jus ad bellum) and the law of conducting war (jus in bello). Under domestic law, the United States must follow the terms of both the Constitution and the various statutory authorizations for, and restrictions on, the use of military force.[13] The United States under Obama asserted that it is in a non-international armed conflict with Al Qaeda, the Taliban, and associated forces in response to the 9/11 attacks and may use force consistent with the laws of war and its inherent right to self-defense. Under this theory, the Obama administration construed the Islamic State (IS) to be a successor to Al Qaeda, as a splinter or offshoot of the Al Qaeda core, that had entered the fight against the United States alongside other armed groups in such active theaters of battle as Afghanistan, Iraq, and Syria.[14] As a matter of international law, the United States claimed to be participating militarily in Syria against IS based not on Bashar al-Assad's consent, but rather in collective self-defense of Iraq. By contrast, until its recent disengagement, Russia said it had been invited to fight in Syria against IS by Assad's government.[15]

The Obama administration never rejected law enforcement tools in favor of exclusive use of tools of war. Instead, it combined a law-of-war approach with law enforcement and other strategies to bring all available tools to bear against Al Qaeda. Thus, if the United States had encountered an Al Qaeda leader like Osama bin Laden in Afghanistan—or as it turned out, in Abbottabad—a law-of-war approach might be appropriate. But if America had instead found him in London or New York, where law enforcement officers were ready and willing to arrest him, a law enforcement approach would have been required. To trigger either response, the relevant question would not be one of *labels*—i.e., "should we call this person an 'enemy combatant'?"—but rather one of *facts*: "Do the facts show that this particular person is actually part of Al Qaeda or its 'associated forces'?"

The Obama administration anticipated that its work would be carried on by a Hillary Clinton administration. But executive branch policies do not bind future administrations in the same way as executive branch determinations about the applicability of international legal rules. Based on recent reporting, many of the legal principles that the Obama administration painstakingly articulated are now up for grabs. It remains unclear how scrupulously these legal and policy rules—particularly the "near-certainty" rules to ensure that civilians are not targeted by drone strikes or other military action—are now being followed by the Trump administration[16] As many have pointed out, the number of civilians whom the Pentagon actually admits to having killed in Iraq and Syria is implausibly low. Some commentators believe that the actual number of civilian dead may be as much as thirty-one times higher than the coalition's figures, because of a flawed methodology that requires that, simply to open an investigation, the Pentagon must first determine by a "preponderance of the evidence" whether a strike has resulted in a civilian death.[17] Nor did President Trump's 2017 speech regarding his Afghanistan strategy clarify much beyond his amorphous intention to maintain an unspecified number of troops there for the indefinite future.[18]

Since Trump took office, his counterterrorism strategy has doubled down on the use of hard power. In September 2017, the Trump administration finally announced its replacement of Obama's presidential policy guidance with a new, apparently looser framework.[19] Inside reporting now strongly suggests that both the drone rules and the detention standards have been significantly loosened.[20] Despite Trump's decision to lift the Obama "near certainty" rules for Somalia, the U.S. military commander for the African Command apparently continued to apply this rigorous standard against civilian deaths.[21] Trump declared large chunks of Yemen and Somalia to be "areas of active hostilities," thereby exempting them from Obama's 2013 rules just before a disastrous raid in Yemen that killed many civilians.[22] In Afghanistan, Trump gave more operational authority to military leaders and in April 2017, the U.S. military deployed a giant GBU-43 (the so-called "mother of all bombs") on an IS tunnel to send a strong signal about the new president's willingness to use aggressive force.[23] In the battle against IS, America has also vividly demonstrated its vaunted capacity to exercise hard power, which the world had already witnessed in both Gulf Wars.[24] But Trump's anti-IS plan was hardly his; an almost-identical use of hard power against IS in these strongholds had also formed a key piece of Hillary Clinton's plan for fighting IS, a strategy that included nullifying these strongholds by intensifying the air campaign and stepping up support for local forces on the ground.[25]

In his January 2018 State of the Union speech, Trump heralded military victories over IS in Mosul, Iraq, and Raqqa, Syria, but asserted that he was battling a still-dangerous foe.[26] The United States' impending completion of its hard-power mission against IS has only surfaced new, vexing questions: where, for example, should captured IS fighters be detained so as not to create a new extremist "Islamic State 2.0," birthed in the detention camps of Syria or Iraq? As the intense 2018 battle for Afrin showed, the United States is now torn between its reliance on armed Kurdish forces on the ground and the determination of its Turkish NATO partner to continue its endless conflict with Kurdish militants, now operating within Syrian territory.

What remains sadly underdeveloped or missing from the Trump administration's program are the *smart-power pieces* of the Clinton strategy. In particular—as I will say more about at the end of this chapter—Trump offers no identifiable diplomatic strategy to resolve Syria's civil war and Iraq's sectarian conflict between Sunnis and Shias—both of which have contributed to the rise of IS. Nor is it clear what steps, if any, the Trump administration is taking to cut off IS's supplies, money, arms, propaganda, and fighters.

As presidential candidate Hillary Clinton recognized, the conflict against IS is taking place not just in Iraq and Syria but also online and in the homelands of North America and Europe. She urged that the United States mobilize smart-power cybertools and public diplomacy to lead a concerted effort to discredit IS ideology online: stopping digital recruitment strategies; hardening homeland defenses; using an "intelligence surge" to build resilience at home; and making concerted individual and collective law enforcement efforts to discover and disrupt terrorist plots before they occur. Obviously, executing this broader smart-power approach would require the new administration to maintain and deepen strong alliances, particularly with Canada and Europe. But far from doing so, from his earliest diplomatic conversations, Donald Trump has placed those alliances under extraordinary strain, including with many of his actions already described: the Muslim Ban, "withdrawal" from the Paris Agreement and the Iran Nuclear Deal, and hostile trade diplomacy.

Going forward, the canary in the coal mine will be how the Trump administration distinguishes criminal acts from acts of war, when treating homegrown sympathizers allegedly "inspired" by Al Qaeda or IS. The Obama administration made clear that the United States is not at war with any idea or religion. Nor is it at war with mere propagandists or journalists, or with every sad individual—like the Boston Marathon bombers—who may become radicalized, inspired by Al Qaeda's ideology, but who never actually join or become part of Al Qaeda. Such persons may be exceedingly dangerous, but they should be dealt with through tools of civilian law enforcement, not military action, because they are not part of any enemy force recognizable under the laws of war. For that reason, under Obama's theory, such self-radicalized individuals were considered imitators, not "members" of these terrorist organizations and hence better-suited for criminal prosecution than military action.[27] The United States has long successfully prosecuted horrific acts of terrorism within our civilian criminal justice system, with U.S. attorneys' offices in New York and Virginia achieving unblemished records of convictions.[28]

In the months ahead, we should be most wary of the "self-generated 9/11." Suppose Trump's Travel Ban inspires a Muslim-American residing in the United States to get a gun, shoot up a nightclub or shopping mall, and then post on Facebook that he supports Al Qaeda and IS. Our criminal justice system has a long and well-established history of swiftly trying and punishing such acts in civilian courts. That scenario would present absolutely no reason to bestow any new authorities on the executive branch, to send that person to Guantánamo, or to try that person before the struggling military commissions on the false claim that we cannot trust "so-called judges" to protect our safety. The most obvious motivation behind Trump's frequent attacks on independent Article III federal judges is to enable him, at some point in the future, to call for disobedience of adverse court orders on the grounds that federal judges are partisan political actors who cannot be trusted to protect us from such "bad hombres" as terrorists or immigrants.

It would be perverse indeed if homegrown attacks inspired by Trump's own discriminatory actions enabled him to successfully call for new accretions of, and deference to, his executive power. It would be even more perverse if a *new* round of homegrown IS attacks responding to the bellicosity of an extreme U.S. administration were used to justify revival of such failed counterterrorism measures as Guantánamo, military commissions, extraordinary rendition, or illegal interrogation by torture. Recent history only confirms that self-radicalized criminals are best subject to domestic law enforcement, not laws of war. Oklahoma City bomber Timothy McVeigh plotted and executed an attack that killed three hundred people, but was given due process, represented, tried, convicted, and executed, all within a civilian setting.[29] Similarly, Dzhokhar Tsarnaev, the younger Boston Marathon bomber, was fully represented, convicted, tried, and sentenced in an Article III court, during a period in which the cumbersome, constitutionally challenged post-9/11 military commission system achieved no meaningful convictions.[30]

In short, even—perhaps especially—if Trump favors swift punishment of terrorist suspects, he would be better off sticking to Obama's smart-power counterterrorism framework. Going forward, the broader U.S. counterterrorism approach cannot maintain its effectiveness unless it preserves its perceived legality. As the Trump administration's counterterrorism strategy evolves, its ability to pass muster under both international and domestic law will prove key to whether other transnational actors will continue to support the broader U.S. approach or rather, choose to challenge its legality before a variety of courts and other transnational fora.

B. ENDING THE FOREVER WAR

President Obama's 2013 NDU speech recognized that the armed conflict that began against Al Qaeda and its co-belligerents "like all wars, must end."[31] By so saying, he acknowledged that the United States is not committed to fighting everyone, everywhere—past, present, and future—who ever has or will dislike the United States or wish it harm. Instead, ever since Congress passed its 2001 Authorization for the Use of Military Force one week after September 11, the United States has engaged in an armed conflict with a knowable enemy that does not limit its activities to a single country's borders.[32]

But this was never intended to be a conflict without end. Admittedly, hard-power strategies are critical to end the conflict through military victory over such hard-core terrorist groups as Al Qaeda and IS. As the successful campaign against

IS has shown, such victories are possible. Jeh Johnson, then general counsel of the United States Department of Defense, argued six years ago:

> [T]here will come a tipping point ... at which so many of the leaders and operatives of Al Qaeda and its affiliates have been killed or captured, and the group is no longer able to attempt or launch a strategic attack against the United States, such that Al Qaeda as we know it, the organization that our Congress authorized the military to pursue in 2001, has been effectively destroyed.
>
> At that point, we must be able to say to ourselves that our efforts should no longer be considered an "armed conflict" against Al Qaeda and its associated forces; rather, a counterterrorism effort against *individuals* who are the scattered remnants of Al Qaeda, or are parts of groups unaffiliated with Al Qaeda, for which the law enforcement and intelligence resources of our government are principally responsible, in cooperation with the international community—with our military assets available in reserve to address continuing and imminent terrorist threats.[33]

To truly end the Forever War, U.S. counterterrorism policy should include three critical but achievable elements: (1) disengaging from Afghanistan; (2) closing Guantánamo and the military commissions; and (3) formally ending the war with Al Qaeda and its co-belligerents by narrowing and repealing two Authorizations for Use of Military Force that were enacted nearly two decades ago to authorize quite different wars.

1. Disengaging from Afghanistan

For Trump, the first goal—disengaging from Afghanistan—should be both easier and harder than it looks. It should be easier, because leaving Afghanistan's problems to others most squares with Trump's "America First" philosophy. But it is harder because there is no meaningful hard power solution in Afghanistan of the kind that Trump favors.

At this writing, the U.S. military has more than 15,000 troops in Afghanistan, a number that could soon increase.[34] The Obama administration tried and failed to get out of Afghanistan, and after reviewing the issue early in his term, Trump decided to retain a significant U.S. force there, while putting more diplomatic pressure on Pakistan and its Inter-Services Intelligence by withholding aid.[35] A full-scale initiative to leave Afghanistan in tolerable condition would require not just a security transition but also a political and economic transition, e.g., creation of a New Silk Road. Those transitions would require combining declining U.S. military engagement with a sustained diplomatic surge to create a regional architecture able to support a secure, stable Afghanistan, along with enhanced civilian engagement to develop the Afghan economy and civil society.

Starting under the late Afghanistan/Pakistan (AfPak) Coordinator Richard Holbrooke, the Obama administration began the diplomatic surge in 2010 in Lisbon, and intensified it in 2011 in Istanbul and Bonn, culminating in 2012 at the Chicago NATO and Tokyo Economic Summits. Through that robust diplomatic sequence, Afghanistan and its international partners charted a blueprint for a full transfer of security responsibility, which led to the 2012 Strategic Partnership Agreement, Afghanistan's designation as a major non-NATO ally of the United States, and the negotiation of agreements on bilateral security, detention transfer, and the like. Other efforts followed, particularly the 6+1 process (involving Afghanistan, Pakistan, Iran, China, Russia, and the United States), and most recently the Kabul Process, but each failed to establish a viable negotiating track because it did not include the Taliban.

These diplomatic strands remain available for Trump to pick up and pursue should he decide to pursue meaningful diplomacy with the government of Afghanistan, other strongly affected nations, and the Taliban itself. Before he died, Holbrooke and his team began secret talks with the Taliban.[36] But when, in February 2018, the Taliban issued an open letter to the American public requesting direct talks with the United States, Trump responded: "[T]here's no talking to the Taliban. We don't want to talk to the Taliban. We're going to finish what we have to finish."[37]

But if Trump is serious about leaving, there is no other way to create viable conditions for U.S. disengagement. As one of the most astute observers of this region has noted, "[s]talemated civil wars like Afghanistan's can last a very long time. They end only through negotiations with the enemy."[38] For an Afghan diplomatic effort to succeed, as Secretary Clinton described in her February 2011 speech to the Asia Society, the Taliban should accept, as necessary preconditions, three "unambiguous red lines for reconciliation . . . : [1] They must renounce violence; [2] they must abandon their alliance with al-Qaida; and [3] they must abide by the constitution of Afghanistan . . . [as] necessary outcomes of any negotiation."[39]

Under Trump's second Secretary of State, Mike Pompeo, the Trump administration could build on its recent willingness to open a secret negotiating track with North Korea to enlist some of the State Department's many AfPak hands to revive the back channel first created by Holbrooke to the Taliban Political

Commission, based in Doha, Qatar. The Taliban would have to accept involving the Afghan government in other aspects of the deal. The United States would need to signal that it is prepared, under the right conditions, to discuss the timeline and details of American troop withdrawal as part of a broader political settlement.[40] And all sides would need to consider whether accepting some small continuing American military presence would help contain insurgent splinter groups and Islamic State militants who might reject the peace process.

International economic support from the forty-two allied nations that joined in the Afghanistan mission would be needed to help stabilize the country economically and politically.[41] The key would be to build upon advances in Afghan civil society that have occurred in the last two decades. Ordinary Afghans must come to believe that even if some of the Taliban return, their society need not regress to the bleak days before September 11. A U.N. report showed that Afghanistan has made faster gains in human development over the last fifteen years than virtually any other country in the world.[42] When Afghan civil society development resumed a decade ago, there were few men, and almost no women, in school. Now there are nearly ten million attending school, almost evenly divided between men and women. Kabul is the fifth fastest-growing city in the world. Since 2003, the gross domestic product of Afghanistan has nearly quintupled. Health facilities like hospitals have quadrupled. Access to electricity has tripled. Life expectancy is up 50 percent. In the last decade, more roads have been built than in the entire previous history of the country. Cellphone contracts have gone from 20,000 to several million, and access to the Internet has gone from nonexistent to more than 5.7 million users.[43]

This, in short, is what a smart-power strategy looks like. As more and more Afghans become convinced that they, and not the

Taliban, control their political, economic, and security future, they can see U.S. disengagement as necessary to give them ownership of their own country and to bring civil society closer to self-reliance, self-determination, and self-governance. But to make this a genuinely regional discussion, the negotiations would need to expand to include China, India, Iran, Pakistan, Russia, and perhaps some Central Asian neighbors. Each of the parties has a stake in finally ending the endless war. For the United States simply to leave would surrender large parts of the country to the Taliban and the Islamic State, squandering the sunk costs in terms of American money and lives. Unlike IS, the Taliban does not appear to have regional or global aspirations for spreading jihad. China has a strong incentive to stabilize Afghanistan to further its ambitious Belt and Road Initiative in Pakistan and Central Asia. Pakistan has an interest in Afghanistan becoming more stable without an expanded Indian presence and in restarting millions of dollars in suspended U.S. foreign military aid. China, Iran, and Russia all share a common interest in preventing fleeing IS fighters from flooding into Afghanistan. Presidential elections are scheduled for 2019, which creates an opening to bring the Taliban into the political process, should the peace process bear fruit.

The discussion could begin with such consensus issues as Afghan sovereignty and ending foreign intervention, and move on to identifying key confidence-building measures. Understandably, human rights defenders fear that such negotiations may end up condoning regression in some parts of the country to grotesque Taliban abuses. Obtaining the prenegotiation pledges described above from the Taliban would be key to addressing this concern, and requiring intense human rights monitoring will be critical. In addition, in any such discussions, the United States must ensure that any transfers of detainees comply with our obligations under international law not to return detainees to persecution or torture, and that future detentions will comply with fair process and treatment obligations.

Although the diplomatic challenge is huge, the potential rewards are great. If, as Trump claims, he is genuinely interested in dealmaking, Afghanistan presents him with a rare opportunity to make a historic one. But to do so would require him to invest deeply in the kind of high-level, smart-power diplomacy he has largely eschewed thus far. It would require that he work closely with allies he has constantly rebuffed, seek funding to help build a foreign economy, and be patient and humble in the face of reversals, none of which are instincts that he has exhibited in abundance.

2. Closing Guantánamo and Ending Military Commissions

Perhaps the most surprising, yet obvious, step that Trump could take to signal that he is ending the war with Al Qaeda and IS would be finally to close Guantánamo, where only forty detainees now remain. To be sure, Trump hailed Guantánamo, promised to bring more detainees there, and made much in his first State of the Union speech of his executive order directing the Secretary of Defense to keep Guantánamo's detention facilities open.[44] But having visited Guantánamo repeatedly since 1991—first as a human rights lawyer and later as a government policymaker and lawyer—I have repeatedly seen policymakers initially perceive Guantánamo as an answer to their problems, only to realize later that using it creates far more problems than it solves. This time around, the camp has been open since 2002, with the number of detainees now down twenty-fold from the 780 who were brought there at various points during the George W. Bush administration. Even Bush acknowledged in his memoir that he had started to close it, because "the detention facility had become a propaganda tool for our enemies and a distraction for our allies."[45] For Trump to close Guantánamo would be like Richard Nixon going to China, not to mention the clearest example of his ability to achieve something Obama could not.

President Obama first announced the policy of closing Guantánamo in January 2009, reiterated it at the National Archives in 2010, reaffirmed it in March 2011 and May 2013, and then repeatedly restated the promise until the end of his presidency. As he once cogently summarized: "Guantánamo is not necessary to keep America safe. It is expensive. It is inefficient. It hurts us, in terms of our international standing. It lessens cooperation with our allies on counter-terrorism efforts. It is a recruitment tool for extremists."[46] Many of the detainees are repeatedly on hunger strike, and some are being force-fed, which Obama had acknowledged was "not sustainable" and "contrary to who we are."[47] A number have died in detention. Others have been held so long that they now exhibit the medical problems associated with old age, with the oldest captive now over seventy. The cost to house a single detainee for one year is a shocking $11 million.[48]

Closing Guantánamo would carry with it the virtue of closing, or at least moving, the military commissions, which hold their proceedings there. By any measure, the commissions have been a failure, even after they were revamped, following the Supreme Court's declaration that their first iteration was unconstitutional.[49] Since the establishment of the Guantánamo military commissions over fifteen years ago, they have achieved only eight convictions, half of which have been either overturned or partly invalidated, and each of which included purely domestic charges, which may yet be held to exceed the constitutional reach of the commissions' jurisdiction.[50] Defense Secretary Mattis recently fired the official in charge of overseeing the trials, after that official had explored the possibility of a plea deal.[51] And even if Trump wants to keep military commissions as an option for particular cases, there is no good reason why he should not "domesticate" them, by bringing them back to the American mainland. There could be no clearer case of the tail wagging the dog than for Guantánamo to remain open in order that military commissions cases could be heard there. This is particularly true because such cases could be more effectively heard on the continental United States, for example, at the military base in South Carolina where the first post-9/11 trials were held. The overriding, incurable defect of such commissions is that even if particular trials were perfectly executed, they would never provide *credible* justice, in the sense of ever persuading anyone in the Muslim world that real justice had actually been done.[52]

What should make closing Guantánamo easier for Trump is that Obama brought the closure project so close to the finish line. So Trump needs no new policy to close Guantánamo; he just needs to put the full weight of his office behind finishing what Obama started, proceeding in four steps.

First, Trump could charge Defense Secretary Mattis to actually make Guantánamo closure happen. Over his long military career, including leading U.S. Central Command, Mattis opposed the involvement of the U.S. military in long-term detention. Mattis and his subordinates should lead the administration's three-pronged efforts to close Guantánamo: through diplomatic *transfers* of those individuals who could be safely transferred, *prosecution* of those who can be tried, and *periodic review* of so-called "law-of-war detainees" to see if any can be released because of changes, either in their own attitude or in the conditions of the country to which they could be transferred. Of the current population, five who have been "cleared for transfer" by the U.S. government— i.e., identified as eligible for repatriation or resettlement by an administration task force that exhaustively reviewed each prisoner's file—are expected to be transferred from Guantánamo, leaving just thirty-five behind.

Second, Defense Secretary Mattis should work with Congress to make closure possible. Starting in 2010, Congress used authorization bills to impose a series of counterproductive restrictions on the transfer of Guantánamo prisoners. But some of those restrictions are subject to waiver requirements that a conservative Congress could well modify if asked by Trump, particularly if presented with the president's authority as commander-in-chief to regulate the movement of law-of-war detainees. Where Guantánamo once aroused passion, it now arouses largely apathy.[53] More fundamentally, it now connotes wildly expensive "detention without exit," which has reduced the number of its fervent congressional advocates. It may be possible to reach consensus on legislation to allow long-distance plea bargains for military commission defendants and other Guantánamo detainees in Article III courts. These detainees would agree by videoconference from Guantánamo to plead guilty to criminal charges in civilian court, and then be sent to other countries to serve any resulting sentences—with time off for time already served—the entire time never setting foot on the continental United States. Apparently, Republican legislators were intrigued by this possibility, for which there was support within the Obama administration, and defense counsel for many detainees were eager to pursue it, but the move was blocked by the Department of Justice, which reportedly voiced concerns, including about the voluntariness of the resulting pleas.

Third, those on Guantánamo who can be prosecuted should be prosecuted in civilian courts where possible, and plea bargains negotiated wherever feasible. As two seasoned New York federal prosecutors have exhaustively documented, cases like Warsame of

Al Shabaab, the "Shoe Bomber" Richard Reid, the "Christmas Day Bomber" Abdulmutallab, and the "Times Square Bomber" Faisal Shahzad all show that civilian courts are more than able to handle and punish complex terrorism cases.[54] The so-called "Warsame protocol"—developed by the Obama administration to enable lawful military interrogation followed by a civilian prosecution—has succeeded in gathering crucial intelligence without sacrificing convictions or robust sentences.[55] Nor is there any reason why U.S. civilian judges could not be sent to Guantánamo to try the triable so that Guantánamo can be closed.[56]

Fourth and finally, the administration should keep conducting periodic review for the two dozen or so detainees who are not presently under charges, but who an interagency task force concluded should remain held under rules of war that allow detention without charge for the duration of hostilities. In theory, this small group could now be moved en bloc to the mainland United States, but many human rights advocates understandably oppose creating a new system of indefinite detention without charge for terrorism suspects on American soil. If Al Qaeda should become so decimated that the armed conflict could be deemed over, that would eliminate the legal justification for holding these law-of-war detainees without charge and further the claim that after so many years in custody, such long-term detainees should simply be released.

Perhaps most important, it is in both Trump's and Mattis's interests to ensure that no new IS detainees are brought to Guantánamo. Because IS did not even exist at the time of the September 11 attacks, and because Guantánamo detainees have the right to challenge their detention in court through habeas corpus actions, any IS detainees brought to Guantánamo could challenge the entire legal justification for U.S. military operations against IS in Syria and beyond, potentially jeopardizing the legal basis for the broader war effort. There seems little reason to bring such prisoners to Cuba, especially if they can be kept in or near the theater where they were originally captured. The attendant danger, of course, is that local partners, like the Iraqis and the Kurds, may not hold large numbers of IS detainees in a humane fashion. But again, that risk can be mitigated by negotiating agreements requiring assurances against torture and inhumane treatment, which the Torture Convention requires the United States to do anyway to prevent illegal transfers to torture.

In May 2018, Trump surprised many by transferring, over minimal dissent, his first prisoner off of Guantánamo to Saudi Arabian custody.[57] The case could serve as a model for future transfers after plea bargains before military commissions: that prisoner will serve out abroad the nine years remaining on a thirteen-year sentence initially received after a guilty plea before a military commission. Despite his campaign to "load [Guantánamo] up with some bad dudes,"[58] Trump has already shown awareness of the detention facility's limitations. In declining calls to send the New York City bomber to Guantánamo, Trump tweeted: "Would love to send the NYC terrorist to Guantánamo but statistically that process takes much longer than going through the Federal system," which "[s]hould move fast, and "[t]here is also something appropriate about keeping him in the home of the horrible crime he committed."[59]

While closing Guantánamo might not play to Trump's base, as time passes, that option might increasingly appeal to Trump himself. Closing Guantánamo would save time and money and give Trump the bragging rights over Obama that he so clearly craves. More important, it would represent the most visible, achievable step he could take to demonstrate that he has meaningfully started to reduce American overstretch and to end the many burdens of the Forever War.

3. Narrowing and Repealing the AUMF

President Obama's 2013 NDU speech made clear his intent to work with Congress to "refine and ultimately repeal" the 2001 Authorization for Use of Military Force (AUMF) against Al Qaeda.[60] He also proposed to modify the 2002 AUMF in Iraq, which expressly authorizes the president "to use the Armed Forces of the United States as he determines to be necessary and appropriate in order to ... defend the national security of the United States against the continuing threat posed by Iraq."[61] Nevertheless, some argue that these AUMFs must continue, or even be expanded, claiming that repealing the 2001 AUMF in particular will leave legal "gaps" in both the president's targeting and detention authorities that will prevent the executive from successfully protecting America and our allies from known and future terrorist threats.

These concerns are ill-founded. There is a growing bipartisan consensus that the ongoing conflict against IS, which relies on the 2001 and 2002 AUMFs, rests on uncertain legal footing. Senator Tim Kaine has said on numerous occasions that he believes the conflict against IS is unauthorized under current law, and he has repeatedly introduced bipartisan legislation to provide specific authorization for the conflict. The Obama administration also proposed draft IS-specific legislation, but it attracted little support on either side of the aisle. A federal appeals court has heard a service member's challenge to the sufficiency of the existing legal authority, but that suit was initially dismissed on standing, rather than decided on the merits.[62]

The 2001 AUMF was enacted seventeen years ago to prevent Al Qaeda and its co-belligerents from attacking the United States, not to enable a distant battle against IS, a terrorist group that did not exist at that time and that has now clearly split from Al Qaeda.

The 2002 AUMF for Iraq targeted the national security threat in Iraq, but was directed not against IS but against Saddam Hussein and the unfounded fear that he possessed weapons of mass destruction. President Obama acknowledged that IS posed no immediate threat to the U.S. homeland—the signature feature of bin Laden's Al Qaeda—limiting his administration's capacity to argue under either domestic or international law that he was acting against IS in U.S. national self-defense.[63] Instead, his administration argued that it could lawfully wage war against IS as a "splinter group" that had spun off from the Al Qaeda core.[64] This "splinter" theory introduced a dangerous methodology that effectively invites current and future presidents to cite "factual evidence of common AQ DNA" to declare war against a succession of groups increasingly far removed from the Al Qaeda that Congress declared war against after September 11, 2001. If current and future presidents can claim on weak factual grounds that every terrorist organization that comes along—including groups that do not yet exist—are "AQ splinters" or successors, and thus covered by the 2001 AUMF, then we have stopped trying to end the "Forever War" and will have instead reverted to a perpetual Global War on Terror.

Successive presidents cannot fight endless wars based on outmoded statutes or shaky constitutional authority. We need a bespoke statutory framework based on shared responsibility between the legislative and executive branches for national security matters. Both legal authority and political legitimacy would be maximized if Congress and the president could work together to ensure that the authority given to the president reflects the current threat actually facing the United States. As Justice Jackson's famous concurrence in the *Steel Seizure* case makes clear, when the president goes to war based on express statutory authorization, his "authority is at its maximum, for it includes all that he possesses in his own right plus all that Congress can delegate."[65]

Going forward, the key issue of legal interpretation will be whether new groups that rise up to commit acts of terror can reasonably be considered "associated forces" of Al Qaeda with whom we are already at war.[66] Just because someone hates America or sympathizes with Al Qaeda does not make them a lawful enemy. An "associated force" must be (1) an organized, armed group that (2) has actually entered the fight alongside Al Qaeda against the United States, thereby becoming (3) a co-belligerent with Al Qaeda in its hostilities against America.[67] If government lawyers are too loose in deciding who is "associated with" Al Qaeda going forward, then the United States will always have new enemies, and the Forever War will continue forever.

Legal authority must obviously be sensitive to conditions on the ground. As President Obama noted in his NDU speech, the "future of terrorism" is "lethal yet less capable Al Qaeda affiliates; threats to diplomatic facilities and businesses abroad; homegrown extremists"—a threat that would require a range of tools to combat. Ideally, Congress should narrow, then repeal the 2001 AQ AUMF and the 2002 Iraq AUMF. If Congress wants to play a proactive role in clarifying presidential war-making authorities, it could narrow the AUMF's mandate to recognize the evolving nature of the threat facing the United States by shifting from an "armed conflict" theory to a "current threat" theory. Congress could tighten the language of the current AUMF to narrow its substantive scope and improve accountability. Instead of continuing to rely on the broadly worded 2001 AUMF to codify a permanent state of war, Congress could narrow targeting and detention authority to match policy by codifying the standards stated in President Obama's December 2016 Law and Policy Frameworks Report. So doing would give Congress greater say in authorizing force and bolster the constitutional legitimacy of counterterrorism operations by granting the president's current standards a shared legislative and executive imprimatur. Codifying those standards would also enhance the global legitimacy of U.S. counterterrorism operations in ways that would encourage greater information-sharing and multilateral cooperation.

A narrower AUMF should meet five conditions. First, *specificity*: it should be both IS-specific and mission-specific, i.e., limited to the current armed conflict with IS, and specifying the particular objectives and organizations and groups against which Congress is authorizing the use of force. Many previous use-of-force authorizations have included such specifications, and some have required that the president both formally determine when those objectives have been fulfilled and regularly report such determinations to Congress. If the AUMF is intended to authorize the use of force against "associated forces" of IS, it should define that term.

Second, *terminability*: unlike the September 2001 AUMF, an IS-specific AUMF should include a sunset clause, which would periodically require Congress affirmatively to vote whether and under what terms to continue to support the evolving conflict. Adding a sunset clause would also help to ensure that the statutory framework for U.S. counterterrorism operations is regularly updated to reflect the realities of the threats we are facing, and to accurately express the intent and will of the legislative branch. Such a clause would confirm that Congress is not granting the executive another open-ended check, by guaranteeing definite legislative review of the situation at a defined point in the future. A sunset clause would provide increased opportunities for congressional and executive dialogue and force debate and voting at timed intervals. For example, the 1983 Multinational Force in Lebanon Resolution ratified the president's unilateral use of force there but placed important limitations on that statutory authority with respect to both scope and duration.[68] The fact that both the enemy and the conflict may morph in unforeseeable ways is the best reason to include a sunset, because nobody in Congress today can predict precisely what the conflict will entail in three years' time. Nor is a sunset a repeal, or even a proposal to repeal in the future; it is simply a shared congressional–executive agreement to reassess the situation together later, as a nation.

Third, *repeal* of outmoded predecessor AUMFs. Any new AUMF should repeal both the 2001 Al Qaeda AUMF and the 2002 Iraq AUMF. The narrower, more specific, later-in-time bill would then become the president's exclusive lawful authority for fighting IS. Obviously, the precise timing of these repeals remains a decision about which the administration and Congress should agree, based upon conditions as they develop on the ground. The 2001 AUMF can be repealed at the appropriate time, once Al Qaeda has been effectively defeated; the 2002 AUMF can be repealed once IS has been militarily defeated. At that time, repeal should create no "legal gaps." If the United States found an ongoing need to strike back against particular remaining Al Qaeda terrorists and associated forces who pose a continuing and imminent threat to the United States, future strikes could still be justified under both domestic and international law. But a repeal would clarify that current U.S. objectives are quite different from those described in authorizations that were enacted nearly two decades earlier and designed for different armed conflicts against different enemies.

Fourth, *transparency*: to improve public and congressional access to information, Congress could include more stringent transparency and reporting requirements. To ensure that the American public and Congress understand the scope, progress, and costs of military operations on a continuing basis, any new AUMF should mandate that the president report to Congress on a periodic basis. If greater transparency is demanded by interested stakeholders, provisions should be included: (1) describing the progress toward the mission's objectives; (2) identifying any groups or nations other than IS that have joined the armed conflict; (3) providing detailed information about civilian and combatant casualties on all sides; and (4) sharing with Congress, and to the extent possible with the public, any significant legal analyses regarding the scope and legal authority for U.S. uses of force. Because similar reports are regularly given in the context of the War Powers Resolution, it should not unduly burden the executive to require that similar information be revealed.

Nor is there good reason why President Trump should not be required to issue a regular public report on the number of combatants and civilians killed by the United States' use of targeted lethal force abroad. As noted above, publicly released civilian casualty statistics in Iraq and Syria have been criticized by many in the human rights community as unrealistically low. Reaching public agreement on shared principles on targeting with key allies would blunt criticism and place the U.S. use of drones on a sounder footing. Such transparency would also help rebut a wave of drone reports—by Human Rights Watch and Amnesty International, and by the U.N. Special Rapporteur on Counter-terrorism and Human Rights and Extrajudicial Killings—that have questioned whether the strict standards stated in President Obama's NDU speech are in fact being consistently and rigorously applied by Trump. These are serious charges that deserve serious public responses from our government.[69]

Fifth and finally, *third-party review*. The executive should not make all of these decisions alone. A responsible force authorization would explore and implement some form of ex post review mechanism—judicial or otherwise—for evaluating targeting, particularly with respect to American citizens. In his 2013 NDU speech, President Obama asked his lawyers to consider a special court or an executive review board as possible ways to extend oversight of lethal actions outside of the Afghan theater. Obama's own guidelines stated that targeting policies should be reviewed for legality. Because European courts are showing increased initiative in reviewing European cooperation in targeting operations for compliance with domestic and international law, some form of ex post judicial review of these actions may prove inevitable in the near future, whether American officials like it or not.[70]

In the name of reasserting Congress's authority over war making, two leading senators have proposed the bipartisan Kaine-Corker bill to replace the 2001 and 2002 authorizations.[71] Unfortunately, of the five safeguards described above—specificity, terminability, repeal, transparency, and third-party review—this bill offers only one. The bill would repeal the 2001 and 2002 AUMFs but declares that the new AUMF "provides uninterrupted authority" to continue using force as those two laws had authorized.

But the Kaine-Corker bill is not IS-specific. It authorizes the president to use force not just against Al Qaeda and the Taliban but also against six groups not named in the 2001 authorization: IS, Al Qaeda in the Arabian Peninsula, Al Shabaab, Al Qaeda in Syria, Al Qaeda in the Islamic Maghreb, and the Haqqani Network of Afghanistan and Pakistan. The Kaine-Corker bill expands the authorization for the use of force to Libya, Somalia, Syria, and Yemen, and authorizes a future president to carry out operations against more "associated forces" and countries, just by informing Congress within forty-eight hours of listing them. The Kaine-Corker bill would thus perpetuate, not end, the Forever War by codifying Congress's abdication of its constitutional duty to declare war each time a new conflict begins. In effect, it would reverse the constitutional structure by allowing the president to declare new wars, then shift the burden to Congress to muster the two-thirds vote in each house necessary to block them.

Second, the bill does not include a real sunset clause. It forces a floor debate on reauthorization at least every four years but does not require enactment of new legislation for the authority to continue. Third, while the bill has transparency, oversight, and reporting provisions, most of the reporting is classified and does not ensure that the public will receive clear notification that a new group has been added to the enemies' list. Such a proposal to expand and extend the AUMF's mandate would be exceedingly unwise. The Kaine-Corker bill authorizes the president to identify a new group as "associated forces" and to send Congress a classified report within forty-eight hours explaining why that group has been added to the list. In form, this looks uncomfortably like the State Department's Foreign Terrorist Organization (FTO) designation process. Under that process, Congress charges the secretary of state—pursuant to specific statutory standards, in consultation with other departments, and following a notification period to Congress—to designate particular groups as terrorist organizations, thereby creating statutory consequences for those groups and their members.

For nearly four years as Legal Adviser, I engaged regularly with the FTO designation process, which I did not find to be a good one. By and large it has become a buck-passing, list-making exercise that should not be replicated elsewhere. Congress adopts a standard for generating lists that, through the vagaries of the legislative process, is hard to construe. It then delegates to the executive the responsibility to make and tier lists with various sanctions attached to the various tiers. The incentive created for everyone in the process is to be overly inclusive: a participant can only get into trouble if a terrorist group that is involved in a strike was *not* on the list. Sometimes the friendly government of the country where the group operates opposes the designation on the ground that recognition through FTO designation by a country the size and stature of the United States would give that organization the very visibility and status it seeks, perversely strengthening the terrorist organization by helping with recruiting, raising resources, and the like. These designations are hard to change, forcing the executive to try to carve out exceptions from the sanctions when the inflexibility of the process bites in unanticipated ways: witness, for example, the lengthy struggle to lift the FTO designation for the African National Congress when it meant denying a visa to Nelson Mandela.[72] Importing that process here would not foster meaningful congressional engagement or oversight, but would likely expand and perpetuate, not help narrow and eventually end, the Forever War.

A better option, presented by Senator Jeff Merkley in May 2018, would offer four of the five safeguards described above—specificity, terminability, repeal, and transparency (omitting only third-party review).[73] The bill authorizes for three years the use of force—only in Iraq and Afghanistan—against the Taliban, Al Qaeda, and IS "to protect the United States and its compelling interests from attack" by those three entities, but it would create expedited procedures whereby the president could come to Congress to add new groups and countries to the list. The proposal requires that the United States adhere to international law, includes comprehensive, largely unclassified reporting requirements to both Congress and the public with respect to the numbers and preventive mechanisms for civilian casualties, and repeals the 2002 Iraq AUMF immediately and sunsets the 2001 AUMF after six months. The president would retain existing authority if necessary to use force outside theaters of armed conflict against senior leaders. And if the president ever needed additional authority—because a situation quickly turned from one that required self-defense to respond to an immediate threat into one that genuinely demanded an ongoing conflict with a new armed group that threatened the United States—his straightforward solution, with or without the Merkley bill, would be to ask Congress to authorize military force against that group, making the specific case for why a new AUMF is needed. Unless the United States can clearly define just who its new enemies are—and why existing legal authorities are insufficient to defend ourselves against them—it has no good basis for passing new laws that would perpetuate the Forever War against shadowy foes whose association with those who attacked the Twin Towers on 9/11 cannot be proven.

These issues are hard. Reasonable people can disagree. Everyone is weary of war and tired of fighting. But that is all the more reason to keep our eye on the real issue: how to end the Forever War. Collaboration is key, and we should put partisanship aside. Whatever our differences regarding the future of war, we should all be able to agree that war must be both lawful and terminable. The president and Congress must together enact sufficient authority to win a war that must end. But if force is to be legislatively authorized, it should look more like the Merkley bill than the Kaine-Corker bill. If Congress follows the Kaine-Corker path, and overbroadly authorizes a fight against IS that mutates endlessly to include new enemies, we will have tipped the balance toward perpetual war.

As President Obama noted at the National Defense University: "the choices we make about war can impact—in sometimes unintended ways—the openness and freedom on which our way of life depends."[74] The conflict originally triggered on September 11 was neither perpetual nor global. Even in a time of terror, it should still be possible to defend our security consistent with our values and the rule of law. As noted above, ending foreign engagements was one of Trump's key foreign policy planks. If he is serious about that, it should still be possible for even a President Trump to end the Forever War.

C. SYRIA

That brings us finally to Syria, the greatest humanitarian tragedy of our time. Nearly seven years of civil war have witnessed half a million Syrian deaths, six million internally displaced, and five million refugees, some two million of them children.[75] I have elsewhere detailed at some length a broader approach to this complex problem, which includes at least five elements:[76] (1) fighting IS; (2) pursuing accountability for Assad and other leading war criminals; (3) responding to Assad's attacks on civilians and the use of chemical weapons; (4) energizing the peace process; and (5) meaningfully grappling with the refugee crisis, which has strained the frontline states and disrupted Europe.

Simply put, this debacle has grown out of Assad's brutality and multiple Russian vetoes, which have obstructed any viable peace process. During the 2016 presidential campaign debates, three of the four national candidates—Hillary Clinton, Tim Kaine, and Mike Pence—argued that the United States should use limited military force in Syria to create a humanitarian corridor and no-fly zone.[77] An intensely divided Obama administration claimed that a no-fly zone would not achieve the humanitarian results that those who supported it desired, but continuously reviewed the possibility of various forms of direct intervention in Syria.[78]

The absence of a threat of lawful force has crippled effective diplomacy and created a mismatch between broader policy objectives and available soft-power tools. Thus, a key policy question has been whether to add a lawful hard-power element to motivate diplomacy, without undermining the broader smart-power strategy to solve the overall crisis. Is doing nothing really the only option? Or is there a lawful option that would enable the United States to use Richard Holbrooke–style "diplomacy backed by force" if the goal were entirely humanitarian: to prevent outrageous and illegal attacks on civilians—particularly those employing chemical weapons—and to jump-start diplomacy, achieve a durable ceasefire, with an eye toward negotiating a Syrian version of the Dayton Peace Accords?

Candidate Trump argued vociferously against further involvement in Syria. But in April 2017, following reports that Assad had again used chemical weapons against civilians, including small children, the new president abruptly reversed course and launched missile strikes against Assad's forces.[79] When in April 2018, he did it again, striking targets in Syria associated with the chemical weapons capabilities, U.S. Ambassador to the United Nations Nikki Haley said that the Trump administration is "locked and loaded" to target Syria if the "regime is foolish enough to test our will. When our president draws a red line," she intoned, "our president enforces a red line."[80] But precisely what red line did Trump draw?

Clearly, Trump did not draw a red line against Assad's attacking innocent Syrian civilians or children. For implicit in the Trump administration's actions was its willingness to allow Assad to keep exterminating Syrian innocents by conventional means, so long as he does not use chemical weapons.[81] If Trump were genuinely moved by the plight of innocent Syrian children, why not exempt Syrians from the Travel Ban, increase humanitarian aid, or admit into the U.S. more than the tiny number of Syrian refugees that he has admitted? Nor was Trump's red line clearly directed against those who would *support* the use of chemical weapons in Syria. For even while Trump chastised the Russians for complicity in the use of chemical weapons, he made clear that he shares his main goal in Syria with both Putin and Assad: namely, using America's "small force [in Syria] . . . to eliminate what is left of ISIS." Trump restated his objective as "doing what is necessary to protect *the*

American people," underscoring that "America does not seek an indefinite presence in Syria, *under no circumstances.*"[82]

Significantly, both of Assad's April chemical attacks followed closely on similar Trump statements proclaiming his disengagement from and disinterest in solving any longer-term problems in Syria. And when Assad again used chemical weapons in early 2018, the United States responded with only a toothless "warning" from Secretary of Defense Mattis.[83] For that reason, Trump's most recent strikes—standing alone—seem unlikely to achieve his own stated goal: to "establish a strong deterrent against the production, spread, and use of chemical weapons." Plainly, the strongest deterrent against Assad's renewed use of chemical weapons would not be sporadic missile strikes but *sustained U.S. participation in a long-term solution to the Syrian crisis.* But Trump's real red line seems to be calibrating a strike that would not trigger retaliation, so as to avoid getting sucked any deeper into the Syrian civil war, keeping U.S. forces in Syria, or offering to catalyze or commit to any kind of serious multilateral diplomatic strategy to end the seven-year Syrian catastrophe.[84]

All of these policy considerations may matter little to those legal commentators who subscribe to what I have called the "never-never rule": the absolutist notion that, absent a U.N. Security Council resolution, military intervention taken in the name of humanitarian goals can never be legal under either domestic or international law.[85] This "never-never rule" exhibits the absolutist, formalist, textualist, originalist quality Americans usually associate with the late Justice Antonin Scalia. It relies on absolutist readings of texts as "originally understood," claiming that a nation may not engage in unilateral humanitarian intervention because of prohibitive wordings of Article 2(4) of the U.N. Charter[86] and Article I of the U.S. Constitution.[87] But under both domestic and international law, this simplistic, absolutist reading cannot be squared with state practice, interbranch practice, or the broader object and purpose of the document the reader claims to be interpreting.

As a matter of international law, the never-never rule cannot be squared with the object and purpose of the U.N. Charter, whose broad purposes include "promoting and encouraging respect for human rights."[88] The absolutist position would allow each of the five permanent members of the U.N. Security Council (P5) to commit genocide against their own citizens with no lawful basis for any other actor to intervene to protect the population at risk. It seems equally untenable for a P5 member like Russia to invoke international law as an excuse to invoke twelve consecutive U.N. Security Council vetoes to protect a client state like Assad's Syria, when it commits war crimes and crimes against humanity against its own citizens. Against the manifest rigidity of the never-never rule, state practice has offered many prominent counterexamples of de facto humanitarian intervention:[89] India–Bangladesh;[90] Tanzania–Uganda;[91] Vietnam–Cambodia (Khmer Rouge); the United States and the United Kingdom creating no-fly zones over Iraq to protect the Kurds and the Shias;[92] and of course, NATO's famous Kosovo episode of the late twentieth century.[93] If international lawyers believe that international law should serve human purposes—including the protection of human rights, and not just the territorial sovereignty of states—then an immutable never-never rule cannot survive as the legal rule governing unilateral humanitarian intervention in the twenty-first century.[94]

Nor is it consistent with the design of the U.S. Constitution to claim—in the face of a long history of consistent executive branch practice to the contrary—that a limited, unilateral executive strike genuinely motivated by humanitarian purposes constitutes a "war" that, constitutionally, Congress must always declare. As I have chronicled elsewhere, the Framers plainly intended to have a strong executive operating within a strong constitutional system capable of responding effectively to emergent external threats.[95] Because of the superior institutional capacity of the executive to respond quickly, over time, interbranch practice has inevitably shifted discretion to the president to respond in many bona fide emergency situations, eroding the domestic face of the never-never rule through institutional acquiescence.

With respect to Trump's April 2018 strikes, one never-never adherent, Professor Kevin Jon Heller, for example, recently illustrated the absolutist approach by categorically asserting *before* Trump's action that "the coming attack on Syria will be unlawful," no matter what form it might take, or what its stated purpose might be.[96] But to those international lawyers who take a more nuanced view, context and motivation matters. Whether Trump's action should be adjudged legal depends on the stated rationale and its actual likelihood of achieving the broader humanitarian objective of the mission that was supposedly "accomplished."

Obviously, I am no fan of the Trump administration. But neither do I believe that, absent a Security Council resolution, humanitarian intervention is never legally available under either domestic or international law. I have argued that under emerging international law, the Trump administration's initial April 2017 strikes against Syria were not illegal.[97] In so arguing, I applied a legal test I had previously proposed for judging the international lawfulness of claimed humanitarian interventions:

(1) If a humanitarian crisis creates consequences significantly disruptive of international order—including proliferation of chemical weapons, massive refugee outflows, and events destabilizing to regional peace and security—that would likely soon create an imminent threat to the acting nations (which would give rise to an urgent need to act in

individual and collective self-defense under U.N. Charter Article 51);

(2) a Security Council resolution were not available because of persistent veto; and the group of nations that had persistently sought Security Council action had exhausted all other remedies reasonably available under the circumstances, they would not violate U.N. Charter Article 2(4) if they used

(3) limited force for genuinely humanitarian purposes that was necessary and proportionate to address the imminent threat, would demonstrably improve the humanitarian situation, and would terminate as soon as the threat is abated. In particular, these nations' claim that their actions were not wrongful would be strengthened if they could demonstrate:

(4) that the action was collective, e.g., involving the General Assembly's Uniting for Peace Resolution or regional arrangements under U.N. Charter Chapter VIII;

(5) that collective action would prevent the use of a per se illegal means by the territorial state, e.g., deployment of banned chemical weapons; or

(6) would help to avoid a per se illegal end, e.g., genocide, war crimes, crimes against humanity, or an avertable humanitarian disaster, such as the widespread slaughter of innocent civilians, for example, another Halabja or Srebrenica.

To be credible, the legal analysis of any particular situation would need to substantiate each of these factors with persuasive factual evidence of: (1) Disruptive Consequences likely to lead to Imminent Threat; (2) Exhaustion; (3) Limited, Necessary, Proportionate, and Humanitarian Use of Force; (4) Collective Action; (5) Illegal Means; and (6) Avoidance of Illegal Ends.[98]

In April 2018, significantly, Trump failed to present an adequate case on either the facts or the law. He did not offer sufficient factual evidence to conclude that his second strikes satisfied Parts 3 through 6 of this proposed standard:

(3) While the latest strikes clearly aimed at destroying much of Assad's chemical weapons capacity, Assad undeniably continues to possess chemical weapons. What evidence did the Trump administration have that its strike would not lead Assad to *intensify* his conventional slaughter of those Syrian civilians still surviving in Douma, Idlib, and elsewhere?

(4) While Trump's 2018 Syrian strikes were coordinated with France and the United Kingdom, that joint effort did not approach the kind of concerted collective action that we saw with the nineteen-nation coalition that conducted the 1999 intervention in Kosovo.

(5) Was the Trump administration's real goal deterring the use of nerve agents, like sarin gas, or all chemical weapons, including chlorine, which is equally banned but less deadly?

(6) Precisely what kind of humanitarian disaster was the Coalition trying to avoid? Here the United States was intentionally threading a needle, to reduce what many thoughtful observers recognized was a real risk of escalation with a nuclear adversary.[99] It is far harder for the United States to claim that its actions will relieve humanitarian suffering if it intentionally inflames a war that will only end up increasing the level of human suffering.

Trump's April 2018 strikes again show the glaring need for the United States to articulate its long-overdue legal justification for using military intervention for genuinely humanitarian purposes. Too many observers already suspect that Trump's strikes were actually driven by political impulses. To be sure, a legal explanation won't remove all skepticism about the motivations of a president who has done so much to encourage it. But such an explanation would at least tie the United States' present actions to a broader set of principles that explain why the United States believes it is acting lawfully. Such principles would also clarify the future circumstances in which the United States believes it is legally empowered to act, potentially furthering the very deterrent goals that the president claims to want to advance.

While legal academics have been largely critical of both of Trump's April strikes, state practice has been more accepting: only the Russians and Syrians went so far as to call the attacks unlawful.[100] Within academia, my approach has been largely criticized from the left, with some mischaracterizing my view as favoring unilateral humanitarian intervention. To be clear, I have not broadly endorsed unilateral humanitarian intervention as a matter of either law or policy. Nor does my test preauthorize humanitarian intervention. Instead, it would allow a humanitarian claim to be asserted as an affirmative defense that would exempt certain actions that meet rigorous standards from legal wrongfulness.[101] I argue only that humanitarian intervention is not always unlawful under all circumstances under both domestic and international law, particularly when a U.N. Security Council resolution has been persistently blocked by twelve Russian vetoes. Whether or not you accept my test, surely it is past time for the U.S. government, and its NATO allies, to articulate and agree upon a better rule governing whether and under what narrow circumstances limited intervention for humanitarian purposes may be lawful.[102] The U.S. government missed its chance to state that legal rationale during the Kosovo intervention nearly two decades ago, instead listing amorphous "factors" that it believed made that intervention "illegal but legitimate."[103] After Kosovo, the international legal community went some distance to define a legal standard to govern the lawfulness of Responsibility to Protect (R2P). Twenty years after Kosovo, it is time to finish the job.

In his 2009 Nobel Prize address, President Obama declared that he believed in humanitarian intervention, but mistakenly, his administration never publicly stated a legal test.[104] But faced with a renewed use of outlawed chemical weapons, the United States failed again to state that rationale in 2013, when President Obama did not defend his own announced "red line" in Syria. In the days following the 2017 and 2018 U.S. strikes in Syria, the Trump administration again declined to offer any meaningful analysis defending the legality of those missile strikes.

This silence only exacerbates the growing debate about the lawfulness of any continuing U.S. military engagement in Syria under domestic and international law. Whatever domestic legal basis could be derived from the existing 2001 and 2002 AUMFs for operations against IS—as a splinter or "offshoot" group with common DNA as the Al Qaeda core—cannot plausibly be extended to authorizing U.S. troops to remain in Syria to fight against various proxies of Iran, after IS's collapse. Similarly, the fall of Raqqa and Mosul now makes it implausible for the United States to assert an international law claim of collective self-defense as its basis for continuing the use of military force to hold former IS territory in Syria. While a few senators—particularly Cory Booker,[105] Bob Corker, Jeff Flake, and Tim Kaine—have wisely raised the domestic constitutional issues, they have not adequately thought through how to avoid, in former U.S. Syrian envoy Fred Hof's words, "inadvertently building a legal justification for consigning the people of eastern Syria to the ministrations of a homicidal regime in Damascus."[106] How can the United States lawfully and politically participate in an effective effort to stabilize eastern Syria by excluding Assad's forces and Iranian-led Shia foreign fighters from occupying liberated IS territories?

The glaring absence of an official U.S. legal justification for humanitarian intervention has reached a crisis point. Trump cannot simply bomb on impulse within Syria, invoking the defense of innocent Syrian children, without a plausible legal theory. Trump declared, "We are prepared to sustain this response until the Syrian regime stops its use of prohibited chemical agents." But unlike the United States, the United Kingdom, Denmark, and Belgium have all articulated the conditions under which they believe humanitarian intervention to be lawful.[107] So if the same troika—the United States, France, and the United Kingdom—were again to strike against Assad's renewed use of chemical weapons, we could expect the British at least to proffer a legal opinion to explain why they believe their actions to be lawful.[108] But absent any kind of public legal rationale from the Trump administration, U.S. soldiers and the world watching them will not know whether America's commander-in-chief is ordering them to act in violation of their oaths to act lawfully, under both domestic and international law.

Some claim that a humanitarian exception to the U.N. Charter would permit any state to invoke claims of treaty violation or regional instability to use unilateral executive force pretextually, in order to commit aggression based on a claimed need for humanitarian intervention.[109] But surely states can craft a legal rule that—particularly when applied to agreed facts—would distinguish exceptional situations from pretextual justifications.

At this point, there should be little doubt that Syria presents a situation of unusual and exceptional severity. Assad has used chemical weapons in blatant violation of a century-old global prohibition against the use of chemical weapons, and European and Middle Eastern stability has been genuinely threatened by the Syrian civil war and the ensuing refugee crisis. Others fear that legally permitting unilateral humanitarian intervention in exceptional circumstances will lead down a slippery slope. But having lived through Rwanda, Kosovo, Sierra Leone, and East Timor, as a human rights policymaker, I have seen the slippery slope run both ways. Certainly, able international lawyers should be able to develop narrow legal tests that hold harmless the running of red lights by ambulance drivers without granting broad license for abuse to ambulance *chasers*.

Some commentators would split the difference by treating some forms of unilateral humanitarian intervention as "illegal but legitimate," a position that seemed dubious at the time of Kosovo and even less acceptable now. Where else in the field of human rights do we accept "illegal but legitimate" as the permanent judgment of history? We did not say, for example, that regrettably, same-sex and interracial marriage were "illegal but legitimate." Instead, we brought our very best lawyerly skills, craft, and commitment to bear in a concerted effort to make lawful what we believed to be morally legitimate. Not to do so simply corrodes respect for the rule of law.[110]

Because the absolutists offer no alternative to the notion that humanitarian intervention is always illegal, they offer no policy suggestion as for how we should stop the continuing horrible slaughter in Syria, which is only intensifying as IS retreats.[111] Repeatedly doing nothing in the face of horrific cruelty promotes a skewed bilevel policy bias toward passivity in the face of gross abuses at both the international and domestic level. The consequences of that legal bias falls on innocent civilians and undercuts meaningful atrocities-prevention. When all the world seems already to have intervened in Syria, it is a fiction to assert an absolutist norm against intervention as a prevailing governing norm. As a matter of policy, sticking with that anti-interventionist legal fiction has become a de facto pro-slaughter position. As a policy matter, the never-never rule guts the possibilities for smart-power diplomacy backed by the *threat* of force of the kind that might motivate a "Syrian Dayton" peace process that could resolve the festering crisis.

All this again shows why it is a mistake to isolate international law analysis solely within its own bubble, entirely distinct from policy. In the international realm, law and policy are inevitably and inextricably intertwined. Most transnational players use policy arguments to try to change international law, or make international law claims to force governments to change their policies. Academics inevitably miss half the picture if they constantly insist on artificially separating the two.

To build an enduring smart-power solution, the United States must engage, translate, and leverage. To solve Syria, the United States must join other nations—including Russia—in building a sustainable peace process, organized around a durable legal arrangement, and leverage that lawful core into a broader policy solution that contains and manages the sprawling crisis. In arguing for a public legal rationale for humanitarian intervention, I am not suggesting that lawyers should provide excuses for unconstrained use of force in places like Syria. Nor have I advocated use of force in Syria to engage in broader regime change. But neither should international lawyers take the smart-power policy option of diplomacy backed by force off the table by claiming that a collective exercise of the Responsibility to Protect is always legally unavailable. If the Holbrookeian option of diplomacy backed by force is legally available, that could give the West greater leverage for meaningful diplomacy to solve the Syrian crisis than diplomatic talk alone.

It is no coincidence that Russia and Assad have been most willing to engage seriously at the diplomatic table when the United States has credibly threatened force: after President Obama's

2013 "red line" episode (which prompted the removal of a significant stockpile of chemical weapons) and after Trump responded to Assad's chemical weapons attack in 2017. In the so-called "Astana process," the Russians have expressed receptivity to the notion that Iran, Russia, and Turkey would become guarantors of so-called "de-escalation zones" within Syria, authorized to use any necessary force to prevent civilian harm within those zones.[112] This proposal has many evident flaws: it does not mention chemical weapons, provide any legal rationale, or offer a credible group of guarantors. But it would make sense for the Trump administration's special Syrian envoy to seize on Russia's seeming concession that these "de-escalation zones" within Syria are both a legally and politically available policy option in search of a more durable solution.

The most serious objection to my position comes from those in America and elsewhere who simply do not trust Donald Trump and his administration to get this right. As should be clear by now, I share their skepticism. But in the international order, there remains only one United States, which, regardless of who is its president, plays a critical role as a balance wheel of the international system. The first years of the new administration have shown that the United States is much bigger than Donald Trump. As this book has demonstrated on many fronts, Donald Trump will shift on many aspects of his stated foreign policy aims if subjected to enough political pressure.[113]

It is past time to demand from the Trump administration a *Syrian policy and strategy*, not just a set of military strikes. We should demand a pivot toward a broader smart-power diplomacy that might resolve the underlying Syrian crisis. If the president wishes to pursue such sensitive diplomacy, he would also be well advised to revise other aspects of his chaotic foreign policy: to do a better job talking and listening to our allies and working with critical organizational partners like NATO and the European Union; to dial back his bombastic rhetoric in situations of growing tension with hostile countries like North Korea; and to be more careful about telling the truth and respecting our intelligence agencies, so that listeners will actually believe our government when we accuse Russia of complicity in a future Assad chemical weapons strike. If Trump cannot make these adjustments on his own, concerted pressure from litigation, Congress, allies, media, and public opinion will be needed to make him change his position.

Solving the festering crisis in Syria will require far more sustained and coherent diplomacy than we have seen to date from the Trump administration. During his brief, disappointing tenure as secretary of state, Rex Tillerson oversaw a baffling and troubling hollowing out of the State Department career services.[114] An institutional State Department populated by the kind of extraordinary U.S. diplomats who brought about Dayton, Paris, and the Iran Nuclear Deal is more than capable of finding and concluding creative, durable diplomatic solutions even to nightmarish problems like Syria. The open question is whether this president and his current secretary of state will give them the mandate and discretion to do so.

Chapter 6

What's at Stake

A. EARLY LESSONS

From this rapid tour d'horizon, three early lessons should emerge. First, America's observance of law, international and constitutional, is preserved not just by the federal political branches and the leaders who lead them at any particular time, but also by an ongoing transnational legal process whose diverse stakeholders elected officials do not control. Second, institutional habits, once formed, prove surprisingly hard to break. For that reason, with respect to international organizations and regimes, as the old song goes, breaking up is hard to do. Third, in the twenty-first century, the best way to produce good foreign policy outcomes remains engage–translate–leverage, not disengage–black hole–hard power.

When Donald Trump took office, he found himself enmeshed in a complex web of international and domestic rules that created a persistent default path to compliance with preexisting norms. Once in place, this web of law became a "guardrail" keeping certain political and policy decisions traveling along previously agreed-upon paths. As his first term approaches its midpoint, all signs are that most of those guardrails are still holding. A new president cannot simply have his way. Domestic constituencies and interests with institutional authority to push back are doing

The Trump Administration and International Law. Harold Hongju Koh.

so, as are foreign allies with shared interests in preserving rules of law within a painstakingly constructed international system. Government bureaucracies long devoted to pursuing solutions to climate change or promoting diplomacy as a principal tool of foreign policy do not turn on a dime.[1] The United States has become deeply enmeshed in many multilateral regimes, and exit from those regimes is neither immediate nor easy.

More fundamentally, many Americans want what many of the global regimes offer, whether it be a nuclear-free Iran or clean energy. So even if abrupt exit is attempted, it will be challenged by transnational actors committed to continuing the default agenda. If exit and change are made difficult, the administration will have to ask itself, how much capital can we afford to spend on this particular issue? The real question becomes: how crucial, really, is any particular policy change or institutional exit to Trump's core agenda? How much does his administration care about, say, separating migrant children from their parents, when the resisters remain ready to fight against it, from both the outside and the inside? So even for an administration obsessed with saying that it kept its campaign promises, enough internal and external resistance to change can shift the administration's path of least resistance to staying in and underperforming within existing legal regimes, rather than absorbing the costs of actually breaking standing international rules and exiting from standing international institutions.

B. A HISTORICAL TIPPING POINT?

As the battle unfolds across this landscape of issues, what's really at stake? We find ourselves at a potentially dramatic crossroads: a moment of transition from our long-standing post–World War

II system of Kantian global governance to a cynical system of authoritarian spheres of influence. As time goes on, it becomes clearer that the Trump administration is repudiating not just a prior administration's foreign policy strategy but the broader political philosophy of international cooperation that philosopher Immanuel Kant supported in *To Perpetual Peace*.[2] Those who attack Kantian global governance as "world government" are attacking a straw man. Kant never advocated world government; he proposed instead that "The Law of Nations Shall be Founded on a Federation of Free States"[3]: a community of democracies, if you will. Law-abiding nations try to live together in a law-governed international society, where sovereign states collectively explicate shared moral commitments to democracy, the rule of law, individual freedom, and the mutual advantages derived from peaceful intercourse. These free states engage in mutual discourse, based on respect for domestic and international rule of law, to achieve shared outcomes: i.e., they engage, translate, and leverage.

Since World War II, Kantian global governance provided the international system that—across administrations of both political parties—the United States helped to create and has fought to sustain. It formed the basis for our United Nations system to end war and promote human rights, our treaty structure for mutual security (e.g., NATO), and our system to end global depression and poverty: the Bretton Woods system to govern international monetary flows, trade, and development through the International Monetary Fund (IMF), World Trade Organization (WTO), and World Bank. A shared commitment to Kantian global governance enabled the United States to lead a group of like-minded nations to organize an ambitious multilateral assault on all manner of global problems: e.g., climate change, denuclearization, intellectual property, and global health. For more than seventy years, the United States acted as the driver and balance wheel of this Kantian

2nd use - what this does mean?

governance system. But all of these historical experiments, like the Brexit-led attack on the European Union, have come under threat of displacement by a countermodel of Orwellian spheres of influence.

We can now understand Donald Trump less as a cause than as a symptom of this anti-globalist countermovement. Everywhere we look, open societies are under siege. As German Foreign Minister Sigmar Gabriel warned, "a longing for order, clarity, hierarchy and control is now emerging. Diversity and individuality, equality and inclusion are being derided and called into question by representatives of populist parties as an expression of excessive 'political correctness.'"[4] The heyday of democracy in the 1990s unleashed global economic forces and technological shifts that some believed killed jobs, froze wages, and forced the migration of manufacturing, leaving the middle class feeling abandoned and betrayed. As inequality grew, so, too, did middle-class anger against the globalist forces that robbed them of their jobs and future, building into a broad nationalist and authoritarian countermovement against such perceived liberal orthodoxies as diversity, inclusion, and multiculturalism. Populist politicians fed off these resentments to form anti-European political parties. Then the Syrian refugee crisis of 2015 overwhelmed local authorities and caused racism and xenophobia to feed off each other to bring an end to compassion for outsiders. Europe now faces an existential threat from three directions: refugees, regional disintegration, and stalled economic development.

This infectious countermovement has fostered proliferation of a group of "closed democracies" that now thrives on identifying enemies. The new global authoritarians seem to play by the same basic playbook. They demonize immigrants, cow legislators, disparage multilateral bureaucrats, intimidate the judiciary, reward cronies, intimidate the media, and claim that constitutional checks and balances must give way to the "will of the people." The populist movements supporting Trump in America, Orbán in Hungary, and Kaczyński in Poland share a common emotional language of marginalization, anti-elitism, economic nationalism, and militarism. Stung by a failed coup attempt against him, Tayyip Erdoğan, leader of the once-democratizing Turkey, has veered wildly toward authoritarianism, becoming the world's leading jailer of journalists, judges, and politicians, while his thugs beat demonstrators in Washington, D.C., and his soldiers wage war against Kurdish nationalists in northwest Syria. In Venezuela, where Nicholas Maduro's populist governance has crippled the courts and the legislature, quality of life has disintegrated, crime is rampant, and corruption is pervasive. In sub-Saharan Africa, the deep dissatisfaction currently fueling populism grows out of a conviction that the elite cosmopolitan human rights movement has insufficiently focused on realizing economic, social, and cultural rights and benefits for their own people.

These trends have had a devastating effect on human rights, which have come under global challenge from both the left and the right.[5] Increasingly, courts are being used as tools of oppression. The language of human rights and democratic sovereignty is increasingly being turned against the whole notion of external monitoring of domestic compliance with international law.[6] Pressure on human rights defenders has grown visibly, not just in these states but in other ostensibly democratic states throughout Europe and South and Central Asia.

Unlike Kant, Trump, whose election was part of this global countermovement, does not seem to believe in universal rights or accept the notion that everyone can rise together. His "America First" strategy, repeated in his first U.N. speech and his first State of the Union speech, views America's interactions with the world as grimly zero-sum, an approach that inevitably promotes reciprocal self-centeredness on the part of other powerful nations. While this book has argued that in Donald Trump's America, legal guardrails may be keeping the traffic of power more or less on the road of law, in other countries with weaker democratic institutions and civil societies, the news is darker. China, Russia, and such illiberal democracies as Hungary, Poland, the Philippines, Turkey, and Venezuela are emerging not just as spoilers but as active predators within the liberal international order.

What this disheartening picture recalls is the alternative vision to Kant's: George Orwell's haunting *1984*. Orwell famously described a nasty and brutish world in which cynical global megapowers—virtually indistinguishable from one another in their authoritarianism and totalitarianism—violate human rights and the rule of law within their own spheres. They make today's adversaries tomorrow's allies by making cynical alliances and manipulating public opinion and disseminating disinformation and "fake news."[7] So as Trump taunts his G-7 allies as creating national security threats, yesterday's demon Kim Jong-un becomes today's "very talented" summit partner. Depending on the day, the Chinese, Russians, and Europeans alternate between being sworn enemies and welcome partners. The value of the Kantian smart-power system has been its capacity generally to dampen such impetuous mood swings to maintain policy and legal consistency across political transitions. In the years ahead, the challenge for our civil society institutions and postwar alliance system will be to show that they have the resilience to build techniques of resistance robust enough to check such authoritarian opportunism, so as to keep our democracy within the guardrails.

More fundamentally, the case studies above suggest that Trump's strategy rests on a false diagnosis. Contrary to his assertions, America's synergistic relationship with other countries is far from a zero-sum game. Through expansion of trade, globalization can make the American working class better off, so long as global integration of the United States and the world economies is carefully managed through a combination of smart diplomacy abroad and wise domestic policy at home. In that management exercise, immigrants represent a crucial part of a transnational solution to labor gaps, global awareness, and national revitalization. This complex management task calls on the United States to lead and intensify—not abandon—the mechanisms of global governance. So dealing with the problems of other nations is not a waste of America's energies. Rather, it is an essential task to preserve the common values of democracy, human rights, and rule of law that have driven the post–World War II global order.

It would be a fundamental error for the United States to resign from global leadership. Instead, America must improve its capacity for such leadership by doing more homework, less bombing, and more listening and talking, toward the broad strategic goal of improving long-term multilateral regime-building. Seen in this light, the resisters' game of rope-a-dope—a counterstrategy hastily improvised to blunt and push back against the myriad initiatives of a new and impetuous president—has proven both appropriate and necessary. Collectively, this toolkit of resistance is designed to ensure that Trump does not lead America permanently down the wrong track.

C. TECHNIQUES OF RESISTANCE

Increasingly lame —

Will we head in this Orwellian direction? Will Donald trump international law? Will he change the process or will it change him? Will consistent rope-a-dope resistance force him to adapt and change course to a more international law-friendly direction? And as his fragile coalition comes under stress, will it solidify or crumble?

The answer to all of these questions, of course, is: we shall see. But the story I have told here should give some ground for cautious optimism. As this review has chronicled, in some issue areas, bold public acts of resistance are playing a critical role in blocking Trump's initiatives. In other areas, bureaucratic inertia, path dependence, overly high opportunity costs, and the realities of international realpolitik have posed powerful constraints. In many of these areas, both heroic and mundane constraints can be seen at work. In some areas, the constraint is legal, based in domestic or international law, or a blend of the two. In other areas, the constraint is political or policy-based. But the common element is that these constraints create paths of lesser and greater resistance, depending on which path Trump chooses to go. So the challenge for those who wish to join forces to resist actively is to search for, find, and apply political pressure to those critical pressure points within transnational legal process that can be *strategically leveraged* by those who resist Trump's policy misdirection.

The discussion above has shown the strengths and weaknesses of various techniques of civil resistance. These techniques include such public international law strategies as alliances, international regimes and institutions, and treaty invocation; litigation strategies such as injunctions and delay granted by domestic and international courts; and bureaucratic strategies like inertia, slow-walking political commands, and outright refusals to obey. They embrace partnership strategies to make up for shortfalls in federal government performance, including partnerships with and among subnational entities, foreign governments, private entities, and committed individuals and networks; media strategies, such as leaking, blogging, and investigative reporting; and legislative initiatives to promote greater accountability, democratic participation, and oversight.

As the immigration context shows, the most obvious technique of resistance—litigation against the U.S. government—can be a double-edged sword. Over time, it may harden the executive's resolve to defend and continue negative behavior or trigger normatively undesirable litigation positions. But smart litigators know they must be thoughtful about who and how they sue. Sometimes—for example, when a new administration issues a thinly disguised Muslim Ban after just one week—the government throws down a gauntlet by publicly declaring that the president's authority will not be questioned. Under such circumstances, rule-of-law litigators have little option but to generate interactions and interpretations in the smartest possible way: to choose the right cases and the most advantageous fora, making arguments sensitive to the range of positions the U.S. government has taken in the past in an effort to advance better interpretations of international law.

Whatever the ultimate outcome, such litigation serves a critical signaling and public education function. The Travel Ban case, for example, has signaled to government litigators that there are limits to the arguments they can press. It has reminded beleaguered public servants that the legal interpretations they were fighting for within the bureaucracy resonate with the courts and the public at large. Especially when combined with street demonstrations, court injunctions remind policymakers that they cannot unilaterally change the status quo while the whole world is watching. Perhaps most important, prudent persistent litigation has taught the public that resistance is not futile and reminded Muslim-American communities that they are not alone.

I make no claim to have offered a complete account of the forms of political response required to deal with Trump and the new populist authoritarians. Nothing I say should be read to suggest that concerned citizens around the world should not also be in the streets demonstrating or that grassroots efforts should not also be trying to win back the statehouses and institutions of formal government power. Such populist counterresponses are exactly what people can and should do and are, in fact, what we are seeing. Nor do I propose an "elite project" of transnational lawyering in response to what is plainly a populist rejection of just such elite policymaking. In fact, the best antidote to underinformed populism seems to be *more enlightened populism*, combined with carefully chosen legal and political action. Lawyers will never relieve average citizens of the burdens of politics, but they certainly can—and, I believe, should—constantly create acts of political pressure that promote the rule of law through legal training and techniques that simply are not available to others.

Some commentators may be more sanguine about this story, seeing the "distributed checks and balances" that constrain any president as a kind of "self-correcting synopticon," in which the visibility of the president's actions subjects him to constant accountability.[8] I see this moment instead as a call for greater action, not complacency. There is a very big difference between a system that self-corrects and a system where concerted human agency and political struggle repeatedly force an underinformed, recalcitrant president back from the brink of illegality. In this latter kind of system, the domestic constitutional constraints that check the president are deeply intertwined with the international norms that have permeated U.S. domestic law in the Kantian era. At both the domestic and international level, these constraints have enhanced American power by strengthening its legitimacy.

Other commentators dismiss human rights lawyers who oppose U.S. government initiatives as engaged in disruptive "lawfare," unsettling policy by constraining America's Gulliver with a web of Lilliputian bonds. I believe, to the contrary, that what we are witnessing in the Trump era is only the latest iteration of the historic "LawFair" begun during the civil rights era, as carried forward into equality movements on behalf of women, racial and sexual minorities, and newcomers to America. The strategic parrying and counterpunching that has thus far limited the damage done by the Trump administration has been waged by a series of public interest law campaigns designed to ensure that outsiders (especially immigrants), the media, allies, subnational and national governments, courts, and elected legislators all have a seat at the table to express their constituents' views. It is this unprecedented level of social and political mobilization and contestation, not Trump's nativism, that has again shown America and the world "what democracy looks like."

In sketching this snapshot, I am intensely mindful that we are still in the early rounds of this fight. Inevitably, a rope-a-dope strategy wears down both sides. While the resistance has won impressive early victories, the constant battering by the Trump administration is corroding the long-term health and well-being of our democratic institutions. Over time, Trump's policy impulses may gain greater legal legitimacy, particularly if accompanied by legislative victories and judicial—particularly Supreme Court—confirmations. The more often we rely on the stickiness of transnational legal process to limit Trump's options, the greater the risk that the entire system will start to come unglued. But I am not simply betting that the stickiness of transnational legal process is stronger than the forces trying to unglue it. I believe that our job as lawyers is to make sure that it is stronger.

Some have expressed surprise at what they call a "move from the descriptive to the normative": my treating transnational legal process not just as a descriptive theory but as a call to arms or prescriptive counterstrategy.[9] In fact, this normative component has been a key part of transnational legal process theory from the beginning. My original lecture sketching this approach more than two decades ago closed by saying:

It is sometimes said that someone who, by acquiring medical training, comes to understand the human body acquires as well a moral duty not just to observe disease, but to try to cure it. In the same way, I would argue, a lawyer who acquires knowledge of the body politic acquires a duty not simply to observe transnational legal process, but to try to influence it.[10]

In short, I am not claiming, as a predictive matter, that Trump and his kind will inevitably be checked by transnational legal process. Rather, I am asking as a normative matter, for committed international lawyers to keep fighting to invoke that process—repeatedly, if need be—to preserve and advance the imperfect world we have inherited.

D. THE TALLY TO DATE

Is the rope-a-dope working? While we are still in the first half of the Trump administration's term, here's the foreign policy tally so far. More than sixty executive orders with little real impact. Over thirty senior officials resigned and many others fired. A Travel Ban narrowly upheld by the Supreme Court, but returning for further litigation to the lower courts, which it has already been thrice blocked. Torture order: never issued and the torture ban reaffirmed by senior officials. Climate: a claimed withdrawal that will not go into effect until after the next presidential election. Trade agreements: still intact, with the United States sidelined from or seeking re-entry to the most recent arrangements. Iran nuclear deal: America withdrawn, but the battered deal still in place. North Korea: rhetorical saber-rattling, hasty summitry, and the value of that diplomacy still to be proven. Russian hacking: continued turmoil, many active investigations, indictments issued, and more coming. Ukraine: mobilizing transnational legal process on its own. Al Qaeda: Trump relaxing the Obama framework, with no visible strategy to close Guantánamo or end the Forever War. Islamic State and Syria: borrowing from Hillary Clinton's playbook, but still lacking the smart-power plan that might achieve durable diplomatic outcomes. Not to mention many strained alliances, with foreign governments, international organizations, Trump's Republican allies, Congress, the law enforcement and intelligence communities, and the national and global media. Little progress on Trump's core agenda. And all this less than halfway into a four-year term.

As time goes on, this tally will change. But the basic outlines have already emerged. Since Trump's election, I have frequently been reminded of a joke once told by comedian Mel Brooks, playing the fictional 2000-Year-Old Man. That superannuated individual is asked, "Before the Almighty, did you believe in any superior being?" His answer: "Well, there was this guy, Phil. We used to plead, 'Oh Phil, don't kick us; don't beat us; don't hurt us.' Until one day, lightning came out of the sky and struck Phil down. At which point we all realized, *There's something bigger than Phil!*"[11]

Well, in the same way, there's something bigger than Donald Trump. And that is transnational legal process. He does not own it. He is just another player in it. What this book should remind you is: so are all of us.

So the game is on, and the stakes are high. The fight is still in its early rounds, and the transnational legal saga is just beginning. As the Reverend Dr. Martin Luther King, Jr., used to remind us, the moral arc of history is long, but it bends toward justice.[12] But it doesn't bend by itself. We are all participants in transnational legal process. As the continuing saga of the Trump Administration and International Law unfolds, authoritarian and antiglobalist forces will push hard to bend that arc in one direction. Isn't it up to us who care about international law to push even harder in the other direction?

BIOGRAPHICAL NOTE

Harold Hongju Koh is Sterling Professor of International Law, former Dean (2004–2009), and co-founder of the Rule of Law Clinic at Yale Law School, where he has taught since 1985. He served as Legal Adviser, U.S. Department of State from 2009 to 2013; Assistant Secretary of State for Democracy, Human Rights, and Labor from 1998 to 2001; Attorney-Adviser, Office of Legal Counsel, U.S. Department of Justice, from 1983 to 1985; and law clerk to Associate Justice Harry A. Blackmun of the United States Supreme Court from 1981 to 1982. He has testified regularly before Congress and has argued at the U.S. Supreme Court, the International Court of Justice, and many other domestic and international courts. An Honorary Fellow of Magdalen College, Oxford, and a Fellow of the American Philosophical Society and the American Academy of Arts and Sciences, he has received seventeen honorary degrees, more than thirty human rights awards, and the Wolfgang Friedmann Memorial Award from Columbia Law School's *Journal of Transnational Law* and the Louis B. Sohn Award from the American Bar Association's International Law Section for his outstanding lifetime contributions to international law.

ACKNOWLEDGMENTS

This book began life on November 8, 2016, the day that Donald Trump was elected president. To that point, my career had divided into four lifestreams: thirty-five years as a law professor; nearly thirty as a human rights lawyer; five as a law dean; and ten in the U.S. government, serving first in the Reagan Justice Department's Office of Legal Counsel, then later in the Clinton and Obama administrations' State Departments, as Madeleine Albright's Assistant Secretary for Democracy, Human Rights, and Labor and as Hillary Clinton's Legal Adviser, respectively. As a supporter of Secretary Clinton for president, one of her State Department team, and a member of her transition team, I obviously did not vote for Trump, but neither did I wish him ill. I did expect him to follow his oath: to preserve, protect, and defend the Constitution and laws of the United States of America, including treaties and customary international law.

One day after the election, at an open forum at Yale Law School, a number of students asked what those who believe in the rule of law should do next. I answered first that we should form a Rule of Law Clinic to participate in the wave of litigation that seemed sure to come. I recalled the remarks of my former professor, former Legal Adviser Abram Chayes, who said after he had sued the U.S. government as a private citizen, "I have always thought there is nothing wrong with an American lawyer holding the United States to its own best standards." So a few weeks later we founded the "11/9 Clinic"—named to distinguish it from the similar "9/11 Clinic" that we had founded soon after September 11, 2001, to help preserve human rights in the wake of America's aggressive counterterrorist response. My dear friends

The Trump Administration and International Law. Harold Hongju Koh.
© Oxford University Press 2019. Published 2019 by Oxford University Press.

Mike Wishnie, Phil Spector, Hope Metcalf, Mitzi Steiner, Eugene Rusyn, Denisha Bacchus, and Sameer Jaywant helped me establish that vibrant public interest law clinic, which has since enlisted more than fifty committed Yale law students to file dozens of briefs and documents to support the rule of law on a number of issues discussed in this book, including the Travel Ban, the Foreign Emoluments Clause, the transgender ban in the military, climate change, gerrymandering, Muslim discrimination, and the Twenty-Fifth Amendment to the U.S. Constitution. In my private capacity, I have also served as counsel to Ukraine in a number of the international litigation matters discussed in Chapter 4.

More broadly, I urged that we try to figure out what Trump's broader strategy would be, so that our Clinic's work could fit into a coherent counterstrategy of response. For Thanksgiving 2016, I was asked by my friends, *Just Security*'s editors Ryan Goodman, John Reed, and Kate Brannen, to publish a short post on their blog outlining that counterstrategy. As I spoke on the lecture circuit over the next fifteen months, I expanded and honed that message in a series of lectures delivered at Harvard, Columbia, Stanford, Buffalo, Penn State, Vermont, and the University of California at Irvine; the Whitney Center, the Lowy Institute of Sydney, Australia; the Geneva Centre for Security Policy; the Lady Margaret Lecture at Christ's College, Cambridge; the Lauterpacht Centre for International Law, Cambridge; and the Blavatnik School of Public Policy, Oxford.

In March 2017, I delivered the Foulston Siefkin Lecture at Washburn University School of Law in Topeka, Kansas, the historic location of *Brown v. Board of Education*, a case decided the year I was born and that has framed my career as a public lawyer. Dean Thomas Romig, the Foulston Siefkin law firm of Topeka, my good friend Professor Craig Martin, and Cristen Hintze, Claire Hillman, and James Latta all helped me turn my lecture into an article published in 56 *Washburn Law Journal* 413 (2017) as part of two symposia: a paper symposium with Professors Margaret McGuinness, Clare Frances Moran, and David Sloss and a virtual symposium on the *Opinio Juris* blog with Professors Craig Martin, Laura Dickinson, Bill Dodge, Kevin Jon Heller, and Frederic Sourgens. John Louth, Blake Ratcliff, David Lipp, and Meera Seth of Oxford University Press then ably helped me to translate that article into this book.

Parts of the discussion here derive from earlier writings:

- *The Emerging Law of 21st Century War*, 66 EMORY L.J. 487 (2017), http://law.emory.edu/elj/_documents/volumes/66/3/koh.pdf
- *The War Powers and Humanitarian Intervention*, 53 HOUSTON L. REV. 971 (2016), https://www.law.ox.ac.uk/sites/files/oxlaw/koh_2016_houston_final_as_published_4-25.pdf
- *Triptych's End: A Better Framework to Evaluate 21st Century International Lawmaking*, 126 YALE L.J. F. 337 (Jan. 17, 2017),

http://www.yalelawjournal.org/pdf/KohMacroedFinal_
b7ccaqrm.pdf [http://perma.cc/QF2K-8XYM]
• *Presidential Power to Terminate International Agreements*, forthcoming in 2018 YALE L.J. F.

A number of the arguments here first saw print on the *Just Security* and
Opinio Juris blogs:

• *Trump's So-Called Withdrawal from Paris: Far from Over*, JUST
SECURITY, June 2, 2017, https://www.justsecurity.org/41612/
trumps-so-called-withdrawal-paris [https://perma.cc/WYM2-
JEU7/] (with Dena Adler, Joanna Dafoe, Peter Posada, Conor
Dwyer Reynolds, and Eugene Rusyn)
• *International Law vs. Donald Trump: A Reply*, OPINIO JURIS,
Mar. 5, 2018, http://opiniojuris.org/2018/03/05/international-
law-vs-donald-trump-a-reply/
• *The Real "Red Line" Behind Trump's April 2018 Syria Strikes*, JUST
SECURITY, Apr. 16, 2018, https://www.justsecurity.org/54952/
real-red-linebehind-trumps-april-2018-syria-strikes/.

I especially thank my wonderful research assistants Catherine McCarthy,
Dylan Kolhoff, Matt Lifson, Wajdi Mallat, Samantha Peltz, Mitzi Steiner,
and Danielle Zucker of Yale Law School, for their excellent work. I am deeply
grateful to my friends and colleagues Lea Brilmayer, Sarah Cleveland, Paul
Dean, Mary-Christy Fisher, Russ Feingold, Chris Fonzone, Joel Goldstein,
Avril Haines, E. Scott Gilbert, Steve Herz, Michael Ignatieff, Rebecca Ingber,
Paul Kahn, Steve Koh, Sarah Labowitz, Elisa Massimino, Jim O'Brien,
Steve Pomper, Mike Posner, David Pozen, Charlie Savage, Phil Spector,
Julia Spiegel, Todd Stern, David Zionts, and the members of the Yale Law
School and University of Buffalo School of Law Faculty Workshops for their
thoughtful comments. As the manuscript deadline approached, Master Sir
Gregory Winter and the Fellows of Trinity College Cambridge, Master Jane
Stapleton and the Fellows of Christ's College Cambridge, Vice-Chancellor
Stephen Toope, Dean Richard Fentiman and the Faculty of Law at the
University of Cambridge, and Director Professor Eyal Benvenisti and the
Lauterpacht Centre for International Law at Cambridge all graciously gave
me the solitude and resources to finish the manuscript while serving as
Cambridge University's Goodhart Visiting Professor of Legal Science.
Through it all, my beloved family—my wife, attorney Mary-Christy
Fisher; my children, Emily Jennings Youngyon Koh and William Hagan
Wonlim Koh; my mother, Dr. Hesung Chun Koh, and mother-in-law, Sarah

J. Fisher; and my siblings Carolyn, Howard, Edward, Jean, and Richard, and siblings-in-law, Jane and Bill Fisher, and their families—all loved and supported me beyond measure. In Seoul, my beloved brother-in-law, Dr. Woong Kil Choo, courageously battled a debilitating illness until just before this book saw print. And deep in my heart, my late father Dr. Kwang Lim Koh reminds me every day how much I owe America and why there is always reason for hope, if you are ready to fight for it. It is to our continuing life together that I dedicate this book.

New Haven, Connecticut and Cambridge, England
June 2018

NOTES

Introduction

1. *See generally* Harold Hongju Koh, *Transnational Legal Process*, 75
   NEB. L. REV. 181 (1996); Harold Hongju Koh, *Why Do Nations Obey
   International Law?*, 106 YALE L.J. 2599 (1997); Harold Hongju Koh, *The
   1998 Frankel Lecture: Bringing International Law Home*, 35 HOUS. L. REV.
   623 (1998) [hereinafter Koh, *Bringing International Law Home*]; Harold
   Hongju Koh, *How Is International Human Rights Law Enforced?*, 74 IND.
   L.J. 1397 (1999).

Chapter 1

1. Aaron Blake, *Stephen Miller's Authoritarian Declaration: Trump's National
   Security Actions "Will Not Be Questioned"*, WASH. POST, Feb. 13, 2017,
   https://www.washingtonpost.com/news/the-fix/wp/2017/02/13/
   stephen-millers-audacious-controversial-declaration-trumps-national-
   security-actions-will-not-be-questioned [http://perma.cc/B8HP-EQYW].
2. Of course, under some circumstances, coercive techniques can and do
   play an important role in enforcing legal norms. *See generally* FREDERICK
   SCHAUER, THE FORCE OF LAW (2015).
3. *See generally* TOM R. TYLER, WHY PEOPLE OBEY THE LAW (1990).
4. *President Obama's Address to Congress*, N.Y. TIMES, Feb. 24, 2009, http://
   www.nytimes.com/2009/02/24/us/politics/24obama-text.html [http://
   perma.cc/WT94-Q2RT].

The Trump Administration and International Law. Harold Hongju Koh.
© Oxford University Press 2019. Published 2019 by Oxford University Press.

5. *Senate Confirmation Hearing: Hillary Clinton*, N.Y. TIMES, Jan. 13, 2009, http://www.nytimes.com/2009/01/13/us/politics/13text-clinton. html [http://perma.cc/MY73-WFLX]. *See generally* HILLARY RODHAM CLINTON, HARD CHOICES (2014).

6. BARON DE MONTESQUIEU, THE SPIRIT OF THE LAWS (Thomas Nugent trans., 1st ed. 1900). *See also* Harold Hongju Koh, *The Spirit of the Laws*, 43 HARV. INT'L L.J. 23 (2002).

7. *Cf.* Lawrence Lessig, *Fidelity in Translation*, 71 TEX. L. REV. 1165 (1993) (arguing that any complete account of interpretation must "translate," by allowing for changes in readings even when there has been no change in the document's text).

8. Harold Hongju Koh, *Preserving American Values: The Challenge at Home and Abroad, in* THE AGE OF TERROR: AMERICA AND THE WORLD AFTER SEPTEMBER 11, at 143, 153 (Strobe Talbott & Nayan Chanda eds., 2001).

9. PAUL KENNEDY, THE RISE AND FALL OF THE GREAT POWERS (1989).

10. *E.g.*, Joseph S. Nye, *Public Diplomacy and Soft Power*, 616 ANNALS OF THE AM. ACAD. OF POL. & SOC. SCI. 94, 107 (2008) ("Power in a global information age, more than ever, will include a soft dimension of attraction as well as the hard dimensions of coercion and inducement. The ability to combine hard and soft power effectively is 'smart power.'").

11. I have labeled such outsiders "transnational norm entrepreneurs" and such insiders "governmental norm sponsors," respectively. *See* Koh, *Bringing International Law Home, supra* Introduction, note 1, at 647–48 (1998).

12. *See generally* Robbie Gramer et al., *How the Trump Administration Broke the State Department*, FOREIGN POL'Y, July 31, 2017, http://foreignpolicy.com/2017/07/31/how-the-trump-administration-broke-the-state-department/ [http://perma.cc/6PYG-PM65].

13. *See* Koh, *Bringing International Law Home, supra* Introduction, note 1 (distinguishing among social, political, and legal internalization).

Chapter 2

1. Trump's January 25, 2018, executive order sought to defund all jurisdictions deemed to be "sanctuaries," a term nowhere defined in the order and apparently used to coerce localities into adopting the aggressive federal immigration agenda. But when the counties of Santa Clara and San Francisco sued to block implementation of the order as unconstitutional, the U.S. District Court for the Northern District of California enjoined nationwide the key defunding provision. *See* City of Santa Clara v. Trump, No. 17-CV-00485-WHO, 2017 WL 1459081 (N.D. Cal. Apr. 25,

2017), *reconsideration denied*, No. 17-CV-00485-WHO, 2017 WL 3086064 (N.D. Cal. July 20, 2017).

2. *See* Reforming American Immigration for Strong Employment Act, S. 354, 115th Cong. (2017).

3. Section 5 of the Executive Order on Sanctuary Jurisdictions, *supra* note 1, sets out the administration's expansive deportation priorities, which include giving immigration officers broad authority to deport any noncitizen even *suspected*, in that officer's opinion, of posing a "safety risk." On September 5, 2017, Trump further announced that he would repeal President Obama's Deferred Action for Childhood Arrivals (DACA) program, which grants work permits to about 800,000 undocumented immigrants brought to the United States as children. After six months' delay, the following Easter, he tweeted, "NO MORE DACA DEAL." *See* Philip Rucker & David Weigel, *"No More DACA Deal," Trump Says as He Threatens to "Stop" NAFTA if Mexico Doesn't Better Secure Border*, WASH. POST, Apr. 1, 2018, https://www.washingtonpost.com/news/post-politics/wp/2018/04/01/deal-on-daca-no-more-trump-says/.

4. Protecting the Nation from Foreign Terrorist Entry into the United States, 82 Fed. Reg. 8977 (Jan. 27, 2017).

5. *See* Sonam Sheth, *Trump Campaign Deletes Statement on Muslim Ban After Reporter Asks About It*, BUS. INSIDER, May 8, 2017, 3:27 PM, http://www.businessinsider.com/trump-campaign-muslim-ban-statement-website-2017-5 [http://perma.cc/Q9FM-AXF8].

6. Convention Relating to the Status of Refugees art. 3, July 28, 1951, 189 U.N.T.S. 150. *See also* Amy B. Wang, *Trump Asked for a "Muslim Ban," Giuliani Says—and Ordered a Commission to Do It "Legally"*, WASH. POST, Jan. 29, 2017, https://www.washingtonpost.com/news/the-fix/wp/2017/01/29/trump-asked-for-a-muslim-ban-giuliani-says-and-ordered-a-commission-to-do-it-legally [http://perma.cc/7HJB-JJQ6].

7. International Covenant on Civil and Political Rights art. 26, Dec. 9, 1966, 999 U.N.T.S. 171 (*ratified* June 8, 1992).

8. Protecting the Nation from Foreign Terrorist Entry into the United States, 82 Fed. Reg. at 8977; Brief for Former National Security Officials as Amici Curiae Supporting Plaintiff-Appellees, Int'l Refugee Assistance Project v. Donald J. Trump, 857 F. 3d 554 (4th Cir. 2017) (No. 17-15589), 2017 WL 1372588.

9. Alex Nowrasteh, *Little National Security Benefit to Trump's Executive Order on Immigration*, CATO INST., Jan. 25, 2017, 3:31 PM, https://www.cato.org/blog/little-national-security-benefit-trumps-executive-order-immigration [http://perma.cc/59ZJ-MUPC].

10. Justin Sink & Ben Brody, *U.S. Exempts Green Card Holders from Trump's Travel Ban*, BLOOMBERG, Jan. 29, 2017, 5:53 AM, https://www.

bloomberg.com/news/articles/2017-01-29/trump-says-u-s-needs-extreme-vetting-after-action-by-judges [http://perma.cc/ZH3L-ZB67].

11. Darweesh v. Trump, No. 17 CIV. 480 (AMD), 2017 WL 388504 (E.D.N.Y. Jan. 28, 2017). *See Rule of Law Clinic Files Amicus Brief in SCOTUS Travel Ban Case*, YALE L. SCH. (Sept. 20, 2017), https://law.yale.edu/yls-today/news/rule-law-clinic-files-amicus-brief-scotus-travel-ban-case [http://perma.cc/P3DY-EYHR].

12. Dissent Channel Memorandum to Edward J. Lacey, Acting Dir. of Pol'y Planning, Alternatives to Closing Doors in Order to Secure Our Borders (Jan. 2017), *available at* https://www.washingtonpost.com/r/2010/2019/WashingtonPost/2017/01/30/Editorial-Opinion/Graphics/Draft_Dissent_on_EOSec3.pdf [http://perma.cc/Y6BT-A67M].

13. Sari Horwitz, *Who Is Sally Yates? Meet the Acting Attorney General Trump Fired for "Betraying" the Justice Department.*, WASH. POST, Jan. 30, 2017, https://www.washingtonpost.com/world/national-security/meet-the-acting-attorney-general-fired-by-trump-and-accused-of-betraying-the-justice-department/2017/01/30/05d4478c-e750-11e6-80c2-30e57e57e05d_story.html [http://perma.cc/HY7Y-3QDQ].

14. *See, e.g.*, Memorandum from the Dep't of Homeland Sec., Citizenship Likely an Unreliable Indicator of Terrorist Threat to the United States (Feb. 2017), *available at* https://www.documentcloud.org/documents/3474730-DHS-intelligence-document-on-President-Donald.html [http://perma.cc/DH7E-BJEA].

15. Indeed, the Canadians offered temporary residence to anyone stranded in Canada by the Order. Ashifa Kassam, *Canada to Offer Temporary Residence to Those Stranded by Trump Travel Ban*, GUARDIAN, Jan. 31, 2017, 10:59 AM, https://www.theguardian.com/world/2017/jan/31/canada-trump-travel-ban-temporary-residence [http://perma.cc/98YU-FHJD].

16. Vets4AmericanIdeals (@Vets4AmerIdeals), TWITTER, https://twitter.com/Vets4AmerIdeals [http://perma.cc/CP6A-Y8MQ].

17. Charlie D'Agata, *Iraqi General Who Works with American Military Kept from Visiting U.S.*, CBS NEWS, Jan. 30, 2017, 7:30 PM, http://www.cbsnews.com/news/iraqi-general-who-works-with-american-military-kept-from-visiting-u-s/ [http://perma.cc/A69A-GHRP].

18. Sean Sullivan & Kelsey Snell, *Angry Republicans Lash Out at Trump for Not Consulting Them on Travel Ban*, WASH. POST, Jan. 30, 2017, https://www.washingtonpost.com/powerpost/angry-republicans-lash-out-at-trump-for-not-consulting-them-on-travel-ban/2017/01/30/3f7db742-e715-11e6-80c2-30e57e57e05d_story.html [http://perma.cc/H6MX-WAWY].

19. Philip Elliott, *The Koch Brothers Oppose President Trump's Immigration Ban*, TIME, Jan. 29, 2017, http://time.com/4652905/koch-brothers-

donald-trump-immigration-Ban-order [http://perma.cc/2FQR-B6H2]; Heather Digby Parton, *George W. Bush's "Torture Lawyer" Turns on Trump—But It May Be Too Late*, SALON, Feb. 7, 2017, 5:15 AM, http:// www.salon.com/2017/02/07/george-w-bushs-torture-lawyer-turns-on-trump-but-it-may-be-too-late [http://perma.cc/AC7W-LFA6]; Justin Wm. Moyer, *Dick Cheney Slams Trump's Muslim Entry Ban*, WASH. POST, Dec. 8, 2015, https://www.washingtonpost.com/news/morning-mix/wp/2015/12/08/dick-cheney-slams-trumps-muslim-entry-ban-and-suggests-u-s-re-invade-middle-east [http://perma.cc/A2NK-KFKU].

20. Dan Levine, *Attorneys General from 15 U.S. States, DC Decry Immigration Order*, REUTERS, Jan. 29, 2017, 12:38 PM, http://www.reuters.com/article/us-usa-trump-attorneygenerals/attorneys-general-from-15-u-s-states-dc-decry-immigration-order-idUSKBN15D0XZ [http://perma.cc/PV9G-XN4C].

21. Brief for Chicago, Los Angeles, New York, Philadelphia, and Other Major Cities and Counties as Amici Curiae Supporting Plaintiffs, Hawai'i v. Trump, No. CV 17-00050 DKW-KSC, 2017 WL 1167383 (D. Haw. Mar. 29, 2017).

22. Katie Reilly, *University Leaders Call President Trump's Immigration Order a Threat to American Higher Ed*, TIME, Feb. 3, 2017, http://time.com/4660098/donald-trump-universities-immigration-ban [http://perma.cc/Z33J-3P24].

23. Brief for Technology Companies as Amici Curiae Supporting Appellees, Hawai'i v. Trump, No. CV 17-00050 DKW-KSC, 2017 WL 1167383 (D. Haw. Mar. 29, 2017).

24. *Worker and Immigrant Rights Advocacy Clinic, Legal Templates*, YALE L. SCH., https://law.yale.edu/studying-law-yale/clinical-and-experiential-learning/our-clinics/worker-and-immigrant-rights-advocacy-clinic/legal-templates [http://perma.cc/6YSP-ZNBX] (last visited Sept. 30, 2017).

25. *Budweiser Focuses on Immigration in Super Bowl Commercial*, CHI. TRIB., Jan. 31, 2017, 6:22 PM, http://www.chicagotribune.com/sports/football/ct-nfl-super-bowl-advertising-anheuser-busch-spt-20170131-story.html [http://perma.cc/GJR8-VX2X].

26. Protecting the Nation from Foreign Terrorist Entry into the United States, 82 Fed. Reg. 13209 (Mar. 6, 2017).

27. *See* Brief for Former National Security Officials as Amici Curiae Supporting Respondents at 3–4, Donald J. Trump v. State of Hawai'i (Nos. 16-1436 & 16-1540), *available at* http://www.scotusblog.com/wp-content/uploads/2017/09/16_1436_16_1540_bsac_Former_National_Security_Officials.pdf [http://perma.cc/97XP-7PMZ] (arguing that "all available evidence suggests that the Order was not based on national

security judgment at all, but rather, on a deliberate political decision to discriminate against a religious minority").

28. *See* Bart Jansen, *Trump's Travel Ban Could Cost $18B in U.S. Tourism, Analysis Shows*, USA TODAY, Mar. 29, 2017, 6:01 PM, https://www.usatoday.com/story/news/world/2017/03/29/trumps-travel-ban-could-cost-18b-us-tourism-travel-analysts-say/99708758/ [http://perma.cc/6DHQ-J2R9].

29. Hawai'i v. Trump, No. CV 17-00050 DKW-KSC, 2017 WL 1167383 (D. Haw. Mar. 29, 2017), *aff'd in part, vacated in part, remanded sub nom.* Hawai'i v. Trump, 859 F.3d 741 (9th Cir. 2017), *cert. granted sub nom.* Trump v. Int'l Refugee Assistance Project, 137 S. Ct. 2080 (2017); Int'l Refugee Assistance Project v. Trump, No. CV TDC-17-0361, 2017 WL 1018235 (D. Md. Mar. 16, 2017), *aff'd in part, vacated in part*, 857 F.3d 554 (4th Cir. 2017), *cert. granted*, 137 S. Ct. 2080 (2017); Washington v. Trump, No. C17-0141JLR, 2017 WL 462040 (W.D. Wash. Feb. 3, 2017), *appeal dismissed sub nom.* Washington v. Trump, No. 17-35105 (9th Cir. Feb. 4, 2017).

30. Trump v. Int'l Refugee Assistance Project, 137 S. Ct. 2080, 2088 (2017) (narrowing the Travel Ban with a stay that barred only those travelers who lacked a "bona fide relationship" to the United States). The Court's stay order allowed the ban to take effect only with respect to those immigrants who had no preexisting "bona fide relationship" with the United States. But that test made little sense, as historically, many refugees have had no prior relationship whatsoever with the countries that admit them.

31. Michael D. Shear et al., *Supreme Court Cancels Hearing on Previous Travel Ban*, N.Y. TIMES, Sept. 25, 2017, https://www.nytimes.com/2017/09/25/us/politics/trump-travel-ban-supreme-court.html [http://perma.cc/U3VW-P9HD].

32. *A Trump Travel Ban We've Seen Before*, N.Y. TIMES, Sept. 25, 2017, https://www.nytimes.com/2017/09/25/opinion/editorials/trump-travel-Ban.html [http://perma.cc/TC7E-QCE9].

33. White House Office of the Press Sec'y, *Presidential Proclamation Enhancing Vetting Capabilities and Processes for Detecting Attempted Entry into the United States by Terrorists or Other Public-Safety Threats*, WHITE HOUSE (Sept. 24, 2017), https://www.whitehouse.gov/the-press-office/2017/09/24/enhancing-vetting-capabilities-and-processes-detecting-attempted-entry [http://perma.cc/XLE5-CNEW].

34. Marbury v. Madison, 5 U.S. (1 Cranch) 137, 177 (1803).

35. *See generally* Harold Hongju Koh, *The Enduring Legacies of the Haitian Refugee Litigation*, 61 N.Y.L. SCH. L. REV. 31 (2016–2017), http://www.nylslawreview.com/wp-content/uploads/sites/16/2017/09/Law-Review-61.1-Koh.pdf (describing relitigation of the *nonrefoulement* issue in the Haitian case before various international tribunals).

36. *See generally* Harold Hongju Koh, *The 2001 Richard Childress Memorial Lecture: A United States Human Rights Policy for the 21st Century*, 46 ST. LOUIS U. L.J. 293 (2002) [hereinafter Koh, *A United States Human Rights Policy for the 21st Century*].

37. Zoë Chapman, *The Early Edition: January 13, 2017*, JUST SECURITY, Jan. 13, 2017, 7:55 AM, https://www.justsecurity.org/36292/early-edition-january-13-2017 [http://perma.cc/M3WB-EHED].

38. Carol Morello, *Did Tillerson and Duterte Discuss Human Rights? Depends on Which Side You Ask*, WASH. POST, Aug. 8, 2017, https://www.washingtonpost.com/world/did-tillerson-and-duterte-discuss-human-rights-depends-on-which-side-you-ask/2017/08/08/6eac13af-1046-4bf1-b971-7a4c8a91e8d1_story.html [http://perma.cc/U6RA-X522]. Duterte's summary executions have since been referred to the Prosecutor of the International Criminal Court for future investigation.

39. Sec'y of State Rex Tillerson, Remarks to U.S. Department of State Employees (May 3, 2017), https://www.state.gov/secretary/remarks/2017/05/270620.htm [http://perma.cc/7N5X-8YDL].

40. *See* Michael Posner, *Tillerson's Degradation of Human Rights Mustn't— and Can't Yet—Be Executive Branch Policy*, JUST SECURITY, May 22, 2017, 8:35 AM, https://www.justsecurity.org/ 41229/tillerson-human-rights-presidential-directive-30/ [http://perma.cc/9FEA-BSFA].

41. *See generally* Koh, *A United States Human Rights Policy for the 21st Century*, *supra* note 36; Michael Posner, *Trump Abandons the Human Rights Agenda*, NEW YORKER, May 26, 2017, https://www.newyorker.com/news/news-desk/trump-abandons-the-human-rights-agenda [http://perma.cc/72ME-L3K5].

42. Michael Gerson, *Rex Tillerson Is a Huge Disappointment*, WASH. POST, Aug. 7, 2017, https://www.washingtonpost.com/opinions/rex-tillerson-is-a-huge-disappointment/2017/08/07/a9918b8e-7ba5-11e7-9d08-b79f191668ed_story.html [http://perma.cc/5KAV-BYEL].

43. Somini Sengupta, *Nikki Haley Calls United Nations Human Rights Council "So Corrupt"*, N.Y. TIMES, Mar. 29, 2017, https://www.nytimes.com/2017/03/29/world/nikki-haley-un-human-rights-council-corrupt.html [http://perma.cc/2Q49-UDVS]/; Avery Anapol, *US expected to withdraw from UN Human Rights Council: report*, The Hill (June 15, 2018), http://thehill.com/policy/international/392418-us-expected-to-withdraw-from-un-human-rights-council-report.

44. Josh Rogin, *State Department Considers Scrubbing Democracy Promotion from Its Mission*, WASH. POST, Aug. 1, 2017, https://www.washingtonpost.com/news/josh-rogin/wp/2017/08/01/state-department-considers-

scrubbing-democracy-promotion-from-its-mission [http://perma.cc/EYZ3-C39Z].

45. Jenna Johnson, *Trump Says "Torture Works," Backs Waterboarding and "Much Worse"*, WASH. POST, Feb. 17, 2016, https://www.washingtonpost.com/politics/trump-says-torture-works-backs-waterboarding-and-much-worse/2016/02/17/4c9277be-d59c-11e5-b195-2e29a4e13425_story.html [http://perma.cc/6D2L-JMRV].

46. Contrary to the president's rhetoric, the draft order cautioned that "[n]o person in the custody of the United States shall at any time be subjected to torture or cruel, inhuman, or degrading treatment or punishment, as proscribed by U.S. law." *Draft Executive Order on the Detention and Interrogation of Enemy Combatants*, WASH. POST, Jan. 25, 2017, http://apps.washingtonpost.com/g/documents/national/read-the-draft-of-the-executive-order-on-cia-black-sites/2288 [http://perma.cc/YH9N-M29U]; Charlie Savage, *Trump Poised to Lift Ban on C.I.A. "Black Site" Prisons*, N.Y. TIMES, Jan. 25, 2017, https://www.nytimes.com/2017/01/25/us/politics/cia-detainee-prisons.html [http://perma.cc/MY34-8EUS].

47. *See, e.g.*, International Covenant on Civil and Political Rights, *supra* note 7, art. 7 ("No one shall be subjected to torture or to cruel, inhuman or degrading treatment or punishment."); Convention Against Torture and Other Cruel, Inhuman or Degrading Treatment or Punishment, Dec. 10, 1984, 1465 U.N.T.S. 85; War Crimes Act, 18 U.S.C. § 2441 (1996) (criminalizing torture); Torture Victim Protection Act, 28 U.S.C. § 1350 (1991) (civil remedy); Alien Tort Claims Act, 28 U.S.C. § 1350 (1988) (civil remedy); National Defense Authorization Act for Fiscal Year 2016, Pub. L. No. 114-92, § 1045, 129 Stat. 726, 977 (2015).

48. The Convention Against Torture states that "[n]o exceptional circumstances whatsoever, whether a state of war or threat of war . . . may be invoked as a justification for torture." The Convention Against Torture Article 2(2). Common Article 3 to the four Geneva Conventions, which is considered customary international law, states as a rule of humanity that there should be no violence to life and persons, including no torture or outrages on personal dignity, or sentences without due process. Geneva Convention Relative to the Treatment of Prisoners of War art. 3, Aug. 12, 1949, 6 U.S.T. 3316. Additional Protocol II amplifies these guarantees and outlaws all forms of violence against noncombatants. Protocol Additional to the Geneva Conventions of 12 August 1949, and Relating to the Protection of Victims of Non-International Armed Conflicts (Protocol II) art. 4, ¶ 2, June 8, 1977, 1125 U.N.T.S. 609.

49. 10 U.S.C. § 855 (1956) ("Punishment by flogging, or by branding, marking, or tattooing on the body, or any other cruel or unusual punishment, may not be adjudged by any court-martial or inflicted upon any person subject to this chapter. The use of irons, single or double, except for the purpose of safe custody, is prohibited.").

50. Al Shimari v. CACI Premier Tech., Inc., 840 F.3d 147, 162 (4th Cir. 2016) (Floyd, J., concurring) ("The fact that the president—let alone a significantly inferior executive officer—opines that certain conduct is lawful does not determine the actual lawfulness of that conduct."); *accord* Harold Hongju Koh, *Can the President Be Torturer in Chief?*, 81 IND. L.J. 1145, 1148, 1156 (2006).

51. *See Hamdan v. Rumsfeld*: Establishing a Constitutional Process, Hearing Before the S. Comm. on the Judiciary, 109th Cong. 51 (2006) (statement of Harold Hongju Koh, Dean, Yale Law School) ("Some have said, well, terrorists have not signed Common Article 3. Well, whales have not signed the Whaling Convention. But it is about how we treat them and how we are obliged to treat them.").

52. 162 Cong Rec. S716 (daily ed. Feb. 9, 2016) (statement of Senator John McCain), *available at* https://www.mccain.senate.gov/public/index.cfm/floor-statements?ID=BEE31A68-99DE-40F6-844E-27482CBA6240 [http://perma.cc/63M5-CBDK].

53. Harold Hongju Koh, Legal Adviser, U.S. Dep't of State, Memorandum Opinion on the Geographic Scope of the Convention Against Torture and Its Application in Situations of Armed Conflict 5–6 (Jan. 21, 2013) (*discussed in* CHARLIE SAVAGE, POWER WARS: INSIDE OBAMA'S POST-9/11 PRESIDENCY 535 (2015)) (emphasis added).

54. Karen DeYoung, *Obama Administration Endorses Treaty Banning Torture*, WASH. POST, Nov. 12, 2014, https://www.washingtonpost.com/world/national-security/obama-administration-endorses-treaty-banningtorture/2014/11/12/b6131e68-6a8c-11e4-9fb4-a622dae742a2_story.html [http://perma.cc/48MA-X2WH] (quoting Assistant Secretary of State for Democracy, Human Rights and Labor Tom Malinowski).

55. PRESIDENT BARACK OBAMA, REPORT ON THE LEGAL AND POLICY FRAMEWORKS GUIDING THE UNITED STATES' USE OF MILITARY FORCE AND RELATED NATIONAL SECURITY OPERATIONS 32 (2016) [hereinafter FRAMEWORKS REPORT], https://www.justsecurity.org/wp-content/uploads/2016/12/framework.Report_Final.pdf [http://perma.cc/SS42-KSGC].

56. President Barack Obama, *Remarks by the President on the Administration's Approach to Counterterrorism*, WHITE HOUSE (Dec. 6, 2016), https://www.whitehouse.gov/the-press-office/2016/12/06/remarks-president-

administrations-approach-counterterrorism [http://perma.cc/Q92S-4B2R].

57. SHANE O'MARA, WHY TORTURE DOESN'T WORK: THE NEUROSCIENCE OF INTERROGATION (2015); *see also* Harold Hongju Koh, *Pain Versus Gain*, JUST SECURITY, June 20, 2016, 3:15 AM, https://www.justsecurity.org/31544/pain-gain/ [http://perma.cc/HW47-U9A2].

58. *See* Douglas Johnson et al., *The Strategic Costs of Torture: How "Enhanced Interrogation" Hurt America*, FOREIGN AFF. (Sept./Oct. 2016), https://www.foreignaffairs.com/articles/united-states/strategic-costs-torture [http://perma.cc/3QXE-BE3B].

59. Paul Koring, *Choice of Panetta to Head CIA Likely to Raise Hackles in Spy Circles*, GLOBE & MAIL, Jan. 10, 2009, https://www.theglobeandmail.com/news/world/choice-of-panetta-to-head-cia-likely-to-raise-hackles-in-spy-circles/article20442915 [http://perma.cc/VHR8-CQZJ].

60. Among other public pressure points, a joint letter from 176 generals and admirals helped to put Trump's cabinet nominees on the record against torture. *See Letter from 176 Retired Generals and Admirals to President-Elect Trump on the Use of Torture*, HUM. RTS. FIRST, Jan. 11, 2017, http://www.humanrightsfirst.org/resource/letter-176-retired-generals-and-admirals-president-elect-trump-use-torture [http://perma.cc/EWB9-GTB5].

61. Kristina Wong, *Pentagon: Mattis Still Opposes Torture Despite Trump Comment*, THE HILL, Jan. 26, 2017, http://www.thehill.com/policy/defense/316356-mattis-remains-opposed-to-torture-pentagon-says [http://perma.cc/7SFL-UCGE]; Caroline Kenny, *CIA Nominee Says He Would Disregard Trump on Torture*, CNN, Jan. 12, 2017, 1:02 PM, http://www.cnn.com/2017/01/12/politics/trump-cabinet-picks-oppose-torture/index.html [http://perma.cc/P8DK-83ZY].

62. Matthew Rosenberg et al., *Gina Haspel Vows at Confirmation Hearing That She Would Not Allow Torture by C.I.A.*, N.Y. TIMES, May 9, 2018, https://www.nytimes.com/2018/05/09/us/politics/gina-haspel-confirmation-hearing-live.html.

Chapter 3

1. Harold Hongju Koh, *International Criminal Justice 5.0*, 38 YALE J. INT'L L. 525 (2013), *available at* http://digitalcommons.law.yale.edu/cgi/viewcontent.cgi?article=1436&context=yjil [http://perma.cc/YJ3L-3V4X]. If anything, the claimed "unsigning"—announced in a letter sent by then-Undersecretary of State John Bolton—only focused the attention of the other International Criminal Court parties on the United States'

continuing obligations as a treaty signatory not to defeat the object and purpose of the Rome Statute under Article 18 of the Vienna Convention on the Law of Treaties.

2. Paris Agreement of the United Nations Framework Convention on Climate Change, art. 28.1, Apr. 22, 2016, T.I.A.S. No. 16-1104 [hereinafter Paris Agreement].

3. Paris Agreement Depository, Status of the Treaty (May 9, 2018), https://treaties.un.org/Pages/ViewDetails.aspx?src=TREATY&mtdsg_no=XXVII-7-d&chapter=27&clang=_en [https://perma.cc/GA8N-EU6K].

4. *See* Press Release, *Communication Regarding Intent to Withdraw from Paris Agreement*, U.S. DEP'T OF STATE (Aug. 4, 2017), https://www.state.gov/r/pa/prs/ps/2017/08/273050.htm [https://perma.cc/V8GP-XD6U] (emphasis added).

5. *See* WEARESTILLIN, https://www.wearestillin.com/about [https://perma.cc/M47V-BWRC].

6. Nikki Haley, U.S. Ambassador to the U.N., Diplomatic Note to the U.N. Secretary-General (Aug. 4, 2017).

7. Geoffrey Smith, *Germany and China Position Themselves as World Climate Leaders*, FORTUNE, June 1, 2017, http://www.fortune.com/2017/06/01/paris-agreement-germany-china-trump [https://perma.cc/V2CC-5EJP]. For example, the Indian Supreme Court has recently backed tougher emissions standards, which may improve its own international bargaining leverage in the years ahead. Amy Kazmin, *Indian Court Backs Drive for Tough Auto Emissions Standards*, FIN. TIMES, Mar. 29, 2017, https://www.ft.com/content/41b4f4bc-1483-11e7-80f4-13e067d5072c [https://perma.cc/8FA2-77BT].

8. *See* Emre Peker, *Trump Administration Seeks to Avoid Withdrawal from Paris Climate Accord*, WALL ST. J., Sept. 16, 2017, 5:16 PM, https://www.wsj.com/articles/trump-administration-wont-withdraw-from-paris-climate-deal-1505593922 [https://perma.cc/4VPP-K83J] (quoting Trump official at diplomatic meeting stating that the United States would stay in under "the right conditions").

9. *Quadrennial Energy Review: Second Installment*, ENERGY.GOV, https://www.energy.gov/policy/initiatives/quadrennial-energy-review-qer/quadrennial-energy-review-second-installment (last visited July 6, 2018).

10. West Virginia v. E.P.A., 136 S. Ct. 1000 (2016).

11. West Virginia v. E.P.A., No. 15-1363 (D.C. Cir. Apr. 28, 2017). The D.C. Circuit has three times extended its holding of the case in abeyance, mandating that the EPA provide regular status reports while the agency considers its path forward. Order, West Virginia v. E.P.A., No. 15-1363 (Mar. 1, 2018).

12. Order, West Virginia v. E.P.A., No. 15-1363 (Aug. 8, 2017) (Millet and Tatel, JJ., concurring). *See also* John H. Cushman, Jr., *Obama's Clean Power Plan: What to Know About the Newest Legal Showdown*, INSIDE CLIMATE NEWS, May 17, 2017, https://insideclimatenews.org/news/16052017/clean-power-plan-epa-lawsuit-trump-obama-climate-change [https://perma.cc/2JK2-L4RH].

13. Repeal of Carbon Pollution Emission Guidelines for Existing Stationary Sources: Electric Utility Generating Units, 82 Fed. Reg. 48,035 (proposed Oct. 16, 2017); State Guidelines for Greenhouse Gas Emissions from Existing Electric Utility Generating Units, 82 Fed. Reg. 61,507 (proposed Dec. 28, 2017).

14. EPA Status Report, West Virginia v. E.P.A., No. 15-1363 (D.C. Cir. May 2, 2018).

15. Mid-Term Evaluation of Greenhouse Gas Emissions Standards for Model Year 2022–2025 Light-Duty Vehicles, 83 Fed. Reg. 16,077 (proposed Apr. 13, 2018).

16. Coral Davenport & Bill Vlasic, *Trump Using Detroit as Stage for Loosening Obama's Fuel Economy Rules*, N.Y. TIMES, Mar. 15, 2017, https://www.nytimes.com/2017/03/15/us/politics/trump-obama-fuel-economy-standards.html [https://perma.cc/FM92-H3WF]. For a comprehensive review of ongoing climate change litigation, see DENA ADLER, *U.S. CLIMATE CHANGE LITIGATION IN THE AGE OF TRUMP: YEAR ONE* (Feb. 2018), http://columbiaclimatelaw.com/files/2018/02/Adler-2018-02-U.S.-Climate-Change-Litigation-in-the-Age-of-Trump-Year-One.pdf.

17. David Hasemyer, *Fossil Fuels on Trial: Where the Major Climate Change Lawsuits Stand Today*, INSIDE CLIMATE NEWS, Apr. 4, 2018, https://insideclimatenews.org/news/04042018/climate-change-fossil-fuel-company-lawsuits-timeline-exxon-children-california-cities-attorney-general (enumerating lawsuits).

18. Hiroko Tabuchi & Coral Davenport, *California Sues Trump Administration over Car Emissions Rules*, N.Y. TIMES, May 1, 2018, https://www.nytimes.com/2018/05/01/climate/california-sues-trump-administration.html [https://perma.cc/E3VD-AKQJ].

19. Camille von Kaenel, *Will Trump Intervene in War over Car Rules?*, E&E NEWS, May 4, 2018, https://www.eenews.net/climatewire/2018/05/04/stories/1060080801 [https://perma.cc/GP5Y-USSR]; Evan Halper & Joseph Tanfani, *Trump Administration Moves on Two Fronts to Challenge California Environmental Protections*, L.A. TIMES, Apr. 2, 2018, http://www.latimes.com/politics/la-na-pol-epa-fuel-standards-20180402-story.html [https://perma.cc/D4MJ-9XLE].

20. Camille von Kaenel, *Trump Admin Draft Proposal Would Freeze Fuel Economy*, E&E NEWS, Apr. 27, 2018, https://www.eenews.net/eenewspm/stories/1060080359 [https://perma.cc/7R33-YCU3].

21. Central Valley Chrysler-Jeep, Inc. v. Goldstene, 529 F. Supp. 2d 1151, 1173 (E.D. Cal. 2007); Green Mountain Chrysler Plymouth Dodge Jeep v. Crombie, 508 F. Supp. 2d 295, 347 (D. Vt. 2007).

22. Lisa Friedman, *Court Blocks E.P.A. Effort to Suspend Obama-Era Methane Rule*, N.Y. TIMES, July 3, 2017, https://www.nytimes.com/2017/07/03/climate/court-blocks-epa-effort-to-suspend-obama-era-methane-rule.html [http://perma.cc/2JZY-VMHH].

23. Rene Marsh, *EPA Ordered to Enforce Obama-Era Methane Pollution Rule*, CNN, Aug. 1, 2017, 12:55AM, http://www.cnn.com/2017/07/31/politics/dc-circuit-epa-methane-rule/index.html [https://perma.cc/W6SS-P33T].

24. The D.C. Circuit initially struck down the EPA's 2015 hydrofluorocarbon rule in 2017, but several parties plan to seek review at the Supreme Court. Amanda Reilly, *HFC Case May Head to Supreme Court*, E&E NEWS, Mar. 14, 2018, https://www.eenews.net/greenwire/2018/03/14/stories/1060076315 [https://perma.cc/SEQ8-9MDY]; Coral Davenport, *Nations, Fighting Powerful Refrigerant That Warms Planet, Reach Landmark Deal*, N.Y. TIMES, Oct. 15, 2016, https://www.nytimes.com/2016/10/15/world/africa/kigali-deal-hfc-air-conditioners.html [https://perma.cc/T38A-Q7SZ].

25. 444 U.S. 996 (1979) (per curiam) (granting, vacating, and remanding with instructions to dismiss complaint).

26. *See Goldwater*, 444 U.S. at 996 (Powell, J., concurring) ("The Judicial Branch should not decide issues affecting the allocation of power between the president and Congress until the political branches reach a constitutional impasse."); *id.* at 1006 (Brennan, J., dissenting) (citing the president's plenary textual recognition power as a basis for affirmance on the merits). Justice Rehnquist, joined by Chief Justice Burger, and Justices Stewart and Stevens found that the case raised a political question. Justices Blackmun and White voted that the case should be set for plenary briefing and argument. Justice Marshall concurred in the result without explanation.

27. *See, e.g.*, Beacon Products Corp. v. Reagan, 633 F. Supp. 1191 (D. Mass. 1986), *aff'd on other grounds*, 814 F.2d 1 (1st Cir. 1987) (concerning the United States' Treaty of Friendship, Commerce, and Navigation with Nicaragua) ("[A constitutional] challenge to the president's power vis-a-vis treaty termination raise[s] a nonjusticiable political question."); Kucinich v. Bush, 236 F. Supp. 2d 1 (D.D.C. 2002) (dismissing as a nonjusticiable political question congressman's challenge to President George W. Bush's decision to withdraw from the Anti-Ballistic Missile Treaty with Russia).

28. Zivotofsky ex rel. Zivotofsky v. Clinton, 132 S. Ct. 1421, 1430 (2012) (reversing the lower court's political question ruling on the ground that the "[r]esolution of [plaintiff's] claim demands careful

examination of the textual, structural, and historical evidence put forward by the parties regarding the nature of the [law in question] and of the [constitutional] powers [in dispute]" and asserting that "[t]he political question doctrine poses no bar to judicial review of this case"). The Chief Justice notably omitted mention of the much-cited six-factor political question test originally introduced in *Baker v. Carr*, 369 U.S. 186 (1962).

29. Marbury v. Madison, 5 U.S. (1 Cranch) 137 (1803); Youngstown Sheet & Tube Co. v. Sawyer (Steel Seizure Case), 343 U.S. 579 (1952); Myers v. United States, 272 U.S. 52 (1925); INS v. Chadha, 462 U.S. 919 (1983); Morrison v. Olson, 487 U.S. 654 (1988); Zivotofsky ex rel. Zivotofsky v. Clinton, 132 S. Ct. 1421 (2012).

30. 549 U.S. 497 (2007). Over Chief Justice Roberts's dissent on the standing issue, Justice Stevens, writing for the Court, held that the state of Massachusetts had standing, due to its "stake in protecting its quasi-sovereign interests," to sue the EPA over potential damage caused to its territory as a result of global warming.

31. 504 U.S. 555 (1992).

32. Curtis Bradley & Jack Goldsmith, *Presidential Control over International Law*, 131 HARV. L. REV. 1201, 1224, 1293 (2018).

33. 462 U.S. 919 (1983). With respect to political questions, Chief Justice Burger wrote for the *Chadha* Court that "[t]he presence of constitutional issues with significant political overtones does not automatically invoke the political question doctrine." *Id.* at 940–41.

   On the merits, the Court was unmoved by the broad past historical use of the legislative veto:

   > the fact that a given law or procedure is efficient, convenient, and useful in facilitating functions of government, standing alone, will not save it if it is contrary to the Constitution.... [O]ur inquiry is sharpened, rather than blunted, by the fact that congressional veto provisions are appearing with increasing frequency in statutes which delegate authority to executive and independent agencies....
   > [P]olicy arguments supporting even useful "political inventions" are subject to the demands of the Constitution, which defines powers and, with respect to this subject, sets out just how those powers are to be exercised.

   Id. at 945 (emphasis added).

34. R (Miller) v. Secretary of State for Exiting the European Union, [2017] UKSC 5, [2017] 2 W. L. R. 583.

35. *See* Democratic Alliance v. Minister of International Relations and Cooperation, High Court of South Africa (Gauteng Division, Pretoria),

Case No. 83145/2016 (Feb. 22, 2017) ("[T]he power to bind the country to the Rome Statute is expressly conferred on parliament. It must therefore, perforce, be *parliament which has the power to decide whether an international agreement ceases to bind the country*."). (emphasis added).

36. STEPHEN BREYER, THE COURT AND THE WORLD: AMERICAN LAW AND THE NEW GLOBAL REALITIES (2015).

37. *See, e.g.*, Julian Ku & John Yoo, *Trump Might Be Stuck with NAFTA*, L.A. TIMES, Nov. 29, 2016, http://www.latimes.com/opinion/op-ed/la-oe-yoo-ku-trump-nafta-20161129-story.html.

38. *Background on the Under2*, UNDER2°, http://under2mou.org/background [https://perma.cc/U79G-MCV6] (last visited July 6, 2018).

39. Eric Wolff, *Washington, California, New York Band Together to Form Climate Alliance*, POLITICO, June 1, 2017, 6:31 PM, http://www.politico.com/story/2017/06/01/climate-alliance-washington-california-new-york-239038 [https://perma.cc/WF7K-35CL].

40. Press Release, *The Global Covenant of Mayors for Climate & Energy Announces Its Global Impact*, GLOB. COVENANT OF MAYORS FOR CLIMATE & ENERGY (Nov. 13, 2016), http://www.globalcovenantofmayors.org/press/global-covenant-mayors-climate-energy-announces-collective-impact-cities-move-paris-agreement-commitment-action [https://perma.cc/6FZG-6JBF].

41. Paris Agreement, *supra* note 2, art. 4.2; *see also* INT'L EMISSIONS TRADING ASS'N, GHG MARKET SENTIMENT SURVEY 2016 at 10 (11th ed. 2016).

42. *See* BREAKTHROUGH ENERGY, http://www.b-t.energy [https://perma.cc/XC53-JKBU]; Kerry A. Dolan, *Bill Gates Launches $1 Billion Breakthrough Energy Investment Fund*, FORBES, Dec. 12, 2016, 1:31 PM, https://www.forbes.com/sites/kerryadolan/2016/12/12/bill-gates-launches-1-billion-breakthrough-energy-investment-fund [http://perma.cc/E5CB-LF7F].

43. *Ambitious Corporate Action Driving Delivery of Paris Goals*, WE MEAN BUS. COALITION, Nov. 9, 2016, https://www.wemeanbusinesscoalition.org/content/ambitious-corporate-action-driving-delivery-paris-goals [http://perma.cc/A8M4-S2YQ].

44. Merrit Kennedy, *Hundreds of U.S. Businesses Urge Trump to Uphold Paris Climate Deal*, NPR, Nov. 17, 2016, 11:54 AM, http://www.npr.org/sections/thetwo-way/2016/11/17/502425711/hundreds-of-u-s-businesses-urge-trump-to-uphold-paris-climate-deal [https://perma.cc/8X78-WW5W]; LOW-CARBON USA, *Business Backs Low-Carbon USA*, http://wwf.worldwildlife.org/site/PageServer?pagename=lowcarbonusa; Samantha Raphelson, *Energy Companies Urge Trump to Remain in Paris Climate Agreement*, NPR, May 18, 2017, 6:32 PM, http://www.npr.org/2017/05/18/528998592/energy-companies-urge-

trump-to-remain-in-paris-climate-agreement [https://perma.cc/FJ36-AZWJ].

45. Hiroko Tabuchi & Henry Fountain, *Bucking Trump, These Cities, States and Companies Commit to Paris Accord*, N.Y. TIMES, June 1, 2017, https://www.nytimes.com/2017/06/01/climate/american-cities-climate-standards.html [https://perma.cc/5C79-WYFU].

46. CASABLANCA (Warner Bros. 1942).

47. Sigmar Gabriel, Foreign Minister, Ger., Speech at the Berlin Foreign Policy Forum at the Körber Foundation: Europe in a Less Comfortable World (Dec. 5, 2017), https://new-york-un.diplo.de/un-en/news-corner/20171205-gabriel-koerberfoundation/1212264.

48. Ana Swanson, *White House Tries to Pull Nafta Back from Brink as Deadlines Loom*, N.Y. TIMES, Apr. 5, 2018, https://www.nytimes.com/2018/04/05/us/politics/nafta-negotiations-trump-canada-mexico.html.

49. Alastair Jamieson, *Trump Praises Kim at Summit, But Takes Aim at Justin Trudeau*, NBC NEWS, June 12, 2018, 7:47 AM, https://www.nbcnews.com/politics/white-house/trump-praises-kim-jong-un-takes-aim-again-justin-trudeau-n882266 (last updated June 12, 2018, 1:23 PM).

50. Tom Philips, *Donald Trump Soft Pedals After Earlier Threats of Trade War with China*, GUARDIAN, Aug. 14, 2017, https://www.theguardian.com/world/2017/aug/15/donald-trump-china-trade-war-investigation.

51. Kevin Carmichael, *Trump's Trade Policies Keep Backfiring*, FIVETHIRTYEIGHT, Nov. 9, 2017, https://fivethirtyeight.com/features/trumps-trade-policies-keep-backfiring.

52. *S. Korea Toughens Stance on Free Trade Deal as U.S. Threatens to Scrap KORUS FTA*, XINHUA, Oct. 11, 2017, http://www.xinhuanet.com/english/2017-10/11/c_136672153.htm.

53. Kanga Kong et al., *U.S. Settles South Korea Trade Dispute Before Summit With North*, BLOOMBERG, Mar. 26, 2018, https://www.bloomberg.com/news/articles/2018-03-25/south-korea-says-agreement-made-with-u-s-on-trade-deal-tariffs.

54. From President Trump's inauguration to November 1, 2017, the Commerce Department launched 77 unilateral investigations, up from 48 a year earlier, an increase of 61 percent. *See* Press Release, *U.S. Department of Commerce Finds Dumping and Subsidization of Imports of Softwood Lumber from Canada*, U.S. DEP'T OF COMMERCE (Nov. 2, 2017), https://www.commerce.gov/news/press-releases/2017/11/us-department-commerce-finds-dumping-and-subsidization-imports-softwood.

55. Paul Krugman, *Oh, What a Trumpy Trade War!*. N.Y. TIMES, Mar. 8, 2018, https://www.nytimes.com/2018/03/08/opinion/trump-trade-tariffs-steel.html.

56. Press Release, *Steel Imports Up 20% Year-to-Date*, AM. IRON AND STEEL INST. (Oct. 25, 2017), http://www.steel.org/~/media/Files/AISI/Press%20Releases/2017/IMP1709.pdf; Dustin Dwyer, *As Vote on ZTE Sanctions Looms, Some U.S. Lawmakers Focus on a Bigger Chinese Telecom*, NPR, June 15, 2019, https://www.npr.org/2018/06/15/620393860/as-vote-on-zte- sanctions- looms-some-u-s-lawmakers-focus-on-a-bigger-chinese-tele.

57. *Current Lumber, Pulp and Panel Prices*, NAT. RESOURCES CAN., Feb. 6, 2018, 6:32 PM, http://www.nrcan.gc.ca/forests/industry/current-prices/13309.

58. The real issue with NAFTA and other free trade agreements is not that trade deals are being badly negotiated but rather that trade adjustment assistance is not "effective in helping displaced workers." Mark Muro & Joseph Parilla, *Maladjusted: It's Time to Reimagine Economic "Adjustment" Programs*, BROOKINGS, Jan. 10, 2017, https://www.brookings.edu/blog/the-avenue/2017/01/10/maladjusted-its-time-to-reimagine- economic-adjustment-programs.

59. Robert Farley, *Trump Wrong About WTO Record*, FACTCHECK.ORG, Oct. 27, 2017, https://www.factcheck.org/2017/10/trump-wrong-wto-record.

60. *United States Files WTO Complaint on China's Protection of Intellectual Property Rights*, WTO, Mar. 26, 2018, https://www.wto.org/english/news_e/news18_e/ds542rfc_26mar18_e.htm.

61. Paul Krugman, *Bumbling into a Trade War*, N.Y. TIMES, Mar. 22, 2018, https://www.nytimes.com/2018/03/22/opinion/trade-war-china-trump.html.

62. Ana Swanson & Jim Tankersley, *As U.S. Trumpets "America First," Rest of the World Is Moving On*, N.Y. TIMES, Jan. 25, 2018, at B1, *available at* https://www.nytimes.com/2018/01/24/us/politics/trump-trade-america-first-davos.html.

63. Tim Daiss, *Trump Pledges to Rip Up Iran Deal; Israelis Say Not So Fast*, FORBES, Nov. 22, 2016, 1:50 AM, http://www.forbes.com/sites/timdaiss/2016/11/22/trumps-iran-deal-rhetoric-israelis-say-not-so-fast [https://perma.cc/Q422-SDWC].

64. For the full text of the JCPOA, which consists of the agreement itself and five technical annexes, see Joint Comprehensive Plan of Action, U.S. Dep't of State, http://www.state.gov/e/eb/tfs/spi/iran/jcpoa [http://perma.cc/875H-XPE9]. The Annexes include: Annex I, Nuclear Related Commitments; Annex 2, Sanctions Related Commitments; Annex III, Civil Nuclear Cooperation; Annex IV, Joint Commission; and Annex V, Implementation Plan.

65. S.C. Res. 1929 (June 9, 2010).

66. *Read the Full Transcript of Trump's Speech on the Iran Nuclear Deal*, N.Y. TIMES, May 8, 2018, https://www.nytimes.com/2018/05/08/us/politics/trump-speech-iran-deal.html.

67. *See* Alex Ward, *Trump Says Iran Is Violating the Nuclear Deal. It Isn't.*, VOX, Aug. 7, 2017, 9:00 AM, https://www.vox.com/2017/8/7/16089848/trump-iran-deal-nuclear-spirit-rip-up [http://perma.cc/5V4H-6ACE].

68. *Statement by IAEA Director Yukiya Amano*, INT'L ATOMIC ENERGY AGENCY, May 9, 2018, *available at* https:// www.iaea.org/ newscenter/ statements/statement- by-iaea-director- general- yukiya-amano-9-may-2018.

69. President Donald Trump, *Remarks by President Trump on Iran Strategy*, WHITE HOUSE (Oct. 13, 2017), https://www.whitehouse.gov/the-press-office/2017/10/13/remarks-president-trump-iran-strategy [http://perma.cc/SPA3-H76E] (citing Iran's violations as "exceed[ing] the limit of 130 metric tons of heavy water, . . . fail[ing] to meet [U.S.] expectations in its operation of advanced centrifuges, . . . [and] intimidat[ing] international inspectors"; President Trump also denounced Iran for violating "the spirit of the deal"); Julian Borger, *Trump's Debut at the UN: Threats, Taunts—and Gasps of Alarm from the Diplomats*, GUARDIAN, Sept. 23, 2017, 4:00 PM, https://www.theguardian.com/us-news/2017/sep/23/donald-trump-united-nations-general-assembly [http://perma.cc/DP5K-EGGA]; Scott Neuman, *State Department Certifies Iran's Compliance with Nuclear Deal*, NPR, July 17, 2017, http://www.npr.org/sections/the-two-way/2017/07/17/537793465/state-department-certifies-irans-compliance-with-nuclear-deal [http://perma.cc/AX57-5QWM].

70. President Donald Trump, *State of the Union Address* (Jan. 30, 2018), https://www.whitehouse.gov/briefings-statements/president-donald-j-trumps-state-union-address ("I am asking the Congress to address the fundamental flaws in the terrible Iran nuclear deal.").

71. Mark Landler & David E. Sanger, *Trump Disavows Nuclear Deal and Denounces Iranian Leadership*, N.Y. TIMES, Oct. 13, 2017, https://www.nytimes.com/2017/10/13/us/politics/trump-iran-nuclear-deal.html [http://perma.cc/4TFZ-J77C]; Jana Winter et al., *Trump Assigns White House Team to Target Iran Nuclear Deal, Sidelining State Department*, FOREIGN POL'Y, July 21, 2017, http://www.foreignpolicy.com/2017/07/21/trump-assigns-white-house-team-to-target-iran-nuclear-deal-sidelining-state-department [http://perma.cc/AA7E-Z5JJ].

72. Daiss, *supra* note 63 (quoting Shemuel Meir, former analyst for the Israeli Defense Forces and researcher at Tel Aviv University); *see also* Carmi Gillon, *The Iran Nuclear Deal Has Been a Blessing for Israel*,

FOREIGN POL'Y, July 13, 2017, http://foreignpolicy.com/2017/07/13/
the-iran-nuclear-deal-has-been-a-blessing-for-israel-jcpoa [http://
perma.cc/TFT5-ECAT] ("[W]hile the majority of my colleagues in the
Israeli military and intelligence communities supported the deal once
it was reached, many of those who had major reservations now acknowledge that it has had a positive impact on Israel's security and
must be fully maintained by the United States and other signatory
nations.").

73. Colin Kahl, *The Myth of a "Better" Iran Deal*, FOREIGN POL'Y, Sept. 26,
2017, http://foreignpolicy.com/2017/09/26/the-myth-of-a-better-iran-
deal [http://perma.cc/DZ76-6YP6].

74. *See* Joshua Keating, *What Happens If Trump Blows Up the Iran
Deal?*, SLATE, Nov. 17, 2016, 3:38 PM, http://www.slate.com/blogs/
the_slatest/2016/11/17/what_happens_if_trump_blows_up_the_
iran_deal.html [http://perma.cc/4GZV-33QC] (noting that "EU
governments . . . recently reaffirmed their commitment to continue
with the deal").

75. INT'L CRISIS GROUP, THE IRAN NUCLEAR DEAL AT TWO: A STATUS
REPORT (Jan. 16, 2018), *available at* https://www.crisisgroup.org/
middle-east-north-africa/gulf-and-arabian-peninsula/iran/
181-iran-nuclear-deal-two-status-report.

76. Oren Dorell, *Could Trump Trash the Iran Deal? Yes, but It's Complicated*,
USA TODAY, Nov. 10, 2016, http://www.usatoday.com/story/news/
world/2016/11/10/could-trump-trash-iran-deal-yes-but-s-complicated/
93568040 [http://perma.cc/RX4C-3WVM].

77. *See* Dan Joyner, *The Trump Presidency and the Iran Nuclear Deal: Initial
Thoughts*, EJIL: TALK!, Nov. 17, 2016, http://www.ejiltalk.org/
the-trump-presidency-and-the-iran-nuclear-deal-initial-thoughts
[http://perma.cc/HC2W-WQAK] ("If the U.S. were to re-impose or
even strengthen secondary banking sanctions on foreign banks, it's
hard to say if this would have any effect on the pace of re-engagement
with Iran by European and Asian businesses, mostly because those
businesses have already had to find ways to work around unclear
U.S. banking sanctions. . . .").

78. *See generally* Kenneth W. Dam, *Economic and Political Aspects of
Extraterritoriality*, 19 INT'L LAW. 887 (1985), *available at* https://www.
jstor.org/stable/40705649?seq=1#page_scan_tab_contents (describing
Soviet pipeline controversy of the 1980s).

79. Jean Galbraith, *The End of the Iran Deal and the Future of the Security Council
Snapback*, OPINIO JURIS, May 10, 2018, http://opiniojuris.org/2018/05/09/
the-end-of-the-iran-deal-and-the-future-of-the-security-council-snapback/.

80. Y.J. Fischer, *Trump Is Going Easy on Iran*, L.A. TIMES, May 6, 2018, http://www.latimes.com/opinion/op-ed/la-oe-fischer-trumps-soft-iran-policy-20180506-story.html.

81. *Trump to Approve Iran Nuclear Deal for Last Time*, BBC, Jan. 12, 2018, http://www.bbc.com/news/world-us-canada-42670577.

82. William J. Burns & Jake Sullivan, *The Smart Way to Get Tough with Iran*, N.Y. TIMES, Sept. 21, 2017, https://www.nytimes.com/2017/09/21/opinion/iran-trump-nuclear-deal-.html [http://perma.cc/7NUE-5VK5].

Chapter 4

1. Merrit Kennedy, *Pence Tells North Korea: "The Era of Strategic Patience Is Over"*, NPR, Apr. 17, 2017, 10:19 AM, http://www.npr.org/sections/thetwo-way/2017/04/17/524316419/pence-tells-north-korea-the-era-of-strategic-patience-is-overtillers [http://perma.cc/GGT7-VGLJ].

2. Anne Gearan & Anna Fifield, *Tillerson Says "All Options Are on the Table" When It Comes to North Korea*, WASH. POST, Mar. 19, 2017, https://www.washingtonpost.com/world/tillerson-says-all-options-are-on-the-table-when-it-comes-to-north-korea/2017/03/17/e6b3e64e-0a83-11e7-bd19-fd3afa0f7e2a_story.html [http://perma.cc/SNB6-YLDD].

3. Jim Sciutto et al., *Trump Promises North Korea "Fire and Fury" over Nuke Threat*, CNN, Aug. 9, 2017, 4:06 AM, http://www.cnn.com/2017/08/08/politics/north-korea-missile-ready-nuclear-weapons/index.html [http://perma.cc/AH2A-MLFS].

4. *At U.N., Trump Singles Out "Rogue" Nations North Korea and Iran*, N.Y. TIMES, Sept. 19, 2017, https://www.nytimes.com/2017/09/19/world/americas/united-nations-general-assembly.html [http://perma.cc/7QTV-6U75].

5. David E. Sanger & William J. Broad, *A "Cuban Missile Crisis in Slow Motion" in North Korea*, N.Y. TIMES, Apr. 16, 2017, https://www.nytimes.com/2017/04/16/us/politics/north-korea-missile-crisis-slow-motion.html [http://perma.cc/GA2Z-TL6D].

6. Steve Coll, *The Madman Theory of North Korea*, NEW YORKER, Oct. 2, 2017, https://www.newyorker.com/magazine/2017/10/02/the-madman-theory-of-north-korea [http://perma.cc/N9HX-2FY4].

7. *See* Lisa Collins, *Beyond Parallel: 25 Years of Negotiations and Provocations: North Korea and the United States*, CSIS, https://beyondparallel.csis.org/25-years-of-negotiations-provocations/ [http://perma.cc/YM4H-NZUK] (last visited July 6, 2018).

8. Susan Rice, *It's Not Too Late on North Korea*, N.Y. TIMES, Aug. 10, 2017, https://www.nytimes.com/2017/08/10/opinion/susan-rice-trump-north-korea.html [http://perma.cc/MX2H-KS3H].

9. *Joint Statement of President Donald J. Trump of the United States of America and Chairman Kim Jong Un of the Democratic People's Republic of Korea at the Singapore Summit*, WHITE HOUSE (June 12, 2018), https://www.whitehouse.gov/briefings-statements/joint-statement-president-donald-j-trump-united-states-america-chairman-kim-jong-un-democratic-peoples-republic-korea-singapore-summit/; Jennifer Williams, *Read the Full Transcript of Trump's North Korea Summit Press Conference*, VOX, June 12, 2018, https://www.vox.com/world/2018/6/12/17452624/trump-kim-summit-transcript-press-conference-full-text.

10. *See* Donald J. Trump (@realDonaldTrump), TWITTER (Oct. 1, 2017, 9:30 AM), https://twitter.com/realDonaldTrump/status/914497877543735296 [http://perma.cc/3TNW-V3CK] ("I told Rex Tillerson . . . that he is wasting his time trying to negotiate with Little Rocket Man . . .").

11. Trump, *State of the Union Address, supra* Chapter 3, note 70.

12. Panmunjom Declaration for Peace, Prosperity, and Unification of the Korean Peninsula, N. Kor.-S. Kor., April 27, 2018, available at Panmunjom Declaration for Peace, Prosperity and Unification of the Korean Peninsula, Reuters (Apr. 27, 2018), https://uk.reuters.com/article/uk-northkorea-southkorea-summit-statemen/panmunjom-declaration-for-peace-prosperity-and-unification-of-the-korean-peninsula-idUKKBN1HY193.

13. *See* David Sanger, *U.S. in Direct Communication with North Korea, Says Tillerson*, N.Y. TIMES, Sept. 30, 2017, https://www.nytimes.com/2017/09/30/world/asia/us-north-korea-tillerson.html [http://perma.cc/ETU2-6XAT] (quoting Secretary Tillerson).

14. 2007 Declaration on the Advancement of South-North Korean Relations, Peace and Prosperity, S. Kor-N. Kor., Oct. 4, 2007, *available at* https://peacemaker.un.org/node/1659 [https://perma.cc/V5MG-GRMW]; South-North Joint Declaration, S. Kor-N. Kor., June 15, 2000, *available at* https://peacemaker.un.org/koreadprk-southnorthdeclaration [https://perma.cc/6ZC7-W9DN]. In 2003, North Korea withdrew from the Treaty on the Non-Proliferation of Nuclear Weapons in defiance of its 2000 declaration, and after the country's 2007 commitment, it nonetheless "continued nuclear tests, ignored requests for returning South Korean detainees, and 'maintained a belligerent rhetoric' regarding events on the Korean peninsula." Adam de Bear, *From Sunshine to Storm Clouds: An Examination of South Korea's Policy on North Korea*, 23 MICH. ST. INT'L L. REV. 823, 857, 864 (2015).

15. Adam Taylor, *What the New U.N. Sanctions on North Korea Mean*, WASH. POST, Aug. 7, 2017, https://www.washingtonpost.com/news/worldviews/wp/2017/08/07/what-the-new-u-n-sanctions-on-north-korea-mean/ [http://perma.cc/B7AE-4ALQ]; Reuters, *Here Are the UN's Harsh New Sanctions on North Korea*, FORTUNE, Nov. 30, 2016, http://fortune.com/2016/12/01/un-sanctions-north-korea-coal-statues/

[http://perma.cc/4M9Q-D8GA] (noting the slashing of North Korea's annual coal export revenue by 60 percent; the reduction of copper, nickel, silver, and zinc exports; and the sale of symbolic statues).

16. William Tobey, *"No Good Options" on North Korea Is a Myth*, FOREIGN POL'Y, July 7, 2017, 8:28 AM, http://foreignpolicy.com/2017/07/07/no-good-options-on-north-korea-is-a-myth [http://perma.cc/XJ3C-KCC9].

17. Antony J. Blinken, *To Win a Nobel, Trump Should Look to the Iran Deal*, N.Y. TIMES, May 2, 2018, https://www.nytimes.com/2018/05/02/opinion/trump-north-korea-nobel-iran-nuclear-deal.html.

18. Michael Fuchs, *The North Korea Deal: Why Diplomacy Is Still the Best Option*, FOREIGN AFF., Dec. 21, 2017, https://www.foreignaffairs.com/articles/north-korea/2017-12-21/north-korea-deal [https://perma.cc/9RFX-2VNM].

19. Jeffrey A. Bader, *Why Deterring and Containing North Korea Is Our Least Bad Option*, BROOKINGS, Aug. 8, 2017, https://www.brookings.edu/blog/order-from-chaos/2017-08-08/why-deterring-and-containing-north-korea-is-our-least-bad-option [http://perma.cc/3JUV-H8UB].

20. Jake Sullivan, *The Other Risk from Trump's Talks with North Korea*, WASH. POST, Apr. 6, 2018, https://www.washingtonpost.com/news/global-opinions/wp/2018/04/06/the-other-risk-from-trumps-talks-with-north-korea/ [https://perma.cc/H887-4K5F].

21. Office of the Dir. of Nat'l Intelligence, ICA 2017-01D, *Background to "Assessing Russian Activities and Intentions in Recent US Elections": The Analytic Process and Cyber Incident Attribution* ii (2017), *available at* https://www.dni.gov/files/documents/ICA_2017_01.pdf [http://perma.cc/BZG6-U65J].

22. Remarkably, we learned that an FBI counterintelligence probe has been on-going *since July 2016* to determine the extent of Russian interference and possible collusion with U.S. persons. Julian Borger & Spencer Ackerman, *Trump-Russia Collusion Is Being Investigated by FBI, Comey Confirms*, GUARDIAN, Mar. 20, 2017, https://www.theguardian.com/us-news/2017/mar/20/fbi-director-comey-confirms-investigation-trump-russia [http://perma.cc/B5ZK-36HJ]. But then-FBI Director Comey did not report publicly on this, choosing instead to publicize various matters around Hillary Clinton's emails. Natasha Bertrand, *Comey Successfully Dodged the Biggest Question Looming over the Trump-Russia Probe*, BUS. INSIDER, May 4, 2017, 6:03 PM, http://www.businessinsider.com/comey-did-not-disclose-trump-russia-probe-testimony-2017-5 [http://perma.cc/H9SK-W33B].

23. Brief for Former National Security Officials as Amici Curiae Supporting Neither Party at 4–5, 8–9, Cockrum v. Donald J. Trump for President, Inc. (D.D.C. filed July 12, 2017), *available at* https://cases.justia.com/federal/district-courts/district-of-columbia/dcdce/1:2017cv01370/187894/37/0.pdf?ts=1513147021 (dismissed on grounds of personal jurisdiction and venue July 3, 2018).

24. Mike Allen, *1 Big Thing: The Public Case Against Trump*, AXIOS AM, May 12, 2018, https://www.axios.com/newsletters/axios-am-212f77ed-3c07-4281-88a7-d4d7c5297dae.html.

25. French President Emmanuel Macron claimed that he was hacked during the French presidential campaign. Aurelien Breeden et al., *Macron Campaign Says It Was Target of "Massive" Hacking Attack*, N.Y. TIMES, May 5, 2017, https://www.nytimes.com/2017/05/05/world/europe/france-macron-hacking.html [http://perma.cc/XGU4-GGGK]. According to Republican Senator Marco Rubio, the Russians also tried to hack him earlier in 2017. Emmarie Huetteman, *Marco Rubio Says His Campaign Was a Target of Russian Cyberattacks*, N.Y. TIMES, Mar. 30, 2017, https://www.nytimes.com/2017/03/30/us/politics/marco-rubio-russian-cyberattacks.html [http://perma.cc/BRZ7-JCPZ].

26. *See generally* Harold Hongju Koh, *International Law in Cyberspace*, 54 HARV. INT'L. L.J. ONLINE 1, 2–7 (2012), http://digitalcommons.law.yale.edu/fss_papers/4854/ [http://perma.cc/4J78-35YG].

27. TALLINN MANUAL 2.0 ON THE INTERNATIONAL LAW APPLICABLE TO CYBER OPERATIONS (Michael N. Schmitt ed., 2d ed. 2017). *See also* Koh, *International Law in Cyberspace, supra* note 26, at 2–7 (stating the U.S. government's legal position that international law applies in cyberspace; that under certain circumstances, the use of cybertools may constitute a "use of force"; and that states are legally responsible for the actions of proxy actors); Michael N. Schmitt, *International Law in Cyberspace: The Koh Speech and Tallinn Manual Juxtaposed*, 54 HARV. INT'L. L.J. ONLINE 13 (2012), http://www.harvardilj.org/wp-content/uploads/2012/12/HILJ-Online_54_Schmitt.pdf [http://perma.cc/T465-NAPH] (noting concordance between positions stated in my official speech and the unofficial *Tallinn Manual*).

28. International Covenant on Civil and Political Rights, *supra* Chapter 2, note 7, at art. 25 ("Every citizen shall have the right and the opportunity . . . without . . . unreasonable restrictions: . . . (b) To vote and to be elected at genuine periodic elections which shall be by universal and equal suffrage and shall be held by secret ballot, guaranteeing the free expression of the will of the electors. . . .").

29. *See* Brian J. Egan, Remarks on International Law and Stability in Cyberspace, Nov. 10, 2016, https://2009-2017.state.gov/s/l/releases/remarks/264303.htm [http://perma.cc/3XH4-DTTW].

30. *See* James Stavridis, *How to Win the Cyberwar Against Russia*, FOREIGN POL'Y, Oct. 12, 2016, https://foreignpolicy.com/2016/10/12/how-to-win-the-cyber-war-against-russia [http://perma.cc/VU5V-PVFK] (suggestions made by the Dean of the Fletcher School of Law and Diplomacy and former U.S. Navy admiral).

31. *See, e.g.,* Donald J. Trump (@realDonaldTrump), TWITTER (May 18, 2017, 4:52 AM), https://twitter.com/realdonaldtrump/status/865173176854204416 [http://perma.cc/UY3L-QQF4]; *see also* Glenn Thrush, *Trump, on Twitter, Targets Obama and Russia,* N.Y. TIMES, June 26, 2017, https://www.nytimes.com/2017/06/26/us/politics/trump-twitter-obama-russia.html [http://perma.cc/7HMN-JV8D].

32. Disinformation: A Primer in Russian Active Measures and Influence Campaigns Panel I, Hearing Before the S. Select Intelligence Comm., 115th Cong., S. Hrg. 115-40, Pt. 1 (Mar. 30, 2017) (statement of Clinton Watts, Senior Fellow, George Washington University Center for Cyber and Homeland Security).

33. Natalie Andrews & Rebecca Ballhaus, *Trump Signs—and Slams—Russia Sanctions,* WALL ST. J., Aug. 2, 2017, 8:35 PM, https://www.wsj.com/articles/president-trump-signs-sanctions-bill-aimed-at-punishing-russia-for-election-meddling-1501685839 [http://perma.cc/QUH4-N766].

34. *Russia Expels 755 US Diplomats in Response to Sanctions,* AL JAZEERA, July 30, 2017, http://www.aljazeera.com/news/2017/07/russia-expels-755-diplomats-response-sanctions-170730201720880.html [http://perma.cc/TT85-TA5M].

35. David Jackson, *New Sanctions Against Russia for Chemical Weapons Attack in Syria Still Possible,* USA TODAY, Apr. 17, 2018, 3:38 PM, https://www.usatoday.com/story/news/politics/2018/04/17/new-sanctions-against-russia-chemical-weapons-attack-syria-still-possible/524950002/ (last updated Apr. 18, 2018, 8:50 AM).

36. Joshua Yaffa, *Why Trump's Expulsion of Diplomats Does (and Doesn't) Unnerve Moscow,* NEW YORKER, Mar. 26, 2018, https://www.newyorker.com/news/news-desk/trump-expulsion-diplomats-does-and-doesnt-unnerve-moscow.

37. I should disclose that I have served as a counsel to Ukraine on a number of these international litigation matters.

38. International Convention for the Suppression of the Financing of Terrorism, 2798 U.N.T.S. 197 (entered into force Apr. 10, 2002).

39. International Convention on the Elimination of All Forms of Racial Discrimination, 660 U.N.T.S. 212 (entered into force Jan. 4, 1969).

40. Application of the International Convention for the Suppression of the Financing of Terrorism and of the International Convention on the Elimination of All Forms of Racial Discrimination (Ukr. v. Russ.), Order on Request for the Indication of Provisional Measures, 2017 I.C.J. paras. 74–77 (Apr. 19), *available at* http://www.icj-cij.org/files/case-related/166/19394.pdf [http://perma.cc/S6C2-D6MF]; Beth Van Schaack, *The ICJ Issues Provisional Measures Against Russia on Ukraine's Racial Discrimination Claims,* JUST SECURITY, Apr. 20, 2017, 2:19 PM, https://

www.justsecurity.org/40138/icj-issues-provisional-measures-russia-
ukraines-racial-discrimination-claims [http://perma.cc/8LUN-GJJ8].

41. Gaiane Nuridzhanyan, *Ukraine vs. Russia in International Courts and
Tribunals*, EJIL: TALK!, Mar. 9, 2016, https://www.ejiltalk.org/ukraine-
versus-russia-in-international-courts-and-tribunals [http://perma.cc/
T3WR-VG2K]. The Permanent Court of Arbitration has ordered Russia
to pay $159 million to a group of real investment companies that owned
expropriated properties in Crimea, but Russia has refused to participate
or to pay. Everest Estate LLC et al. v. Russian Federation, Case Number
2015-36, Permanent Court of Arbitration (*discussed in* International
Arbitration Reporter, May 9, 2018, https://www.iareporter.com/articles/
russia-held-liable-in-confidential-award-for-expropriation-of-hotels-
apartments-and-other-crimean-real-estate-arbitrators-award-
approximately-150-million-plus-legal-costs-for-breach-of-ukraine-bi/).

Chapter 5

1. *See* HAROLD HONGJU KOH, REMARKS AT THE OXFORD UNION: HOW TO
END THE FOREVER WAR? 14 (May 7, 2013), *available at* http://opiniojuris.
org/wp-content/uploads/2013-5-7-corrected-koh-oxford-union-
speech-as-delivered.pdf [http://perma.cc/VPJ5-STC8]; Statement by
Harold Hongju Koh, Sterling Professor of International Law, Yale Law
School, before the Senate Foreign Relations Committee Regarding
Authorization for use of Military Force After Iraq and Afghanistan, May
21, 2014, *available at* https://www.foreign.senate.gov/imo/media/doc/
Koh_Testimony.pdf; Harold Hongju Koh, *Ending the Forever War: One
Year After President Obama's NDU Speech*, EJIL TALK!, May 24, 2014,
https://www.ejiltalk.org/ending-the-forever-war-one-year-after-
president-obamas-ndu-speech/; Harold Hongju Koh, *Obama's ISIL Legal
Rollout: Bungled, Clearly. But Illegal? Really?*, JUST SECURITY, Sept. 29,
2014, 8:03 AM, https://www.justsecurity.org/15692/obamas-isil-legal-
rollout-bungled-clearly-illegal-really [http://perma.cc/4RC2-VRG6].

2. President Barack Obama, *Remarks by the President at the National Defense
University*, WHITE HOUSE [hereinafter "Obama NDU Speech"] (May 23,
2013), *available at* https://www.whitehouse.gov/the-press-office/2013/
05/23/remarks-president-national-defense-university [http://perma.cc/
6J6Y-C3B6].

3. Harold Hongju Koh, Legal Adviser, U.S. Dep't of State, The Obama
Administration and International Law, Keynote Speech at the Annual
Meeting of the American Society of International Law (Mar. 25, 2010),
available at https://www.state.gov/documents/organization/179305.

pdf. *See generally* Ken Anderson, *Readings: The Canonical National Security Law Speeches of Obama Administration Senior Officials and General Counsels*, LAWFARE, Aug. 28, 2012, https://lawfareblog.com/readings-canonical-national-security-law-speeches-obama-administration-senior-officials-and-general.

4. Obama NDU Speech, *supra* note 2.

5. In War Powers Reports to Congress under the Obama administration, for example, the administration correctly took pains to specify that "[t]he U.S. military has taken direct action in Somalia against members of al-Qa'ida, *including those who are also members of al-Shabab, who are engaged in efforts to carry out terrorist attacks against the United States and our interests.*" Letter from President Barack Obama to Speaker of the House, Presidential Letter—2012 War Powers Resolution 6-Month Report (June 15, 2012), *available at* https://obamawhitehouse.archives.gov/the-press-office/2012/06/15/presidential-letter-2012-war-powers-resolution-6-month-report ("[T]he U.S. military has worked to counter the terrorist threat posed by al-Qa'ida and al-Qa'ida-associated elements of al-Shabaab" (emphasis added)). By so saying, the administration made clear that it acted against particular individuals because they themselves were part of or co-belligerents with Al Qaeda, not because the United States was at war with all of Al Shabaab.

6. *See* Jeremy Wright, Attorney Gen., U.K., *The Modern Law of Self-Defence*, Speech to the International Institute for Strategic Studies (Jan. 11, 2017), *available at* https://www.gov.uk/government/speeches/attorney-generals-speech-at-the-international-institute-for-strategic-studies [http://perma.cc/S6AA-Q8QD]. The famous *Caroline* case had permitted self-defense in situations in which the "necessity of that self-defence is instant, overwhelming, and leaving no choice of means, and no moment for deliberation." Letter from Daniel Webster to Lord Ashburton (Aug. 6, 1842) (*quoted in* 2 JOHN BASSETT MOORE, A DIGEST OF INTERNATIONAL LAW 412 (1906)). But the U.K. Attorney General argued that under a very narrow set of modern counterterrorism scenarios, the *Caroline* requirement could also reasonably be read to permit direct strikes as a last resort against groups or individuals who pose a continuing and imminent threat by virtue of: (1) engaging in "a concerted pattern of continuing armed activity" directed against the United Kingdom—i.e., demonstrating a willingness to attack the United Kingdom if given the opportunity; (2) past successful attacks; and (3) "actively planning, threatening, or perpetrating [future] armed attacks" against America. Sir Daniel Bethlehem, *Self-Defense Against an Imminent or Actual Armed Attack by Nonstate Actors*, 106 AM. J. INT'L L. 770, 775 (2012). The U.K.

Attorney General also opined that this elongated understanding of imminence was consistent with Article 51 of the U.N. Charter, which codifies the right of national and collective self-defense.

7. President Obama essentially embraced this concept in his 2013 NDU speech when he said—regarding the use of force outside the Afghan theater—"America does not take strikes to punish individuals; we act against terrorists who pose a continuing and imminent threat to the American people, and when there are no other governments capable of effectively addressing the threat." Obama NDU Speech, *supra* note 2.

8. *Id.*

9. *See* FRAMEWORKS REPORT, *supra* Chapter 2, note 55. In July 2016, President Obama also issued an executive order calling for regular disclosure of civilian casualty statistics. *See id.* at 26–27; United States Policy on Pre- and Post-Strike Measures to Address Civilian Casualties in U.S. Operations Involving the Use of Force, 81 Fed. Reg. 44,485 (July 1, 2016); *see also* Charlie Savage & Scott Shane, *U.S. Reveals Death Toll from Airstrikes Outside War Zones*, N.Y. TIMES, July 1, 2016, http://www.nytimes.com/2016/07/02/world/us-reveals-death-toll-from-airstrikes-outside-of-war-zones.html [http://perma.cc/6CEN-D6UK]. White House, Office of the Press Sec'y, Fact Sheet: New Actions on Guantánamo and Detainee Policy (Mar. 7, 2011), *available at* https://obamawhitehouse.archives.gov/the-press-office/2011/03/07/fact-sheet-new-actions-guant-namo-and-detainee-policy.

10. White House Office of the Press Sec'y, Fact Sheet—Guantánamo and Detainee Policy (Mar. 7, 2011), *available at* https://lawfare.s3-us-west-2.amazonaws.com/staging/s3fs-public/uploads/2011/03/Fact_Sheet_-_Guantanamo_and_Detainee_Policy.pdf. Additional Protocol II, which details humane treatment and fair trial standards that apply in the context of non-international armed conflicts, was originally submitted to the Senate for approval by President Reagan in 1987.

11. Hillary Rodham Clinton, U.S. Sec'y of State, Remarks at the John Jay School of Criminal Justice: Smart Power Approach to Counterterrorism (Sept. 9, 2011), https://2009-2017.state.gov/secretary/20092013clinton/rm/2011/09/172034.htm [http://perma.cc/MC2X-T5ZQ].

12. *Id.*

13. *See, e.g.*, Authorization for Use of Military Force, Pub. L. No. 107-40, § 2(b), 115 Stat. 224, 224 (2001).

14. For more detailed discussion of the administration's legal theory for using force against IS, see FRAMEWORKS REPORT, *supra* Chapter 2, note 55, at 4, 11; Koh, *Obama's ISIL Legal Rollout, supra* note 1.

15. Nick Robins-Early, *Russia Says Its Airstrikes in Syria Are Perfectly Legal. Are They?*, HUFFINGTON POST, Oct. 1, 2015, 5:33 PM, http://www. huffingtonpost.com/entry/russia-airstrikes-syriainternationallaw_us_ 560d6448e4b0dd85030b0c08 [http://perma.cc/LRK4-TQG4].

16. Micah Zenko, *Why Is the U.S. Killing So Many Civilians in Syria and Iraq?*, N.Y. TIMES, June 19, 2017, https://www.nytimes.com/2017/06/19/ opinion/isis-syria-iraq-civilian-casualties.html [http://perma.cc/T5E8-SDS6]; Charlie Savage & Eric Schmitt, *Trump Poised to Drop Some Limits on Drone Strikes and Commando Raids*, N.Y. TIMES, Sept. 21, 2017, https:// www.nytimes.com/2017/09/21/us/politics/trump-drone-strikes-commando-raids-rules.html; Daniel R. Mahanty, Rahma A. Hussein and Alex Moorehead, *The Department of Defense's Report on Civilian Casualties: A Step Forward in Transparency?*, JUST SECURITY, June 13, 2018, https://www.justsecurity.org/57718/department-defenses-report-civilian-casualties-step-transparency/ (noting that on June 1, 2018, the Defense Department reported to Congress its estimate that more than 500 civilians were killed or injured in U.S. military operations in 2017).

17. Ryan Goodman, *The Pentagon Needs a Better Way to Count Civilian Casualties*, N.Y. TIMES, Apr. 26, 2018, https://www.nytimes.com/ 2018/04/26/opinion/civilian-casualties-pentagon-military.html [https://perma.cc/P9ZC-XL65].

18. President Donald Trump, *Remarks by President Trump on the Strategy in Afghanistan and South Asia*, WHITE HOUSE, Aug. 21, 2017, https://www. whitehouse.gov/the-press-office/2017/08/21/remarks-president-trump-strategy-afghanistan-and-south-asia [http://perma.cc/7ZXU-QR3E].

19. *See* Charlie Savage & Eric Schmitt, *Trump Poised to Drop Some Limits on Drone Strikes and Commando Raids*, N.Y. TIMES, Sept. 21, 2017, https:// www.nytimes.com/2017/09/21/us/politics/trump-drone-strikes-commando-raids-rules.html [http://perma.cc/SVX5-G4LB].

20. *See* Luke Hartig, *Trump's New Drone Strike Policy: What's Any Different? Why It Matters*, JUST SECURITY, Sept. 22, 2017, 8:01 AM, https://www. justsecurity.org/45227/trumps-drone-strike-policy-different-matters [http://perma.cc/7QSY-73JT].

21. Helene Cooper, *Navy SEAL Who Died in Somalia Was Alongside, Not Behind, Local Forces*, N.Y. TIMES, May 9, 2017, https://mobile.nytimes. com/2017/05/09/world/africa/somalia-navy-seal-kyle-milliken.html [http://perma.cc/P6TL-73VZ].

22. Eric Schmitt & David E. Sanger, *Raid in Yemen: Risky from the Start and Costly in the End*, N.Y. TIMES, Feb. 1, 2017, https://www.nytimes.com/ 2017/02/01/world/middleeast/donald-trump-yemen-commando-raid-

questions.html [http://perma.cc/9SKF-V2EH] (noting that "[a]fter initially denying there were any civilian casualties, Pentagon officials backtracked somewhat on Sunday after reports from the Yemeni authorities begin [*sic*] trickling in and grisly photographs of bloody children purportedly killed in the attack appeared on social media sites affiliated with Al Qaeda's branch in Yemen.").

23. Julia MacFarlane, *Why Is the US Still in Afghanistan?*, ABC NEWS, Feb. 2, 2018, 3:35 PM, https://abcnews.go.com/International/us-afghanistan/story?id=52763044 [https://perma.cc/6WEX-QKYJ].

24. *See* Antony J. Blinken, *The Islamic State Is Not Dead Yet*, N.Y. TIMES, July 9, 2017, https://www.nytimes.com/2017/07/09/opinion/islamic-state-mosul-iraq-strategy.html [http://perma.cc/ZKU6-CM5Y].

25. *Hillary Clinton's Comprehensive Plan to Defeat ISIS and the Threat of Radical Jihadism*, HILLARYCLINTON.COM, https://www.hillaryclinton.com/briefing/factchecks/2016/09/07/hillary-clintons-comprehensive-plan-to-defeat-isis-and-the-threat-of-radical-jihadism [http://perma.cc/4XH8-E869].

26. Michael R. Gordon, *U.S.-Backed Forces Close to Trapping ISIS Holdouts in Raqqa*, N.Y. TIMES, July 2, 2017, https://www.nytimes.com/2017/07/02/world/middleeast/us-backed-forces-close-to-trapping-isis-holdouts-in-raqqa.html [http://perma.cc/7VMQ-5NCC].

27. *See* David Remnick, *Going the Distance: On and Off the Road with Barack Obama*, NEW YORKER, Jan. 27, 2014, https://www.newyorker.com/magazine/2014/01/27/going-the-distance-david-remnick ("'The analogy we use around here sometimes, and I think is accurate, is if a jayvee team puts on Lakers uniforms that doesn't make them Kobe Bryant,' Obama said.").

28. *See* William Finnegan, *Taking Down Terrorists in Court*, NEW YORKER, May 15, 2017, https://www.newyorker.com/magazine/2017/05/15/taking-down-terrorists-in-court.

29. Douglas O. Linder, *The Oklahoma City Bombing and the Trial of Timothy McVeigh: A Chronology*, FAMOUS TRIALS, http://www.famous-trials.com/oklacity/715-chronology [http://perma.cc/SXN4-8HKN]. The recent case of the 2017 New York Halloween killer, Sayfullo Saipov, strongly evokes the hypothetical case described in text.

30. Andy Thibault et al., *Tsarnaev Sentenced to Death in Boston Bombing Trial*, NBC NEWS, May 15, 2015, 4:50 PM, http://www.nbcnews.com/storyline/boston-bombing-trial/boston-bombing-trial-jury-reaches-verdict-penalty-phase-n359731 [http://perma.cc/L9T2-6EPP].

31. Obama NDU Speech, *supra* note 2.

32. The AUMF authorized the president "to use all necessary and appropriate force against those nations, organizations, or persons he determines planned, authorized, committed, or aided the terrorist attacks that occurred on September 11, 2001 . . . *in order to prevent any future acts of international terrorism against the United States by such nations, organizations or persons*" (emphasis added).

33. Jeh Charles Johnson, Jr., General Counsel, U.S. Dep't of Def., Speech at the Oxford Union, Oxford University: The Conflict Against Al Qaeda and its Affiliates: How Will It End? (Nov. 30, 2012), http://www.lawfareblog.com/2012/11/jeh-johnson-speech-at-the-oxford-union/.

34. John Haltiwanger, *The Forever War: U.S. Military Now Has 15,000 Troops in Afghanistan and That Number Could Soon Increase*, NEWSWEEK, Nov. 9, 2017, 10:27 AM, http://www.newsweek.com/forever-war-us-military-now-has-15000-troops-afghanistan-706573 [https://perma.cc/7ALN-W43L].

35. In January 2018, Ambassador Nikki Haley accused Islamabad of "playing a double game for years" with its selective support for various militant groups operating on its soil. *Nikki Haley: Pakistan Playing "Double Game" for Years*, AL JAZEERA NEWS, Jan. 3, 2018, https://www.aljazeera.com/news/2018/01/180103071219690.html.

36. For the definitive account of Holbrooke's effort to negotiate with the Taliban, *see* STEVE COLL, DIRECTORATE S: THE C.I.A. AND AMERICA'S SECRET WARS IN AFGHANISTAN AND PAKISTAN (2018).

37. Patrick Goodenough, *Trump: "We Don't Want to Talk to the Taliban. We're Going to Finish What We Have to Finish"*, CNSNEWS.COM, Jan. 29, 2018, 6:50 PM, https://www.cnsnews.com/news/article/patrick-goodenough/trump-we-dont-want-talk-taliban-were-going-finish-what-we-have [https://perma.cc/L7EQ-8MTT]. But as this book went to press, the Administration announced that it would finally seek direct talks with the Taliban. *See* Afterword.

38. Steve Coll, *We Can't Win in Afghanistan Because We Don't Know Why We're There*, N.Y. TIMES, Jan. 26, 2018, https://www.nytimes.com/2018/01/26/opinion/sunday/united-states-afghanistan-win.html [https://perma.cc/XPR3-JZG].

39. Hillary Rodham Clinton, Sec'y of State, Remarks at the Launch of the Asia Society's Series of Richard C. Holbrooke Memorial Addresses (Feb. 18, 2011), https://2009-2017.state.gov/secretary/20092013clinton/rm/2011/02/156815.htm [https://perma.cc/UKF4-MLDJ].

40. *See* Richard Olson, *Ending the War in Afghanistan: A Diplomatic Perspective*, CSIS, Feb. 28, 2018, https://www.csis.org/analysis/ending-war-afghanistan-diplomatic-perspective [https://perma.cc/EB29-E7QY].

41. Borhan Osman, *The U.S. Needs to Talk to the Taliban*, N.Y. TIMES, Mar. 19, 2018, https://www.nytimes.com/2018/03/19/opinion/america-afghanistan-taliban-talks.html.

42. John F. Kerry, U.S. Sec'y of State, Remarks with President Hamid Karzai After Meeting, Presidential Palace, Kabul, Afghanistan (Mar. 25, 2013), https://2009-2017.state.gov/secretary/remarks/2013/03/206663.htm.

43. Internet Usage Statistics, https://www.internetworldstats.com/asia.htm#af (last visited May 16, 2018).

44. Trump, *State of the Union, supra* Chapter 3, note 70.

45. GEORGE W. BUSH, DECISION POINTS 180 (2011).

46. Lucy Madison, *Obama: Guantánamo Must Close*, CBS NEWS, Apr. 30, 2013, 12:43 PM, https://www.cbsnews.com/news/obama-guantanamo-must-close/.

47. Max Fisher, *Why Hasn't Obama Closed Guantánamo Bay?*, WASH. POST, Apr. 30, 2013, https://www.washingtonpost.com/news/worldviews/wp/2013/04/30/obama-just-gave-a-powerful-speech-about-the-need-to-close-gitmo-so-why-hasnt-he/.

48. Carol Rosenberg, *Guantánamo by the Numbers*, MIAMI HERALD, http://www.miamiherald.com/news/nation-world/world/americas/guantanamo/article2163210.html (last updated May 3, 2018).

49. Hamdan v. Rumsfeld, 548 U.S. 557 (2006).

50. Stephen I. Vladeck, *The Long Reach of Guantánamo Bay Military Commissions*, N.Y. TIMES, Oct. 4, 2017, https://www.nytimes.com/2017/10/04/opinion/the-long-reach-of-guantanamo-bay-military-commissions.html.

51. Aisha I. Saad & Zoe A.Y. Weinberg, *Remember Guantánamo?*, N.Y. TIMES, Mar. 15, 2018, https://www.nytimes.com/2018/03/15/opinion/guantanamo-detainees.html.

52. *See* Harold Hongju Koh, *The Case Against Military Commissions*, 96 AM. J. INT'L L. 337 (2002).

53. Charlie Savage & Adam Goldman, *Following Trump's Lead, Republicans Grow Quiet on Guantánamo*, N.Y. TIMES, Nov. 4, 2017, https://www.nytimes.com/2017/11/04/us/politics/republicans-guantanamo-military-commissions-civilian-courts-terrorism.html.

54. RICHARD B. ZABEL & JAMES J. BENJAMIN, JR., IN PURSUIT OF JUSTICE: PROSECUTING TERRORISM CASES IN THE FEDERAL COURTS: 2009 UPDATE AND RECENT DEVELOPMENTS (2009), *available at* https://www.humanrightsfirst.org/resource/pursuit-justice.

55. DANIEL KLAIDMAN, KILL OR CAPTURE: THE WAR ON TERROR AND THE SOUL OF THE OBAMA PRESIDENCY (2012).

56. Bruce Ackerman & Eugene R. Fidell, *Send Judges to Guantánamo, Then Shut It*, N.Y. TIMES, May 3, 2013, https://www.nytimes.com/2013/05/04/opinion/send-civilian-judges-to-guantanamo-then-shut-it.html.

57. Charlie Savage, *U.S. Transfers First Guantánamo Detainee Under Trump, Who Vowed to Fill It*, N.Y. TIMES, May 2, 2018, https://www.nytimes.

com/2018/05/02/us/politics/guantanamo-detainee-transferred-trump-al-darbi.html.

58. Kurtis Lee, *Donald Trump Wants to Put "Bad Dudes" in Guantánamo Bay*, L.A. TIMES, Feb. 23, 2016, 2:42 PM, http://www.latimes.com/la-na-nevada-republican-c-trump-wants-to-put-bad-dudes-in-guantanamo-bay-1456267357-htmlstory.html.

59. Donald J. Trump (@realDonaldTrump), TWITTER (Nov. 2, 2017, 7:50 AM), https://twitter.com/realdonaldtrump/status/926053970535243777; Donald J. Trump (@realDonaldTrump), TWITTER (Nov. 2, 2017, 7:54 AM), https://twitter.com/realdonaldtrump/status/926054936718307328.

60. Obama NDU Speech, *supra* Chapter 5, note 2.

61. Authorization for Use of Military Force Against Iraq Resolution of 2002, Pub. L. No. 107-243, 116 Stat. 1498.

62. Smith v. Obama, 217 F. Supp. 3d 283 (D.D.C. 2016), which challenged the domestic legality of that legal theory, was dismissed both for lack of standing and as a political question but is currently pending on appeal before the D.C. Circuit. *See* No. 16-843 (D.D.C. Nov. 21, 2016) (mem.); Charlie Savage, *Suit Calling War on ISIS Illegal Is Rejected*, N.Y. TIMES, Nov. 21, 2016, http://www.nytimes.com/2016/11/21/us/politics/judge-lawsuit-war-isis.html [http://perma.cc/8J97-EUUZ]. *But see* Marty Lederman, *Judge Kollar-Kotelly Dismisses Captain Smith's Suit*, JUST SECURITY, Nov. 22, 2016, 8:05 AM, https://www.justsecurity.org/34778/judge-kollar-kotelly-dismisses-captain-smiths-suit [http://perma.cc/DS8H-7F4X] (challenging the court's political question ruling).

63. White House Office of the Press Secretary, Statement by the President [Barack Obama] on ISIL (Sept. 10, 2014), *available at* https://obamawhitehouse.archives.gov/the-press-office/2014/09/10/statement-president-isil-1 ("If left unchecked, these terrorists could pose a growing threat beyond that region, including to the United States. While we have not yet detected specific plotting against our homeland, ISIL leaders have threatened America and our allies.").

64. *See generally* Koh, *Obama's ISIL Legal Rollout, supra* note 1.

65. Youngstown Sheet & Tube Co. v. Sawyer, 343 U.S. 579, 635–36 (1952) (Jackson, J., concurring).

66. While not part of the 2001 AUMF's wording, the term "associated forces" derived from a shared executive and judicial interpretation of the statute's text used to clarify the authority of the AUMF in aftermath of 9/11, which was later codified in the 2012 NDAA.

67. Johnson, Speech at the Oxford Union, *supra* note 33.

68. Multinational Force in Lebanon Resolution, Pub. L. No. 98-119, Oct. 12, 1983.

69. I argued in 2013 that

> the [Obama] administration should make public its full legal explanation for why and when it is consistent with due process of law to target American citizens and residents.... [I]t should clarify its method of counting civilian casualties, and why that method is consistent with international humanitarian law standards. [And] where factual disputes exist about the threat level against which past drone strikes were directed, the administration should release the factual record. By so doing, it could explain what gave it cause to believe that particular threats were imminent, what called for the immediate exercise of self-defense, and what demonstrated either the express consent of the territorial sovereign or the inability and unwillingness of those sovereigns to suppress a legitimate threat.

KOH, HOW TO END THE FOREVER WAR?, *supra* note 1.

70. *See, e.g.*, Marko Milanovic, *European Court Decides Al-Skeini and Al-Jedda*, EJIL TALK!, July 7, 2011, *available at* https://www.ejiltalk.org/european-court-decides-al-skeini-and-al-jedda/.

71. S. J. Res. 59, 115th Cong., 2d Sess. (2018), *available at* https://www.lawfareblog.com/document-draft-counterterrorism-authorization-use-military-force.

72. Robert Windrem, *U.S. Government Considered Nelson Mandela a Terrorist Until 2008*, NBC NEWS, Nov. 2, 2015, https://www.nbcnews.com/news/other/us-government-considered-nelson-mandela-terrorist-until-2008-f2D11708787.

73. Heather Brandon-Smith, *Senator Merkley's Smart New Alternative AUMF Proposal*, JUST SECURITY, May 24, 2018, https://www.justsecurity.org/56987/senator-merkleys-smart-alternative-aumf-proposal/.

74. Obama NDU Speech, *supra* note 2.

75. *Syrian Civil War Fast Facts*, CNN, July 8, 2017, 10:12 AM, http://www.cnn.com/2013/08/27/world/meast/syria-civil-war-fast-facts/index.html.

76. *See* Harold Hongju Koh, *The Emerging Law of 21st Century War*, 66 EMORY L.J. 487, 504–11 (2017).

77. Mark Landler, *Syria Draws a Rare Source of Accord in Debate Between Kaine and Pence*, N.Y. TIMES, Oct. 5, 2016, https://www.nytimes.com/2016/10/06/us/syria-vice-presidential-debate.html [http://perma.cc/V7VF-T9L7].

78. *See* THE FINAL YEAR (HBO 2018) (chronicling recommendations for greater action in Syria by Secretary of State John Kerry and U.S. Ambassador to the United Nations Samantha Power).

79. Michael R. Gordon et al., *Dozens of U.S. Missiles Hit Air Base in Syria*, N.Y. TIMES, Apr. 6, 2017, https://www.nytimes.com/2017/04/06/world/

middleeast/us-said-to-weigh-military-responses-to-syrian-chemical-attack.html [http://perma.cc/D76A-LNAR].

80. Nicole Gaouette et al., *Haley Says US "Locked and Loaded," Prepared to Maintain Pressure on Syria*, DAILY BEAST (last updated Apr. 14, 2018), https://www.thedailybeast.com/nikki-haley-us-is-locked-and-loaded-to-strike-syria-again.

81. *Amb. Nikki Haley on Trump administration's Syria strategy*, FOX NEWS, Apr. 15, 2018, http://www.foxnews.com/transcript/2018/04/15/amb-nikki-haley-on-trump-administrations-syria-strategy.html.

82. Jen Kirby, *Read Trump's Statement on Syria Strike: "They Are Crimes of a Monster,"* VOX, Apr. 13, 2018, https://www.vox.com/2018/4/13/17236862/syria-strike-donald-trump-chemical-attack-statement.

83. Ryan Browne, *Mattis Warns Syria Against Using Chemical Weapons*, CNN, Feb. 2, 2018, https://www.cnn.com/2018/02/02/politics/mattis-syria-chemical-weapons-warning/index.html [https://perma.cc/7LTJ-6DUF].

84. Robin Wright, *The Hypocrisy of Trump's "Mission Accomplished" Boast About Syria*, NEW YORKER, Apr. 14, 2018, *available at* https://www.newyorker.com/news/news-desk/trumps-dangerous-mission-accomplished-boast-about-his-syria-strike.

85. Harold Hongju Koh, *Humanitarian Intervention: Time for Better Law*, 111 AJIL UNBOUND 287 (2017), https://www.cambridge.org/core/journals/american-journal-of-international-law/article/humanitarian-intervention-time-for-better-law/05B23622D7C19B2B3BF4BD05D693BD0F [http://perma.cc/VS62-4VEE].

86. U.N. Charter art. 2(4) ("All Members shall refrain in their international relations from the threat or use of force against the territorial integrity of political independence of any state, or in any other manner inconsistent with the Purposes of the United Nations.").

87. U.S. CONST. art. I, § 8, cl. 11 ("Congress shall have Power . . . to declare war.").

88. U.N. Charter pmbl., art. 1.

89. *See generally* MICHAEL W. DOYLE, THE QUESTION OF INTERVENTION: JOHN STUART MILL AND THE RESPONSIBILITY TO PROTECT 110 (2015) (explaining that since Kosovo, the R2P concept "has been invoked explicitly and implicitly, successfully and unsuccessfully, in cases ranging from Myanmar and Kenya in 2008, to Guinea in 2009, and . . . Libya in 2011"); ANNE ORFORD, INTERNATIONAL AUTHORITY AND THE RESPONSIBILITY TO PROTECT (2011).

90. *See* Gary J. Bass, *The Indian Way of Humanitarian Intervention*, 40 YALE J. INT'L L. 227 (2015).

91. *See* Daniel G. Acheson-Brown, *The Tanzanian Invasion of Uganda: A Just War?*, 12 INT'L THIRD WORLD STUD. J. & REV. 1 (2001).

92. *See* Ryan Goodman, *Humanitarian Military Options for Syrian Chemical Weapons Attack: "Illegal but Not Unprecedented,"* JUST SECURITY, Apr. 6, 2017, 9:56 AM, https://www.justsecurity.org/39658/ humanitarian-military-options-syrian-chemical-weapons-attack-illegal-unprecedented [http://perma.cc/NH2W-65PK].

93. *See* Harold Hongju Koh, *The War Powers and Humanitarian Intervention,* 53 HOUS. L. REV. 971, 976–80 (2016).

94. In other areas, for example, state practice has helped nations to develop an elongated concept of the "imminence" prerequisite to the exercise of national self-defense. *See supra* note 6.

95. *See generally* HAROLD HONGJU KOH, THE NATIONAL SECURITY CONSTITUTION: SHARING POWER AFTER THE IRAN-CONTRA AFFAIR (1990).

96. Kevin J. Heller, *The Coming Attack on Syria Will Be Unlawful,* OPINIO JURIS, Apr. 12, 2018, http://opiniojuris.org/2018/04/12/the-coming-attack-on-syria-will-be-unlawful/.

97. Koh, *War Powers and Humanitarian Intervention, supra* note 93; Harold Hongju Koh, *Not Illegal: But Now the Hard Part Begins,* JUST SECURITY, Apr. 7, 2017, https://www.justsecurity.org/39695/illegal-hard-part-begins [http://perma.cc/ZVF8-9GQZ].

98. Koh, *War Powers and Humanitarian Intervention, supra* note 93, at 1011 (emphasis added).

99. The Crisis Group, *Can the U.S. Respond to the Syria Chemical Weapons Attack without Risking Escalation?,* Apr. 10, 2018, https://www. crisisgroup.org/middle-east-north-africa/eastern-mediterranean/ syria/can-us-respond-syria-chemical-weapons-attack-without-risking-escalation.

100. *See* Julian Ku, *Almost Everyone Agrees That the U.S. Strikes Against Syria Are Illegal, Except Most Governments,* OPINIO JURIS, Apr. 12, 2017, http://opiniojuris.org/2017/04/07/almost-everyone-agrees-that-the-u-s-strikes-against-syria-are-illegal-under-international-law-except-for-most-governments [http://perma.cc/M4PE-TTJR]; Alonso G. Dunkelberg et al., *Mapping States' Reaction to the Syria Strikes of April 2018: A Comprehensive Guide,* JUST SECURITY, May 7, 2018, https:// www.justsecurity.org/55790/update-mapping-states-reactions-syria-strikes-april-2018/.

101. One can analogize this situation to the Good Samaritan principle in domestic tort law, which rarely preauthorizes bystanders to use force for humanitarian motives, for fear that they will abuse this license. But if those bystanders do act in a careful fashion, for the limited purpose of preventing a significantly worse outcome, the law will hold them exempt from wrongfulness after the fact. In such cases, we fully recognize

the tension that the conduct raises with the letter of the law but invoke an affirmative defense so as not to render illegal socially desirable conduct.

102. *See* Koh, *Humanitarian Intervention, supra* note 85.

103. Ashley Deeks, *How Does the Syria Situation Stack Up to the "Factors" that Justified Intervention in Kosovo?*, LAWFARE, Apr. 7, 2017, https://www. lawfareblog.com/how-does-syria-situation-stack-thefactors-justified-intervention-kosovo.

104. *See* Barack Obama, Nobel Lecture (Dec. 10, 2009), https://www. nobelprize.org/nobel_prizes/peace/laureates/2009/obama-lecture_en.html [http://perma.cc/NS2M-3MDW] ("I believe that force can be justified on humanitarian grounds, as it was in the Balkans, or in other places that have been scarred by war. Inaction tears at our conscience and can lead to more costly intervention later.").

105. Cory A. Booker & Oona A. Hathaway, *A Syria Plan That Breaks the Law*, N.Y. TIMES, Jan. 23, 2018, https://www.nytimes.com/2018/01/23/opinion/syria-tillerson-constitution-trump.html.

106. Frederic C. Hof, *Response to Senator Cory Booker on Syria*, ATLANTIC COUNCIL, Jan. 25, 2018, http://www.atlanticcouncil.org/blogs/syriasource/response-to-senator-cory-booker-on-syria.

107. Koh, *War Powers and Humanitarian Intervention, supra* note 93, at 980.

108. *Syria Air Strikes: UK Publishes Legal Case for Military Action*, BBC, Apr. 14, 2018, http://www.bbc.com/news/uk-43770102.

109. *See, e.g.*, Jack Goldsmith, *The Constitutionality of the Syria Strike Through the Eyes of OLC (and the Obama Administration)*, LAWFARE, Apr. 7, 2017, 7:31 AM, https://www.lawfareblog.com/constitutionality-syria-strike-through-eyes-olc-and-obama-administration [http://perma.cc/KW9M-W24V].

110. *See* Rebecca Ingber, *International Law Is Failing Us in Syria*, JUST SECURITY, Apr. 12, 2017, 11:06 AM, https://www.justsecurity.org/39895/international-law-failing-syria [http://perma.cc/D2VH-XBWP].

111. Anne Barnard & Hwaida Saad, *It's Hard to Believe, but Syria's War Is Getting Even Worse*, N.Y. TIMES, Feb. 8, 2018, https://www.nytimes.com/2018/02/08/world/middleeast/syria-war-idlib.html.

112. Patrick Henningsen, *The Astana Process: A Possible Solution to an Impossible Situation in Syria*, 21ST CENTURY WIRE, May 10, 2017, http://21stcenturywire.com/2017/05/10/the-astana-process-a-possible-solution-to-an-impossible-situation-in-syria [http://perma.cc/CS88-TW5P].

113. *See* Emily Holden et al., *Trump, the Indecisive*, POLITICO, Sept. 26, 2017, 5:04 AM, http://www.politico.com/story/2017/09/26/trump-business-climate-indecision-243074 [http://perma.cc/QXS4-UET4].

114. Robbie Gramer et al., *How the Trump Administration Broke the State Department*, FOREIGN POL'Y, July 31, 2017, http://foreignpolicy. com/2017/07/31/how-the-trump-administration-broke-the-state-department [http://perma.cc/AL82-7V5M].

Chapter 6

1. Every U.S. government official, high or low, takes a solemn oath not to obey any particular president but to uphold the Constitution and laws of the United States of America, including the "international law [that] is part of our law." *The Paquete Habana*, 175 U.S. 677, 700 (1900). Those officials have myriad ways of saying "Yes, Minister": i.e., signaling political obedience, while continuing along the previous bureaucratic path. *See* Harold Hongju Koh, *The Next Four Years: A Thanksgiving Strategy*, JUST SECURITY, Nov. 24, 2016, 8:32 AM, https://www.justsecurity. org/34868/years-thanksgiving-strategy-harold-koh [http://perma.cc/ Y3FK-Z6RT].

2. IMMANUEL KANT, PERPETUAL PEACE: A PHILOSOPHICAL SKETCH (1795).
3. *Id.* at § 2, art. 2.
4. Sigmar Gabriel, *supra* Chapter 3, note 47.
5. For a recent critique from the left, *see, e.g.*, SAMUEL MOYN, NOT ENOUGH: HUMAN RIGHTS IN AN UNEQUAL WORLD (2018).

X 6. Compare President Trump's recent "sovereignty first" statements with *Rohingyas Illegal Immigrants, Not Refugees: Rajnath*, PRESS TR. OF INDIA, Sept. 21, 2017, http://www.ptinews.com/news/9089318_Rohingyas-illegal-immigrants—not-refugees—Rajnath.html [http://perma.cc/YCX7-S4EX] (statement of Indian Home Minister) (" 'We have to think about the human rights of our own people before talking about the human rights of people from other countries,' he said. Any sovereign country, the minister said, was free to take a decision on what kind of action it should take against illegal immigrants. 'The issue of national security is involved with regard to illegal immigration which our country can't undermine,' he said.").

7. GEORGE ORWELL, 1984 (1949).
8. JACK GOLDSMITH, POWER AND CONSTRAINT: THE ACCOUNTABLE PRESIDENCY AFTER 9/11, at 49, 232–33 (2012).
9. *See* Craig Martin, *Symposium: The Assumptions of Koh's Transnational Legal Process as Counter-Strategy*, OPINIO JURIS, Feb. 26, 2018, http:// opiniojuris.org/2018/02/26/symposium-the-assumptions-of-kohs-transnational-legal-process-as-counter-strategy/ [https://perma.cc/ BY76-AG6E].
10. Koh, *Transnational Legal Process, supra* Introduction, note 1, at 207.

11. ZachsMind, *Fave Jokes: 2000 Year Old Man*, WORDPRESS: ZACHSMIND, Feb. 2, 2012, https://zachsmind.wordpress.com/2012/02/02/fave-jokes-2000-year-old-man [http://perma.cc/8NLQ-TBVB].

12. Martin Luther King, Jr., "Where Do We Go from Here?," Annual Report Delivered at the 11th Convention of the Southern Christian Leadership Conference in Atlanta, GA (Aug. 16, 1967), *available at* http://kingencyclopedia.stanford.edu/encyclopedia/documentsentry/where_do_we_go_from_here_delivered_at_the_11th_annual_sclc_convention/ [http://perma.cc/8UGK-LDU6].

AFTERWORD

As Donald Trump's presidency careens into its second autumn, thoughtful observers are experiencing exhaustion, whiplash, and bewilderment. Each day brings new, at times wildly contradictory, assessments of the progress of Trump's myriad initiatives.

On global matters, Trump has visibly reveled in shaking free of his handlers. An unpredictable tweet-driven policy has emerged, subsumed under the amorphous slogan "America First." Trump's brutal decision to enforce a "zero-tolerance" immigration policy by separating migrant children from their parents at the border has touched a national nerve and triggered a newly intense round of street demonstrations. Trump's disastrous summit with Putin at Helsinki—historically a symbolic site of American human rights leadership—has confirmed not only his disdain for his own intelligence community, but also his unwillingness to engage seriously on human rights, Ukraine, or Russian election hacking. Both the Paris and Iran deals teeter along, as allies focus on how to fill the void created by Trump's withdrawal of U.S. leadership; meanwhile, Iran has taken matters into its own hands, now suing the United States for breaching the Iran Nuclear Deal before the International Court of Justice.[1] America's wars continue apace: as Bashar al-Assad tightens his grip on Syria, Trump's administration finally

---

1. Rick Gladstone, *Iran Sues U.S. Over Broken Nuclear Deal and Reimposed Sanctions*, N.Y. Times, July 17, 2018, https://www.nytimes.com/2018/07/17/world/middleeast/iran-sues-us-over-sanctions.html.

agrees to direct talks with the Taliban, and new terrorist threats emerge, even as IS keeps losing ground on the battlefield.[2] Trump's premature boast of a diminished North Korean threat has crumbled as it has become clear that, in fact, Kim Jong-un has taken few real steps to denuclearize. And Trump's insistence on confronting NATO and provoking trade wars has created a growing sense of inversion as America battles its traditional allies and embraces its traditional adversaries.

As proof that Trump is in fact gaining ground, some might point to the U.S. Supreme Court's closely watched decision in *Trump v. Hawaii*.[3] Buoyed in that case by the pivotal vote of his first Supreme Court nominee, Neil Gorsuch, Trump finally secured a 5–4 decision upholding Travel Ban 3.0. In July 2018, Justice Anthony Kennedy's resignation handed Trump a game-changing opportunity to shift the Court's balance rightward for a generation, creating a vacancy that Trump promptly sought to fill by nominating Judge Brett Kavanaugh, a young, reliably conservative, international-law skeptic from the D.C. Circuit. Liberals darkly warn that things are finally falling apart and that Trump, backed by his stream of judicial appointments, will now surely secure permanent transformation of the American policy landscape.

But on closer inspection, the latest developments only confirm the broader themes and dangers I have already identified. The Court's 5–4 decision in the Travel Ban case shows that civil society's ability to check Trump's overreaching will depend crucially on the courage and integrity of the courts. In one sense, the decision was predictable, having been signaled by the Court's willingness to stay the lower court's preliminary injunction since December 2017, which ensured that the policy would continue for half a year before the final Supreme Court decision. But Trump's Travel Ban win ultimately turned on the transparently implausible assertion in Chief Justice John Roberts' majority opinion that the infamous Japanese internment case, "*Korematsu* [*v. United States*,[4]] has nothing to do with this case."[5] In *Trump*, Chief Justice Roberts conceded nearly seventy-five years late that *Korematsu* "was gravely wrong the day it was decided, has been overruled in the court of history, and—to be clear—'has no place in law under the Constitution.'"[6] Yet remarkably, in the same breath, he called it "wholly inapt

2. Mujib Mashal & Eric Schmitt, *Pursuing Talks, U.S. Shifts Tack on the Taliban*, N.Y. Times, July 16, 2018, ; Eric Schmitt, *ISIS May Be Waning, but Global Threats of Terrorism Continue to Spread*, N.Y. Times, July 6, 2018, https://www.nytimes.com/2018/07/06/world/middleeast/isis-global-terrorism.html.

3. Trump v. Hawaii, 138 S. Ct. 2392 (2018).

4. Korematsu v. United States, 323 U.S. 214 (1944).

5. 138 S. Ct. at 2423.

6. *Id.*

to liken that morally repugnant order to" Trump's Travel Ban.[7] In fact, the wholly apt resemblance to *Korematsu* should have been enough to invalidate the Travel Ban on its face.

As Justice Sonia Sotomayor's trenchant dissent summarized, the *Trump* Court "blindly accept[ed] the Government's misguided invitation to sanction a discriminatory policy motivated by animosity toward a disfavored group, all in the name of a superficial claim of national security, [in the process] redeploy[ing] the same dangerous logic underlying *Korematsu*. . . ."[8] In both *Korematsu* and *Trump*, the president had invoked an amorphous national security threat to justify a sweeping discriminatory policy limiting the freedom of a particular group. In both cases, the government asserted a grossly overbroad group stereotype that presumed that membership in that group, standing alone, signaled a hidden desire to harm the United States.[9] As Justice Jackson had warned in his prescient *Korematsu* dissent, "once a judicial opinion . . . rationalizes the Constitution to show that the Constitution sanctions such an order, . . . [t]he principle then lies about like a loaded weapon ready for the hand of any authority that can bring forward a plausible claim of an urgent need."[10] Far from rejecting the parallel to *Korematsu*, Trump eagerly seized it as a weapon to justify his call for a "total and complete shutdown of Muslims entering the United States,"[11] claiming that President Franklin Delano Roosevelt "did the same" by interning Japanese-Americans during World War II.[12] Nevertheless, the Court adamantly insisted that *Korematsu* had nothing to do with *Trump*.

The *Trump* majority overlooked that the manifest wrong of both policies stemmed from the U.S. government's insistence on judging and harming people based not on the content of their individual character but on their membership in a supposedly dangerous group—defined by descent, nationality, or religion—whose dangerousness the government had never proven.

7. *Id.*

8. *Id.* at 2448.

9. As Trump said, "Islam hates us. . . . we can't allow people coming into this country who have this hatred of the United States." Anderson Cooper, *Exclusive Interview with Donald Trump*, CNN, Mar. 9, 2016, http://www.cnn.com/TRANSCRIPTS/1603/09/acd.01.html.

10. 323 U.S. at 246 (Jackson, J., dissenting).

11. Jenna Johnson, *Trump Calls for "Total and Complete Shutdown of Muslims Entering the United States"*, WASH. POST, Dec. 7, 2015, https://www.washingtonpost.com/news/post-politics/wp/2015/12/07/donald-trump-calls-for-total-and-complete-shutdown-of-muslims-entering-the-united-states.

12. Meghan Keneally, *Donald Trump Cites These FDR Policies to Defend Muslim Ban*, ABC NEWS, Dec. 8, 2015, 1:01 PM, https://abcnews.go.com/Politics/donald-trump-cites-fdr-policies-defend-muslim-ban/story?id=35648128.

While the Travel Ban nominally barred entry based on country of origin, two of the countries—North Korea and Venezuela—were clearly inserted as window dressing to provide cover for the six Muslim-majority countries that were the Ban's real targets.

To sustain the Ban, the *Trump* majority committed grievous errors of both fact and law. As a matter of fact, the *Trump* majority claimed that there was "persuasive evidence that the entry suspension has a legitimate grounding in national security concerns."[13] But as the amicus brief of former national security officials from both Republican and Democratic administrations chronicled, throughout the fifteen months of the Travel Ban litigation, the U.S. government never offered a sworn declaration from a single executive official who was willing to describe either the national security-based need for the executive orders or the process that had led to their adoption.[14] Nor did the government point to any other evidence of a national security imperative that could remotely justify its unprecedented actions. To the contrary, Trump officials' own dilatory actions in the wake of Travel Ban 1.0 showed that even they never took seriously their own claims of national security urgency.

As a matter of law, the *Trump* majority misread the pivotal statute, the Immigration and Nationality Act, to "exude[] deference to the President in every clause," a description better suited to the Court's own opinion than to the law itself.[15] The Court never plausibly explained why that law, which authorized the president to suspend entry of "immigrants or nonimmigrants," was not modified by a subsequent statutory provision that expressly *prohibited* nationality-based discrimination in the issuance of immigrant visas.[16] The majority uncritically accepted the government's claim that what had undeniably begun life as a Muslim Ban had evolved into "a facially neutral policy denying certain foreign nationals the privilege of admission."[17] But as Justice Sotomayor's dissent clarified—citing chapter and verse from Trump's own Twitter feed—"[t]he full record paints a . . . harrowing picture, from which a reasonable observer would readily conclude that the Proclamation was motivated by hostility and animus toward the Muslim faith."[18] Just weeks earlier, the Court had found that state officials' expressions of hostility to religion toward a baker who had declined to serve LGBT customers violated the

---

13. Trump v. Hawaii, 138 S. Ct. 2392, 2421 (2018).

14. Brief for Former National Security Officials as Amicus Curiae Supporting Respondents, Trump v. Hawaii, 138 S. Ct. 2392 (2018).

15. 138 S. Ct. at 2400.

16. Immigration and Nationality Act of 1965, 8 U.S.C. § 1182(f).

17. 138 S. Ct. at 2423.

18. *Id.* at 2435.

baker's freedom of religion.[19] Yet in *Trump*, the Court dismissed repeated, far more overt anti-Muslim statements from Trump and his senior advisers as irrelevant to the constitutional claims. The Court never acknowledged that the original bigotry that had infected Travel Ban 1.0 carried over to its two successors, which—notwithstanding the government's recitation of a subsequent "worldwide review process undertaken by multiple Cabinet officials"— were thinly disguised to preserve the original Ban's group-discrimination template.[20] As Justice Thomas himself once conceded, "if a policy remains in force, without adequate justification and despite tainted roots . . . , it appears clear—clear enough to presume conclusively—that the [government] has failed to disprove discriminatory intent."[21]

Most troubling, the *Trump* majority upheld the legality of the government's conduct by applying an absurdly deferential standard of review. As one commentary described the Court's reasoning: "even if we know that an immigration policy was motivated by blatant official animus against a religion, the policy should be sustained so long as the government proffers some rational national security basis for it."[22] The majority chose to defer broadly to an executive action that, as the national security officials' brief demonstrated, had not emerged from the considered judgment of executive officials, was not a credible response to a bona fide security threat, and rested on inconsistent, ever-shifting rationales.

In Chapter 2, I offered three reasons why, on closer inspection, the *Trump* Court's ruling decides less than it symbolizes. First, the Court's ruling rested on statutory grounds, so it could be reversed in the legislative arena should Congress change hands in November 2018. Second, as with the other Trump policies reviewed in this book, other transnational actors will surely invoke transnational legal process to contest and limit the impact of the Court's ruling on multiple fronts. Third, the Travel Ban litigation continues; thus far it has failed only to prove the Ban unconstitutional on its face. It still remains to be seen whether, in practice, the elaborate system of individualized exemptions and waivers accompanying the Ban actually allows individual travelers' circumstances to be taken into account in the making of entry decisions. The *Trump* Court remanded the case back to the lower courts so that litigation would proceed without a

---

19. Masterpiece Cakeshop v. Colo. Civil Rights Comm'n, 584 U.S. ___ (2018).

20. 138 S. Ct. at 2402.

21. United States v. Fordice, 505 U.S. 717, 747 (1992) (Thomas, J., concurring).

22. Adam Cox et al., *The Radical Supreme Court Travel Ban Opinion—But Why It Might Not Apply to Other Immigrants' Rights Cases*, JUST SECURITY, June 27, 2018, https://www.justsecurity.org/58510/radical-supreme-court-travel-ban-opinion-but-apply-immigrants-rights-cases/.

preliminary injunction, but it also found that U.S. persons had standing to challenge the Ban's application and that the core issues were effectively justiciable. On remand, discovery can now proceed, and evidence of government discrimination in individual cases can be introduced.[23] As Justice Breyer's dissent pointed out, many different plaintiffs—including "lawful permanent residents, asylum seekers, refugees, students, children, and numerous others"—can now test to see how often the bureaucracy actually awards individualized exceptions to the blanket Ban.[24] If, as Justice Sotomayor suspects, the "waiver program is nothing more than a sham," a court could issue an injunction permanently blocking the Ban for being unconstitutional as applied.[25]

In short, the Travel Ban episode is far from over. One battle does not determine who wins the legal war. The transnational-legal-process struggle will continue on many fronts. One might have hoped that the Court would affirm the many courts that had invalidated the Ban in its relatively early stages. But it is worth recalling that sometimes a favorable court ruling comes at the end, not the beginning, of the legal process. We should not forget that *Korematsu* itself was overruled in the court of public opinion—through concerted action on many fronts—decades before the Roberts Court finally got around to pronouncing it dead.

How willing the courts are to defer to executive authority remains pivotal because the Travel Ban represents only the most prominent Trump administration policy that, in Justice Sotomayor's words, "now masquerades behind a facade of national-security concerns."[26] After all, this president has repeatedly played national security as his trump card. This is the same president who, while separating infants from their parents at the U.S.–Mexico border in the name of national security, bizarrely declared Canada to be a national security threat.[27] This is the same president who, while harshly condemning and using military force in response to Assad's use of chemical weapons against the Syrian people, remains unwilling to lift his nationality-based ban on Syrians entering the United States. And this is the same president whose administration is broadly claiming

23. Noah Feldman, *Take Trump's Travel Ban Back to Court*, BLOOMBERG, June 29, 2018, 12:26 PM, https://www.bloomberg.com/view/articles/2018-06-29/take-trump-s-travel-ban-back-to-court.

24. Trump v. Hawaii, 138 S. Ct. 2392, 2429 (2018).

25. *Id.* at 2445.

26. *Id.* at 2433.

27. Dov S. Zakheim, *Canada as a National Security Threat to the United States*, HILL, June 4, 2018, 1:30 PM, http://thehill.com/opinion/national-security/390527-canada-as-a-national-security-threat-to-the-united-states.

national security justifications for expelling transgender individuals from the U.S. military,[28] imposing steel and aluminum tariffs on allies under Section 232 of the 1962 Trade Expansion Act,[29] and now contemplating, in the name of national security, emergency action under the Defense Production Act and the Federal Power Act to require grid operators to make "stop-loss" purchases from failing coal power plants.[30] Given the *Trump* Court's credulous acceptance that national security concerns justified a Travel Ban, we can soon expect the administration to seek similar judicial validation of these other national security masquerades as well. Surely the confirmation of Judge Brett Kavanaugh to the Supreme Court would shift the Court even more in that direction. But even so, not every struggle gets to the Supreme Court, and those that do rarely get there quickly. So it will still be up to the lower courts, which have proven almost universally hostile to every iteration of the Travel Ban, to determine whether their job is to fortify the administration's national security façades or whether—as Chief Justice Marshall wrote in *Marbury v. Madison*—it is "the province and duty of the judicial department to say what the law is."[31]

At this writing, such judicial pressure is graphically playing out amid the firestorm surrounding Trump's policy of separating children from their parents at the border. Previous administrations handled undocumented family border crossings through civil immigration proceedings. But days after taking office, Trump announced that detention, deportation, and criminal prosecution would become the rule for any undocumented person crossing into the United States, regardless of whether they could ultimately establish the right, under both domestic and international law, to be present

28. Dave Phillipps, *Judge Blocks Trump's Ban on Transgender Troops in Military*, N.Y. TIMES, Oct. 30, 2017, https://www.nytimes.com/2017/10/30/us/military-transgender-ban.html.

29. *Section 232 Tariffs on Aluminum and Steel*, U.S. CUSTOMS AND BORDER PROTECTION, https://www.cbp.gov/trade/programs-administration/entry-summary/232-tariffs-aluminum-and-steel (last updated June 29, 2018); Proclamation 9705 (Mar. 8, 2018) (Adjusting Imports of Steel into the United States); Proclamation 9704 (Mar. 8, 2018) (Adjusting Imports of Aluminum into the United States).

30. Jennifer A. Dlouhy, *Trump Prepares Lifeline for Money-Losing Coal Plants*, BLOOMBERG, May 31, 2018, 8:49 PM, https://www.bloomberg.com/news/articles/2018-06-01/trump-said-to-grant-lifeline-to-money-losing-coal-power-plants-jhv94ghl (last updated June 1, 2018, 9:44 AM); *The Trump Administration's Coal and Nuclear Proposal Undermines the Resiliency of the Grid*, INST. FOR ENERGY RES., June 13, 2018, http://instituteforenergyresearch.org/analysis/trump-administrations-coal-nuclear-proposal-undermine-grid-resiliency-%E2%80%A8/.

31. 5 U.S. (1 Cranch) 137, 177 (1803).

in the United States as a bona fide asylum seeker fleeing persecution at home.[32] Once again, Trump relied on a discriminatory group stereotype. He presumed without proof that every undocumented individual crossing an American border is a criminal, rather than a victim deserving of the protection of American and international refugee laws. The Trump administration then deepened the crisis by abruptly instituting a "zero-tolerance" policy of prosecuting all such undocumented crossing cases.[33] But once again, the administration had overlooked a significant legal impediment. In the 1997 *Flores* litigation, a federal court had entered a settlement directing that children could not be held in detention for more than twenty days.[34] So if detained families are to stay together while awaiting immigration proceedings, under *Flores*, they must stay together outside of jails. To strictly implement the new zero-tolerance policy, border agents picked incarceration over family unity and took the horrifying step of separating children from their parents, who were then held in adult jails pending court appearances.

As wrenching images of small children being forcibly taken from their parents flooded the media, massive street protests erupted, replaying the Travel Ban demonstrations discussed in Chapter 2. The ACLU filed a class-action lawsuit that won a court-ordered deadline from U.S. District Judge Dana Sabraw, a George W. Bush appointee. That order gave the Trump administration two weeks to return separated children younger than five to their parents[35] and thirty days to reunite parents with several thousand older children who had been detained by the government.[36] Administrative chaos ensued as it became clear that the Trump administration could not meet Judge Sabraw's deadlines because, among other obstacles, it did not actually know where many of the children were. Under intense pressure, Trump capitulated and issued an executive order reinstating the principle of family unity.

32. Dara Lind, *The Wall Is the Least Aggressive Part of Trump's Executive Actions on Immigration*, Vox, Jan. 25, 2017, 3:40 PM, https://www.vox.com/2017/1/25/14378474/trump-immigration-order-wall-deport-sanctuary.

33. *Attorney General Announces Zero-Tolerance Policy for Criminal Illegal Entry*, U.S. Dep't of Just., Apr. 6, 2018, https://www.justice.gov/opa/pr/attorney-general-announces-zero-tolerance-policy-criminal-illegal-entry.

34. Stipulated Settlement Agreement, Flores v. Reno, No. CV 85-4544-RJK(Px) (C.D. Cal. Jan. 17, 1997).

35. Margaret Hartmann, *Judge Orders Trump Administration to Reunite Migrant Families Within 30 Days*, N.Y. Mag., June 27, 2018, 5:16 AM, http://nymag.com/daily/intelligencer/2018/06/judge-reunite-migrant-families-in-30-days-end-separations.html.

36. Sarah Nechamkin, *Exactly How Many Separated Immigrant Families Have Been Reunited?*, N.Y. Mag., July 12, 2018, 12:05 PM, https://www.thecut.com/2018/07/how-many-separated-immigrant-families-have-been-reunited-trump.html. *Trump administration*

District court judge Dolly Gee, the judge supervising the *Flores* settlement, then rejected the Justice Department's request to alter the terms of that settlement, meaning that migrant children still cannot be legally detained for more than twenty days. Immigration authorities lack the facilities to detain thousands of families, and so the Trump administration had no choice but to reverse course yet again: it abruptly announced that the reunited migrant families would be released into the United States with the parents wearing ankle monitors. The announcement effectively acknowledged that, pending appeal, the administration would adhere to its "zero-tolerance" immigration policy in name only. So in practice it has now returned to the pejoratively named "catch-and-release" policy that Trump has railed against so often at his political rallies.[37]

Once again, transnational legal process has pushed Trump back. Under pressure from overlapping judicial mandates, Trump officials have reverted to allowing families into the United States to await immigration proceedings, a process that, barring reversal of the policy and given current judicial backlogs, could take years. What Trump and his subordinates again overlooked was that the patchwork of laws and policies they scorn as "catch and release" are in fact part and parcel of transnational legal process. Collectively, these laws are a bulwark of legal protection for certain vulnerable populations such as refugees, children, and families, populations that over time the United Nations, Congress, and the courts have all accorded special solicitude.[38] Trump cannot simply brush those legal protections aside by shouting "end catch and release." Instead, he must do the hard and tedious work of mobilizing his bureaucracy to invoke existing legal mechanisms that will pressure Congress or the courts to change the laws through established legal channels. Because he has not done that work, at this point the law remains unchanged, and the policy has reverted to the status quo ante, after massive public outcry and untold human suffering.

37. Julie Garcia, *Is "Zero Tolerance" Policy for Immigrants Still in Effect? Depends Who You Ask*, CALLER TIMES, June 26, 2018, 8:32 PM, https://www.caller.com/story/news/local/2018/06/26/zero-tolerance-policy-immigrant-families-separated-reunification-process/733912002/; Dara Lind, *"Catch and Release," Explained: The Heart of Trump's New Border Agenda*, VOX, Apr. 9, 2018, 12:50 PM, ("In fiscal year 2017 . . . [m]ost immigrants . . . did show up to their court dates; 60,000 immigrants showed up only to get deported. Thousands more actually won their cases. . . .").

38. *See* Dara Lind, *Why Is the Obama Administration Still Fighting to Keep Immigrant Families Behind Bars?*, VOX, July 29, 2015, 2:20 PM, https://www.vox.com/2015/7/29/9067877/family-detention-immigration-flores; Dara Lind, *The Process Congress Wants to Use for Child Migrants Is a Disaster*, VOX, July 15, 2014, 9:00 AM, https://www.vox.com/2014/7/15/5898349/border-children-mexican-central-american-deport-quickly-2008-law.

On global matters, the same tale of continuity and resilience can be told. On the surface, we see massive turmoil as Trump's tweets superficially signal abrupt shifts in America's policies regarding such countries of concern as China, Iran, North Korea, and Russia and such high-profile issues as immigration, international trade, and the retreat from the two-state solution in the Middle East. Trump's unpredictable bull-in-a-china-shop rhetoric engenders controversy wherever he goes, turning previously routine diplomatic meetings—such as the NATO summit in Brussels or his bilateral visit to the prime minister of Great Britain—into nail-biting high-wire acts. A pattern has emerged whereby Trump signals that he will disrupt a previously settled relationship, the media explodes, U.S. allies push back, Trump partially recants, and policy eventually resettles in roughly the same place that it was before Trump roiled the waters. Foreign policy toward lower-profile nations and issues continues to be governed largely by lower political appointees, career bureaucrats, and standard operating procedures, unless and until those issues rise to the rare level that attracts the White House's political attention and micromanagement. So outside the headlines, key national security and defense policies continue to be made according to long-standing legal and policy principles and frameworks embedded in congressional statutes, executive orders, presidential policy guidance, and institutional custom.[39]

North Korea provides yet more proof that, even with regard to the high-profile countries of concern, Trump is disrupting the status quo without meaningfully changing policies. After issuing a vague 400-word June 2018 Singapore Declaration, Trump tweeted, "I have confidence that Kim Jong Un will honor the contract we signed & even more importantly, our handshake. . . . We agreed to the denuclearization of North Korea."[40] But plainly, he misunderstood that under international law, a handshake is just a handshake; it creates no binding international legal treaty, contract, or agreement. Instead of clarifying a negotiating sequence and timetable, as suggested in Chapter 4, Trump naively concluded that two countries merely talking about "denuclearization" had enough concrete legal meaning to merit tweeting that the North Korean nuclear threat had somehow ended. But in the weeks following the Singapore Summit, things rapidly deteriorated: Secretary of State Mike Pompeo received harsh diplomatic treatment in a Pyongyang visit where he was shunted off to Kim Jong-un's subordinates. The North Koreans

---

39. *See, e.g.*, 2016 Legal and Policy Frameworks discussed in Chapter 5; National Security Strategy of the United States (Dec. 17, 2017); Summary of the National Defense Strategy of the United States (2018) (whose key principles were made public by Defense Secretary James Mattis).

40. Trump, Donald (@realDonaldTrump). July 9, 2018, 10:25 AM. Tweet.

subsequently missed their initial deadline to bring the remains of American soldiers to a meeting at the demilitarized zone.

It has become embarrassingly clear that Kim has played Trump by securing equal billing with a sitting American president, humiliating his secretary of state, and demanding that he adhere strictly to the terms of a Singapore Declaration that contains none of the detail that Trump forgot to write into it. When Trump's aides speak of "denuclearization," they are referring to a far more detailed and sequenced series of steps that Trump apparently never described to Kim—and may not understand himself—that would actually lead to the final "complete, verified, and irreversible denuclearization" (CVID) of the peninsula. Accordingly, the North Korean Foreign Ministry now predictably dismisses Pompeo's request for clarity and sequence as a "unilateral and gangster-like demand. . . . which run[s] counter to the spirit of the Singapore summit meeting and talks."[41]

As Colin Kahl has pointed out, the Barack Obama policy of "strategic patience" toward North Korea always "require[d] a long, hard slog—grinding bilateral and multilateral talks, negotiated freezes, confidence-building steps, and agreements to gradually roll back Pyongyang's [nuclear] program all the while bolstering the U.S. deterrent against North Korean aggression and strengthening regional alliances to manage and mitigate interim risks."[42] These were exactly the smart-power steps the Obama administration followed to build the Iran nuclear deal, which Trump abandoned without a plan B. They are also exactly the steps that Trump has not yet even begun with respect to a future North Korean deal, for which he again seems to have no plan B, apart from a counterproductive return to the bellicose rhetoric of "fire and fury." Once again, Trump's eagerness to claim premature victory, combined with his inability or temperamental unwillingness to do the hard and tedious work of actually mobilizing his bureaucracy to build new and better international legal mechanisms, has led the policy back to an inferior version of the status quo ante.

To be sure, the Trump administration is still in its early days. Significantly, on those rare occasions where the administration has closed ranks with traditional Republicans and worked hand in glove with Senate Majority Leader Mitch McConnell and House Speaker Paul Ryan, it has enjoyed its few

---

41. Jessica Donati & Andrew Jeong, *North Korean Nuclear Talks Are Thrown Off Balance as Accounts by U.S. and Pyongyang Clash*, WALL ST. J., https://www.wsj.com/articles/pompeo-cites-progress-in-north-korea-nuclear-talks-1530967772 (last updated July 7, 2018, 10:53 AM).

42. Colin Kahl, *Trump Has Nobody to Blame for North Korea but Himself*, FOREIGN POL'Y, July 11, 2019, 5:08 PM, https://foreignpolicy.com/2018/07/11/trump-has-nobody-to-blame-but-himself-for-north-korea-nuclear-pyongyang-pompeo/.

meaningful victories, particularly in winning an unpopular tax cut and in the Supreme Court confirmation process. But at the same time, this uneasy coalition of Trumpites and Republicans has twice spectacularly lost legislative efforts to repeal Obamacare, although another round may yet be coming. Over time, the ongoing steady stream of judicial confirmations could well cement Trump's policy changes into law and rewrite established rights and norms. Any meaningful strategy of resistance therefore increasingly turns on driving a wedge between the Trumpites and traditional Republicans, on such "wedge issues" as trade, immigration, and appeasement with Russia.

Should the November 2018 by-elections go strongly in favor of the Democrats and one or both houses of Congress change hands—and should the Special Counsel issue more indictments that cast Trump's political legitimacy into doubt—the Republicans will face a vexing choice: whether to retain Trump as their presidential candidate for 2020 or to replace him with someone more traditional, such as Mike Pence, Nikki Haley, or Mitt Romney. But if replacing Trump as the Republican presidential candidate means alienating Trump's base and keeping his supporters away from the polls, it is an almost certain recipe for electoral defeat in 2020.

In short, as Trump dances further out on the high wire, he may feel freer, but in fact he becomes far more vulnerable to being toppled. As I learned as a human rights policymaker watching many political strongmen fall, when you make everyone happy to see you go, you go quickly. Powerful people who bully those around them end up with few friends, and even fewer who will help save them when they become vulnerable. When you attack as overly constraining the very partnerships, processes, and laws that provide you with a safety net of legitimacy, then without it, you plummet.

As I discussed in Chapter 1, in the penultimate round of Muhammad Ali's famous rope-a-dope fight in Zaire, most observers thought that his opponent, George Foreman, was decisively winning. Foreman pummeled Ali wildly as Ali covered up, absorbed punishment, loudly protested, and counterpunched. In hindsight, we now know that at that moment it was Ali, not Foreman, who was about to prevail. But we also know that the battering took a grave toll on Ali's long-term health and well-being. So who ends up winning in the longer term will depend not just on who is stronger or more determined in the moment but also on who is more resilient in the long run.

The message of this book has been that we are witnessing a similar contest now. And it is happening not just in the United States, but around the world. The global rise of populist authoritarians and the global challenge to human rights and the rule of law have reached crisis proportions. A prominent global rule-of-justice index reported that fundamental human rights have diminished in almost two-thirds of the 113 countries surveyed in 2017; the same index assessed that since 2016, rule-of-law scores had declined in thirty-eight countries.[43] In Poland, once a beacon for emerging democracies, an authoritarian government has conducted a sweeping purge of the Polish Supreme Court, leading tens of thousands to take to the streets in protest.[44] The Philippine Supreme Court nullified the appointment of its chief justice only one month after President Rodrigo Duterte called her his "enemy" for speaking out against his brutal drug war and against his directive that the southern Philippines be placed under military rule.[45] Hungary has adopted openly xenophobic laws that criminalize people for helping asylum seekers.[46] Right-wing governments have taken power in Austria and Italy.[47] Venezuela has experienced an almost complete collapse of the rule of law. In an effort to purge his own "deep state," Turkey's Erdoğan fired 18,000 civil servants for unspecified links to terror groups in advance of his recent inauguration.[48]

In each of these countries, the example America sets over the next few years will be very closely watched. What this book has shown is that thus far, the resilience of American institutions has largely checked Trump at home. But that resilience may finally give way if Trump is re-elected for another term. At the same time, his greatest impact may come from fueling the global rise of authoritarianism and retreat from the rule of law and human rights. His persistent instinct to attack democratic leaders and embrace and emulate authoritarians is emboldening repressive governments elsewhere. His demonization of migrants at home fuels anti-immigrant xenophobia abroad. Concurrently, the arrival to power of Mike Pompeo and John Bolton has

43. *WJP Rule of Law Index 2017–2018*, WORLD JUST. PROJECT, https://worldjusticeproject.org/our-work/wjp-rule-law-index/wjp-rule-law-index-2017%E2%80%932018 (last visited July 14, 2018).

44. Marc Santora, *Poland Purges Supreme Court, and Protestors Take to Streets*, N.Y. TIMES, July 3, 2018, https://www.nytimes.com/2018/07/03/world/europe/poland-supreme-court-protest.html.

45. Andreo Calonzo, *Top Philippine Judge Removed After Attacks on Duterte's Drug War*, BLOOMBERG, May 11, 2018, 2:34 AM, https://www.bloomberg.com/news/articles/2018-05-11/top-philippine-judge-removed-after-attacks-on-duterte-s-drug-war.

46. Patrick Kingsley, *As West Fears the Rise of Autocrats, Hungary Shows What's Possible*, N.Y. TIMES, Feb. 10, 2018, https://www.nytimes.com/2018/02/10/world/europe/hungary-orban-democracy-far-right.html.

47. Jon Henley, *Rise of Far-Right in Italy and Austria Gives Putin Some Friends in the West*, GUARDIAN, June 7, 2018, 12:00 AM, https://www.theguardian.com/world/2018/jun/07/rise-of-far-right-in-italy-and-austria-gives-putin-some-friends-in-the-west.

48. Associated Press, *Turkey Fires Thousands for Alleged Terror Links*, BOSTON GLOBE, July 8, 2018, https://www.bostonglobe.com/news/world/2018/07/08/turkey-fires-thousands-for-alleged-terror-links/W66VkgTMvhxdVqUbMAKaqO/story.html?event=event25?event=event25.

bolstered the Trump administration's concerted effort to undermine the rule-of-law institutions of the postwar legal order—whether the United Nations and its human rights mechanisms, the European Union, or global institutions of trade and security. Indeed, Trump has recently hinted at his desire to withdraw from both NATO and the World Trade Organization, in what now seems to be an intentional pattern, not just impetuous lashing out.[49] As Trump's rhetoric empowers authoritarians antagonistic to the rule of law, the democratic states that would ordinarily push back are being disparaged, the civil society and media institutions within those same states are being squeezed, and the international institutions that would resist are being undermined. Under intense pressure, some of these institutions may break. Some treaty regimes may collapse. Particularly if Trump ends up serving two terms, the longer-term story—as with Muhammad Ali—could be that repeated body-blows to the global body politic contribute to the slow ungluing of the fragile framework of Kantian global governance that has struggled to hold together for seven decades. But if this book shows us anything, it is the resilience of our enduring core institutions: the courts, Congress, the media, bureaucracy, subnational entities, and civil society. With luck and perserverance, these institutions and processes should outlive Trump's deviations and play a critical role in reknitting together our society and our alliances once he is gone.

So going forward, our main question should be, who speaks for America? Donald Trump's tweets and actions? Or our enduring civic institutions, whose founding commitments to upholding human rights and the rule of law have defined America since our country's inception? In his parting opinion that clinched the majority in *Trump v. Hawaii*, Justice Kennedy fretted that "[a]n anxious world must know that our Government remains committed always to the liberties the Constitution seeks to preserve and protect. . . ."[50] Regrettably, in the Travel Ban case, the Court declined to require that commitment. But in the many struggles that still lie ahead, the rest of us must not similarly surrender.

New Haven, Connecticut
June 27, 2018

---

49. Ewen MacAskill, *Trump Claims Victory as Nato Summit Descends into Mayhem*, Guardian, July 12, 2018, 1:16 PM, https://www.theguardian.com/world/2018/jul/12/donald-trump-nato-summit-chaos-germany-attack-defence-spending; Bob Bryan, *Trump Reportedly Wants to Pull the US out of the WTO, a Move that Would Wreck the International Trade System*, Bus. Insider, June 29, 2018, 11:50 AM, http://www.businessinsider.com/trump-leave-world-trade-organization-wto-2018-6.

50. Trump v. Hawaii, 138 S. Ct. 2392, 2429 (2018).

INDEX

Note: Page numbers followed by the italicized letter *n* indicate material found in notes.

The Trump Administration and International Law. Harold Hongju Koh.
© Oxford University Press 2019. Published 2019 by Oxford University Press.